2 -

Here, at last, is a cookbook featuring foods that are naturally—and sometimes surprisingly—healthful, terrifically tasty, and easy to prepare. Almost all recipes, in fact, require little cooking (or little watching) and many baked goods are quick one-bowl jobs. Each chapter contains a history of the food and explains its health benefits. Practical market, kitchen, and storage tips tell you how to select the best fruits, vegetables, fish, and fowl; where and how to store foods; and for how long. You'll also get sound advice on food preparation and cooking techniques—everything you need to make the most of your...

SUPERFOODS

"Imaginative...helpful and intriguing."

—Publishers Weekly

"Virtually a course for smart eating...power-packed with useful information and different, pleasing recipes."

—Lexington News-Gazette (VA)

"Recipes are easy to prepare and offer plenty of variety—and even include heart-healthy meat entrees. In fact, they're so good you'll forget you're doing your body good."

—Longevity

"Full of accessible and useful nutritional facts."

—Fancy Food

"On target in a nutrion-conscious decade."

—Nation's Restaurant News

FOR RICK, AS ALWAYS

Dolores Riccio is the author of eight previously published books, including four cookbooks. She lives in Warwick, R.I., with her husband and is the mother of two grown children.

SUPERFOODS is not intended to offer medical advice. As with any change in your diet, check your plans with your physician.

Copyright © 1992 by Dolores Riccio
All rights reserved.

Warner Books, Inc., 1271 Avenue of the Americas, New York, NY 10020

 A Time Warner Company

Printed in the United States of America
First Trade Printing: March 1994
10 9 8 7 6 5 4 3 2 1
Originally published in hardcover by Warner Books

Library of Congress Cataloging-in-Publication Data
Riccio, Dolores.
    Superfoods: 300 recipes for foods that heal body and
mind / Dolores Riccio
        p.   cm.
        Includes index
        ISBN 0-446-39409-2
        1. Nutrition.   2. Cookery (Natural foods). I. Title.
RA784.R5 1993   92-36868
613.2—dc20   CIP

Cover photograph by Renee Comet
Cover design by Diane Luger

SUPERFOODS

**300 Recipes
For Foods
That Heal
Body And Mind**

DOLORES RICCIO

WARNER BOOKS

A Time Warner Company

CONTENTS

INTRODUCTION

PER CENT' ANNI! . . . MAY YOU LIVE A HUNDRED YEARS!

This robust toast is offered frequently at our house and in other Italian homes—with a glass of good red wine and a meal that nearly always includes pasta, olive oil and garlic, vegetables and fruits. Like many other of the world's great cuisines, Italian home cooking is just naturally rich in the foods that have turned out to be health builders and disease fighters. It's no coincidence that Italians, Greeks, and Japanese have less heart disease than peoples of other countries, according to the revealing Seven Countries Study begun in 1958. Fewer red meat and dairy products, more fish, grains, legumes, and vegetables can be credited. The Japanese diet was very low in fat, but that certainly can't be said of the Italian and Greek diets. Although these Mediterranean folk use olive oil abundantly, to the exclusion of other fats, monounsaturated olive oil actually lowers cholesterol—which explains why it's one of the superfoods in this cookbook.

And there are many other superfoods here, each one chosen because it offers not one but several health benefits and deserves a starring role in your day-to-day menus. They go so well with one another, you'll find these superfoods popping up often in new combinations, just as one might weave primary colors into many different patterns.

It's so important in adopting a healthier diet to stress the positives—what you can and should eat rather than what you must play down or avoid. Since changing your diet for the better should be a permanent change, part of a new lifestyle, it's better for morale to concentrate on the great foods you're enjoying than on those you're giving up. Otherwise, human nature being what it is, temptation will soon overthrow good intentions.

There are so many really *super* foods that prevent or heal illness, lift fatigue, alter mood, and enhance alertness and memory that, once you fit them all into your menus, there won't be much room left on your plate for foods that are better left off it anyway. In this cookbook, the accent will be on using these superstars to the maximum in easy and elegant dishes that really contribute to optimum good health.

Having said that, I do want to mention certain adjustments that have been made so that these dishes will be lighter and more healthful—with less fat, less cholesterol, less salt, and less sugar than their traditional counterparts. For instance, you're not going to find in these pages a broccoli dish that's loaded with heavy cream sauce or a cake in which sugar outweighs flour (as it does in many store-bought cakes).

Olive oil and vegetable oils are the principal fats used, often in lesser amounts than in traditional recipes for similar dishes. Butter is specified only in very small amounts where the flavor is needed; if a low-cholesterol margarine can be substituted, it's so noted. The least amount of salt that will give a good flavor is all that's called for in these dishes. Whenever a recipe reads "salt to your taste," it often can be eliminated entirely. The flavor will come from herbs, spices, onions, garlic, lemon, and other lively taste enhancers. I haven't given up certain salty delicacies like olives or anchovies, however, but where

they're used, no salt is added. I haven't avoided sugar, either, but again, I've experimented to find the least amount needed.

Dairy foods are still an important part of our diets—essential for youngsters, of course, and a good light source of protein for the many women who don't eat enough of it and wonder why they're always tired. Also for women, milk and milk products are rich in that much-needed calcium to help prevent bone deterioration in later life. But our use of dairy foods must be adjusted for what we know now about the dangers of cholesterol. Low-fat or skim milk can be used in all the recipes in this cookbook. Most times I've used low-fat, unsalted soft cheeses, like ricotta, but I haven't entirely renounced the occasional bite of hard cheese. Whenever an egg substitute can be used in place of a whole egg, this option is given.

In most of the recipes calling for ground meat, I've used lower-cholesterol ground turkey rather than beef. (Ground chicken or veal can also be used.) Not all ground turkeys are created equal, however—some of them include the fatty skin, so you always need to check the fat percentage marked on the package. It should form a smaller proportion than the fat in ground beef. But enough about what's been left out!

The important thing is to eat more of the superfoods that fight illness and stress. I was brought up on the philosophy that "you are what you eat," a notion that is continually underscored by recent nutritional research. We all need to be more aware that good food is more than good taste—it builds, repairs, and fuels our bodies and minds. Every food contains chemicals that directly affect our bodies and minds, so when we control our food consumption, we also control our health, energy, and moods—within the perimeters of individual genetic endowment.

Can you get the same benefits from vitamin supplements that you can from fresh, whole foods? Yes, some of them, but never all of them. Fifty essential nutrients have been identified in foods; vitamin supplements supply only a dozen or so. Take the mystery of apples, for instance. Apples contain an abundance of pectin, a soluble fiber that lowers cholesterol. Pectin itself can be isolated in a powder, but studies have shown that eating real apples works better, for reasons that are not entirely clear. The speculation is that this improved performance might have something to do with pectin combining with vitamin C in the whole apple. But there may be other x factors of which we are, as yet, unaware. A multivitamin pill can be good nutritional insurance, but our bodies were designed to operate on whole foods—not on a handful of vitamin supplements washed down with low-calorie sodas.

Can you overdose on good food, as you can on some vitamins? Yes, but it's *very* difficult. Several quarts of carrot juice a day or a liver dinner every night for weeks, for example, could constitute an overdose of vitamin A. But a sensible balance of superfoods will only make you healthier—and certainly will be more enjoyable than a glut of one food to the exclusion of others.

By eating the right healing foods, can we be our own doctors? No! Good nutrition prevents many illnesses and even cures some, but it should never be considered a replacement for medical attention when an illness occurs. Any serious symptom requires consultation with a doctor. You'll find, however, that some doctors give more importance to the role of nutrition than do others, so it's up to us informed patients to choose the foods that may help us to get well faster. In other words, if "a little chicken soup wouldn't hurt," don't wait for the doctor to prescribe it.

Speaking of which, a study was finally done by Dr. Marvin Sackner, a specialist in pulmonary disorders, which proved that chicken soup is indeed effective against the miseries of an upper respiratory infection. Five minutes after ingestion, chicken soup cleared mucus from the nasal passages at the rate of 9.2 millimeters a minute. Your mother would not be surprised!

Doesn't it take a lot of time and effort to prepare these foods? Well, it takes *some* time—more, say, than simply ordering a burger and fries, but it's well worth the little extra effort. My philosophy of cooking is "make it fresh, make it simple, make it fast," and that applies to entertaining as well as family meals. The few long-cooking dishes in this book are the "put it in the oven and forget it for a while" type. Even the more complicated recipes have been streamlined as much as possible.

Besides, cooking is fun! It's just that few of us have the time for it that we would like, so if a few shortcuts in preparation will encourage us not to short-cut nutrition, it makes sense to forgo the homemade stock in favor of tinned low-salt chicken broth, a very useful convenience food.

While you're stocking your shelves for superfood cooking, you'll also need the following: a variety of whole grains and whole-grain flours, which will keep very well in the freezer or refrigerator; pearl barley; old-fashioned (five-minute) oatmeal; brown and white rice; tins of imported Italian whole plum tomatoes; dried legumes like lentils, split peas, and beans, as well as tins of already-cooked chickpeas, cannellini, kidney beans, and shell beans for quick inspirations; lots of garlic, onions, and shallots; a large container of good-quality olive oil; a smaller container of expensive extra-virgin olive oil for special dishes; an assortment of vinegars, such as wine, cider, rice wine, raspberry, balsamic; a variety of nuts (which also keep well in a freezer), preferably shelled; Parmesan cheese for grating; an assortment of pastas; a full complement of herbs and spices; dried shiitake mushrooms; and, to fill in for seasonal deficiencies, frozen, canned (no added sugar), and dried fruits, as well as frozen (but never canned!) vegetables.

As for the many fresh foods featured in this book, market and kitchen tips on their selection and storage are given in each chapter. I do place great emphasis on enjoying these foods in their seasons, when they're abundant, inexpensive, and haven't been shipped from afar. The quality, taste, and nutrition are always superior, especially in locally grown produce.

In general, when organic fruits and vegetables are available, they are well worth their slightly higher cost. Truly organic produce is grown without chemical fertilizers, pesticides, fungicides, or herbicides. It's not treated with wax or any artificial enhancer after harvest. Of course, there have been scams in which produce that contained residues of pesticides has been passed off as organic, but if you buy your organic fruits and vegetables from a reputable whole-foods market, these foods will be safer than conventionally grown produce. I cannot say, however, that organic produce is more nutritious, as this has not been proved, although several studies have been done on the subject. But I do find that the fruits especially taste much better, probably because they are ripened the old-fashioned way rather than gassed and colored. In fact, I'd forgotten how sweet oranges used to be until I met up with the organically grown variety.

In special equipment, a food processor is the most desirable; a blender is also useful, and a microwave oven is a timesaver but not absolutely necessary. For the rest, all you need are the knives, cutting boards, and pans of the ordinary kitchen. I like well-seasoned cast-iron skillets for superior browning and crisping with a minimum of fat. Because they're heavy, cast-iron skillets are also ideal for baking some quick breads and cakes. But as a safely rule, never buy a frying pan so heavy that you can't lift it easily with one hand. A lidded, heavy Dutch oven that can go from range top to oven is invaluable for slow-braised dishes.

I hope you enjoy the recipes that follow and that they lead you to create a high-energy, high-nutrition cuisine of your own, designed to your individual taste and needs—for a lifetime of good eating and good health . . . *per cent' anni!*

APPLES

POTENT PACKAGES OF PECTIN. "An apple a day . . ." The healing properties of apples aren't just folklore anymore, but we should rewrite that well-known proverb to read: "Two or three unpeeled apples a day keep the doctor away." Not as catchy a phrase, perhaps, but more accurate.

It's been shown that two or three apples a day will lower the artery-clogging LDL cholesterol and raise the artery-cleaning HDL cholesterol. The higher a person's LDL cho-

lesterol, the more significant the reduction when apples are added to an otherwise unchanged diet.

Apples may not be as high in vitamins and minerals as other fruits now in the nutritional limelight, but they are impressively high in pectin. If you've ever made jelly, you know that powdered or liquid pectin has to be added to fruits less richly blessed in that substance in order to get the stuff to gel. But it's always a cinch to make apple jelly or apple-combined-with-anything-else, because of the apple's abundant supply of pectin.

That same pectin that gels fruit spreads is also one of the most efficient fibers in lowering the LDL cholesterol level in humans. In a study published in 1983 by R. Sablé-Amplis and others in Toulouse, France, 30 volunteers from the Institut de Physiologie ate two or three raw apples a day. Without any other changes in their diets, there was a marked lowering of this group's LDL cholesterol: Twenty-four subjects showed this improvement, averaging out to a decrease of 14 percent. The biggest drop was seen in those who had the highest levels.

While pure pectin in powdered form does suppress LDL cholesterol, the whole fresh apple has been shown to do so even better! From this we may conclude that there's more to an apple's goodness than just pectin or some advantage to the fruit's combination of elements. We have much more to learn about why the whole apple is such a potent package. In the interim, it makes sense to continue snacking on apples.

Not only are apples a good heart medicine, they also help regulate blood sugar. Despite its natural sweetness, an apple doesn't cause a rapid rise in blood sugar like other sweet foods and therefore doesn't increase the need for insulin. That makes apples a good food for diabetics.

A raw apple is the perfect after-lunch dessert, particularly for those who aren't going to have the opportunity to brush their teeth. Biting into its firm, juicy flesh helps to clean the teeth of sticky foods, like soft breads, that cause plaque buildup. That's why apples are sometimes called "nature's toothbrush."

While apple juice doesn't have the same cholesterol-lowering properties as do whole apples, it has another equally promising effect. Certain viruses put into test tubes with undiluted fresh apple juice or sweet (not hard) cider are rendered inactive. (Grape juice and tea also contain compounds that negate viruses.)

In the Market

The first rule in buying apples is to try to find fruit that hasn't been waxed. Your best efforts to wash waxed fruit won't remove whatever was on the skin before it was coated but will make the fruit look rather mottled where the wax is partially peeled from vigorous scrubbing. Since most of an apple's pectin resides in and just under the skin, you do want to eat the fruit unpeeled when you can. Most supermarket apples are waxed; if you rub the skin with your thumb, you'll feel it, or you can ask the produce manager. Whole-food markets that feature organic produce and farm stands are two places where you may be able to buy unwaxed apples.

Look for relatively unblemished skins. The flesh should be firm; if apples yield to pressure, they may be mealy. Avoid small apples, however attractively priced, unless needed for a specific recipe, for they are liable to be all core and seeds. As in buying most fruit, a pleasant aroma is a reliable clue to good flavor. Three medium-size apples make about one pound.

Thanks to the introduction of Granny Smiths, you can now have good apples in what used to be the off-seasons—late winter, spring, and summer.

In the Kitchen

Fresh, firm apples will keep at room temperature for about a week. After that, you'd better put them in the refrigerator.

When you have any fruits or vegetables that need ripening, such as pears or tomatoes, put them in a bowl with apples for a day or two. Apples give off ethylene gas that accelerates ripening in its neighbors.

Some people just love to eat apples and need no encouragement at all. Apple lovers are less liable to be tense or illness prone, as was shown in a 1961 study done among students at the University of Michigan. For those who are less than apple aficionados, try introducing apples into more entrées, salads, and especially desserts.

In many of the recipes that follow, I have specified not using McIntosh. This isn't because of any special prejudice against the clan. Although the tart and juicy McIntosh is probably America's favorite for eating out of hand, once it's cooked, the McIntosh quickly turns to mush. This is fine if you're making applesauce but won't do if you want the cooked apple to retain its shape, whether whole or sliced. The too-bland flavor of Red or Yellow Delicious apples rules them out for cooking also. Granny Smith, Cortland, and Winesap apples are my choices for cooking. Preference in "eating apples" is strictly a matter of taste. Personally, my favorite is the Macoun, a perfect blend of sweetness, tartness, and juiciness. Macoun apples seem to appear in my home state of Rhode Island for about 24 hours in the fall and then are simply spirited away by their admirers. So naturally I buy as many as I can find and store them in our cellar's "cold room," where unbruised apples will keep for a month or more.

A cold room is any dark unheated room in the cellar that stays between 40 and 50 degrees, about the same temperature as a traditional wine cellar. It's a perfect place for storing apples, grapefruit, potatoes, onions, carrots, squash, and pumpkins when you have acquired an excess either from sales too good to pass up or from your own garden. If you have a real cold room, cherish it! ▬

Chicken with Apples and Radicchio

Makes 4 servings.

Tart red apples are called for in this recipe; Winesap or Cortland would do nicely. Brown rice or baked sweet potatoes go well with this flavorful dish.

2 tablespoons olive oil

4 chicken legs and 4 thighs, skinned

2 large shallots, chopped

1 cup shredded radicchio

2 cups fresh dark cider
(don't substitute apple juice)

½ teaspoon dried thyme leaves

salt and pepper to taste

4 tart apples, cored, unpeeled
(not McIntosh)

1 tablespoon cornstarch

Heat the oil in a 12-inch skillet and brown the chicken pieces over medium-high heat, watching them carefully to avoid burning. If necessary, do this in two batches rather than crowding the pan.

Pour off excess fat, leaving about 2 teaspoons in the pan. Add the shallots and radicchio (between the chicken pieces), and sauté for 1 minute. Add 1 cup of the cider, the thyme, salt, and pepper. Simmer uncovered, turning the chicken once, until the thighs are no longer pink near the bone, about 20 minutes. You should still have ½ cup of pan juices—but if the skillet becomes too dry, add more cider.

Cut the unpeeled apples crosswise into 4 thick rounds each and lay them over the chicken. Cover the pan and simmer 3 to 5 minutes, until the apples are just tender. Don't overcook, or they will be mushy.

Arrange the chicken and apples on a platter, and keep them warm.

Stir the cornstarch into the remaining 1 cup of cider until there are no lumps. Pour the mixture into the pan juices, and cook over high heat, stirring constantly, until the mixture bubbles and thickens. Lower the heat and simmer for 3 minutes. Then pour the sauce over the chicken and apples.

Shrimp with Apple and Celery

Makes 4 servings.

Apples make a tart, crisp complement to this shrimp dish, which can be prepared in 15 minutes if you buy cooked, cleaned shrimp. Serve with white rice, preferably Arborio.

¼ cup olive oil

4 shallots, minced (about ⅓ cup)

1 cup finely diced celery

1 sweet red pepper, seeded and diced

½ teaspoon celery seed

*2 large Granny Smith apples, peeled
and diced small*

6 tablespoons dry white wine

*1 pound cooked, peeled, deveined
medium shrimp*

Heat the olive oil in a large skillet; add the shallots, celery, sweet red pepper, and celery seed. Sauté for about 5 minutes, until the vegetables are softened and fragrant.

Add the apple and 4 tablespoons (¼ cup) of the wine. Steam over medium heat, uncovered, until the apple is cooked but still crisp, about 3 minutes.

Rinse and drain the shrimp.

When ready to serve, add the shrimp and the remaining 2 tablespoons of wine to the skillet. Bring to a boil over high heat, stirring until the shrimp are warmed through.

Remove from the heat, cover the pan, and let it stand 2 minutes.

Apple and Fennel Salad with Cider Vinaigrette

Makes 4 servings.

Fennel (sometimes called anise) is an underused vegetable that crunches like celery and tastes like licorice. Don't throw away the graceful top, called the "hair." Instead, hang bunches of fennel's narrow leaves to dry and use as an herb in salads, sauces, soups, and stuffings. Meanwhile, drying fennel will make your kitchen smell delicious.

2 tablespoons cider vinegar

⅓ cup olive oil

¼ teaspoon sugar (optional)

salt and pepper to taste

*2 small red apples or 1 extra-large (any
tart apple, including McIntosh)*

1 small or ½ large bulb fennel, cored

½ head romaine or red leafy lettuce

1 tablespoon chopped fennel leaves

Put the vinegar, oil, sugar (if using), salt, and pepper in a small jar, cover, and shake to blend. Pour the dressing into the salad bowl.

Core the apples but don't peel them. Slice the apples directly into the dressing and stir. (This will prevent the apples from turning brown before you get the salad to the table.) Slice the fennel into thin wedges and add it to the bowl, stirring again so that everything is well-coated.

Tear the lettuce into bite-size pieces; add the lettuce along with the fennel leaves. But *don't stir again* until you're ready to serve. (This will keep the lettuce crisp.)

Apple-Almond Tart with Apricot Glaze

Makes 6 to 8 servings.

Because tarts have only half the pastry and sugar of regular pies, they are correspondingly lighter, but you'd never guess it from the results. A glazed fruit tart makes a spectacular dessert.

pastry for tart shell (see Basics)
1 egg, separated

For the almond filling:

½ cup blanched slivered almonds
¼ cup sugar
2 tablespoons softened butter or low-cholesterol margarine
½ teaspoon almond extract

For the apple filling:

about 3 Granny Smith or other tart apples (not McIntosh)
1 tablespoon butter, melted
2 tablespoons sugar
cinnamon

For the glaze:

¼ cup apricot preserves

Roll out the pastry, fit it into a 9-inch tart pan with a removable rim, and trim the edge. Brush the inside of the shell with some of the egg white. Chill the crust.

Preheat the oven to 400° F. Purée the almond filling ingredients, with the egg yolk and the remainder of the egg white, in a food processor or blender. Spread the purée gently and evenly over the bottom of the tart shell.

Core, peel, and thinly slice the apples. Arrange in a circular pattern of overlapping slices over the almond filling. Fill in the center also. Brush the apples with 1 tablespoon of melted butter. Sprinkle with 2 tablespoons of sugar and a little cinnamon.

Place the tart pan on a baking sheet and bake on the bottom shelf of the oven until the apples are tender and the crust is golden, about 50 minutes.

Melt the preserves, either in a microwaveable cup in the microwave or in a small saucepan over low heat. Brush the preserves over the warm tart. Cool completely on a wire rack. Remove the tart pan rim and place the tart on a serving plate or cake pedestal.

Dutch Apple Cake

Makes 6 generous servings.

Whole apples filled with blackberry preserves and cooked inside this cake make an attractive presentation. Servings are necessarily large, but no one will mind!

6 small apples, cored and peeled
(any cooking apple—not McIntosh)
1 tablespoon white vinegar or lemon juice
2 cups sifted unbleached all-purpose flour
½ cup sugar
1 tablespoon baking powder
½ teaspoon salt
¾ cup milk
2 eggs or ½ cup prepared egg substitute
¼ cup vegetable oil
½ teaspoon vanilla extract
¼ teaspoon almond extract
about ½ cup blackberry preserves
cinnamon sugar (see Basics)

Preheat the oven to 375° F. Generously butter a 10-inch cast-iron skillet. (If you don't have such a skillet, use a 10-inch-wide, 2-inch-deep flan pan lined with buttered parchment paper, but an iron skillet is much better.)

Core and peel apples; drop them into a bowl of acidulated water (1 tablespoon vinegar or lemon juice per quart of water).

Drain and precook the apples until they are tender-crisp but still hold their shape. *Method one:* Put the apples on a glass pie plate and microwave on high for 4 to 5 minutes. When squeezed, they should give slightly.

Method two: Bake the apples, covered, in the preheated oven for 15 to 20 minutes. Test them with the tines of a fork, which should pierce the flesh easily.

Let the apples cool while preparing the batter. Sift flour, sugar, baking powder, and salt into a large bowl. In a medium bowl, beat together the milk, eggs, oil, and the vanilla and almond extracts. Pour the liquid ingredients into the dry ingredients and stir until blended. Pour the batter into the prepared pan.

Try to take these next steps quickly: Place the apples in a circle in the batter, pushing down slightly. Use a demitasse or grapefruit spoon to fill the cores with blackberry preserves. Sprinkle with cinnamon sugar.

Bake the cake for 35 minutes, or until the top is risen and lightly brown and a cake tester inserted in the center comes out dry. Serve warm from the pan. If there are any leftovers, remove them from the pan before storing.

Micro Apples

Makes 2 servings.
This is the ultimate in last-minute desserts!

2 apples
4 teaspoons brown sugar
2 teaspoons raisins
1 teaspoon butter or low-cholesterol
margarine
cinnamon for sprinkling

Core the apples, but save about ½ inch of the cores to use as plugs to hold in the filling.

Peel just the tops of each apple. Insert the plugs cut from the apple cores at the bottoms. Place the apples in a small casserole or in 2 extra-large custard cups.

Put 1 teaspoon of sugar in each apple, then raisins, then the remaining sugar. Divide the butter, half on each. Sprinkle the cinnamon.

Microwave the apples on high, uncovered, for 4 to 5 minutes, until tender when pierced with a paring knife. Allow them to cool a bit and spoon the melted brown sugar over the tops before serving.

Alternative method: Bake at 350° F. for 30 to 40 minutes, or until quite tender.

For other apple recipes, see the following: Acorn Squash with Apple-Raisin Stuffing; Lucy's Apple Oatmeal Crisp; Spiced Blueberry and Apple Pie; Turnip with Apple and Cardamom; Whole-Wheat, Oatmeal, and Apple Muffins

APRICOTS, PEACHES, AND NECTARINES

SUMMER'S BOUNTY FOR HEALTH AND BEAUTY. The smooth, sweet summer fruits have always been my favorites, and I look forward to their all-too-short season with pleasant anticipation. I've learned to be patient enough to pass by the first hard, greenish peaches and apricots that are rushed to market, knowing they'll never ripen to the golden succulence that nature intended. To really enjoy these luxurious fruits, one must wait for the height of their season. Meanwhile, I content myself with dried apricots or with canned peaches packed in light fruit juice rather than heavy syrup; both of these fruits are chock-full of nutritional goodness.

Apricots, peaches, and nectarines share in the bonus of beta carotene, a precursor of vitamin A that deep yellow and orange fruits and vegetables have in common, and they rank high as cancer-fighting foods, according to the National Cancer Institute. Beta carotene may inhibit cancer of the skin, larynx, and lung.

Of the three fruits, apricots have the highest concentration of beta carotene, particularly dried apricots. This golden orange fruit forms an important part of the diet of Pakistani Hunzas who live in the Karakoram Range of the Himalayas. We don't really know if there's any connection, but Hunzas are famous for their long and active lives. It's not unusual for Hunzas in their eighties and nineties to work in the fields. According to UNESCO, they are the only totally cancer-free people in the world. (We should also note that yogurt and whole grains are other Hunza staples, and that they live in a pollution-free environment, at a heart-strengthening high altitude.) Hunza was the inspiration for the land of Shangri-la in the novel *Lost Horizon*.

Vitamin A, which all three fruits contain in abundance, aids in the repair of body tissue; helps to keep skin smooth, soft, and unblemished; and protects the mucous membranes of the mouth, nose, throat, and lungs as well as the soft tissues of the digestive tract. Even before recent scientific studies revealed the link between a high consumption of beta carotene and a low incidence of cancer, vitamin A was known to aid in the treatment of acne and night blindness.

Although there is considerable disagreement about whether *any* nutritional remedy is useful against colds and viral infections, there is some evidence that vitamins A and C may prevent and/or treat these common ailments. Since foods high in these vitamins are good for us anyway, why not enjoy plenty of them? If they help to prevent colds, too, that's a bonus! Although it *is* possible to overdose on vitamin supplements, overdosing on the vitamins occurring naturally in foods is exceedingly rare.

All three of these delectable fruits are mildly laxative. Like prunes, they are high in magnesium, which is thought to cause this effect. But it's not simply the magnesium, because other magnesium-rich foods, such as fish, tofu, and broccoli, are not necessarily laxative. More likely, it's the whole composition of peaches, apricots, and prunes (plums) that's at work.

Magnesium plays an important role in the healthy functioning of the heart muscle. A deficiency of magnesium has been implicated in coronary vasospasm (which leads to heart attacks and sudden deaths).

Apricots, peaches, and nectarines can come as they are to any dessert party or may be dressed up in marvelous ways. The apricot especially often turns up as an ingredient in classic European pastries. Many a glaze, a sauce, or a filling in fancy baked sweets is made from this versatile fruit. But any of the three may add a touch of elegance to entrées also and be just as good for you as the ubiquitous carrot.

In the Market

Perfect, unblemished *tree-ripened* apricots, peaches, and nectarines are, of course, the ideal but they are almost impossible to find. Fruits that are touted as tree-ripened, packed individually like jewels and priced accordingly, spoil so quickly that it would be like winning a lottery to happen to be standing nearby when they first arrive in the market and are still worth buying. But don't despair—at the

height of the season (late June and July) the great bins of ordinary peaches and nectarines can be quite good.

Look for large fruits with a nice rosy blush and lightly press one with your thumb. The flesh should yield to pressure without caving in. Ripe apricots should be plump and well-formed with slightly yielding flesh and a deep yellow or yellowish orange color. Don't buy green apricots or peaches; they won't ever be sweet. Once picked, apricots and peaches won't get any sweeter, because they don't have enough starch to turn into sugar. (In this respect, they are unlike pears, which have a good supply of starch. Pears are picked green and *do* get sweeter after harvesting.)

In the Kitchen

Handle and wash these summer fruits gently. If the store has pasted code stickers on their thin skins, it's better not to remove them until you're ready to use the fruit because a little piece of skin may come off with the sticker, thus opening the fruit to fast decay. This is so annoying that you may want to find a store that doesn't ruin its soft fruits this way.

"Ripening" apricots, peaches, or nectarines for one or, at the most, two days at room temperature, however, will make them softer and juicier, if not sweeter. After that, store them in the refrigerator, where they will keep for three to four days.

It takes six pounds of fresh apricots to make one pound of the dried fruit, so naturally, the latter are extremely rich in nutrients and flavor. Dried apricots can be reconstituted by simmering in water or used just as they are in recipes. They make a nice snack, too—the dense, sweet-tart apricot taste can be quite addictive.

Peach-Melon Soup with Fresh Mint

Makes 4 to 5 cups.

A cool, refreshing starter for a summer meal.

4 large or 6 medium ripe peaches, peeled and sliced

1 small cantaloupe, chunked (about 4 cups loosely packed)

juice of 1 lime

10 to 12 fresh mint leaves, finely minced

additional mint sprigs for garnishing

In a food processor or a blender in batches, purée the sliced peaches and cantaloupe chunks with the lime juice. Stir in the minced mint. Chill several hours to develop the flavor. Serve in glass bowls; garnish each portion with mint sprigs.

Spice-Coated Pork Chops with Apricots

Makes 4 servings.

Pork chops cooked in a skillet can become too dry unless you cook them very slowly and remove them from the heat the moment they are cooked through. It's okay if there's a vestige of pink juice (but not pink meat) at the center.

4 pork chops (¾ to 1 inch thick, not "thin cut")

1 teaspoon each ground cumin seed, coriander, and ginger

1 tablespoon olive oil

2 large shallots, minced

¾ cup slivered dried apricots, loosely packed

¾ cup dry white wine

Trim off all visible fat from the chops.

Mix the spices and coat the chops with the mixture, pressing it into the meat.

Heat the oil in a 12-inch skillet (cast iron is the best for this dish) and fry the chops slowly so that they are cooked through by the time they're brown on both sides, 5 to 7 minutes per side. The only test for doneness is to cut a chop, which then becomes the cook's portion. During the last 3 minutes, add the shallots to the pan.

Meanwhile, combine the apricots and wine in a small saucepan, and simmer the mixture for 5 minutes. Turn off the heat and let the apricots stand while finishing the chops.

Remove the chops from the pan and keep them warm. If there is any excess fat, pour it off, but keep the shallots. Deglaze the hot pan by pouring in the apricot-wine mixture. After it boils for 1 minute, remove the sauce from the heat. Combine with any meat juices exuded from the chops while they were kept warm. Divide the apricot sauce among the chops before serving.

Broiled Veal Loin Chops with Quick Peach Chutney

Makes 4 servings.

Not all preserves have to simmer for hours. This quick chutney can be ready in the time it takes you to get the rest of the dinner together.

4 large veal loin chops (½ pound each)

For the chutney:

one 1-pound can of peaches, packed without sugar, drained, or 3 large fresh peaches, peeled
½ of a sweet red pepper, finely diced
¼ cup minced shallots
2 tablespoons each golden raisins, rice vinegar, and brown sugar
2 dried hot red peppers
1 slice fresh ginger, peeled and minced, or ½ teaspoon ground ginger
¼ teaspoon each ground cinnamon and turmeric
⅛ teaspoon ground cloves

Dice the peaches. Combine all the chutney ingredients in a 1½-quart casserole, and microwave on high for 12 minutes, stirring once in the middle of the cooking time. Let the chutney cool to room temperature. Remove the dried red peppers.

Alternatively, put all the ingredients in a saucepan, adding ¼ cup of the juice from the peaches (or water if you are using fresh peaches), and simmer over low heat for 30 minutes, stirring often. If the chutney starts to stick, add more juice or water by the tablespoonful.

Broil the loin chops in a preheated broiler for 5 minutes per side. Put each chop on a plate and top it with about ¼ cup chutney.

Note: Leftover chutney is terrific on baked beans.

Baked Chicken Breasts with Yogurt Crust and Peaches

Makes 4 servings.

From start to finish, you can have this "peachy" entrée on the table in 30 minutes.

*1½ cups herb stuffing mix
(not the stovetop variety)*

*2 whole skinless, boneless chicken breasts,
each cut in half*

about ½ cup plain yogurt

*2 large ripe peaches (or 4 small),
peeled and halved*

cinnamon sugar (see Basics)

Preheat the oven to 375° F. In a food processor or blender, reduce the stuffing mix to coarse crumbs. Pour them onto a sheet of wax paper.

Coat one piece of chicken breast with yogurt as thickly as possible (admittedly, this is a messy step), then dip it into the crumbs to coat. Lay the chicken in an oiled baking dish large enough to hold chicken and peaches in one layer. Repeat with the remaining chicken.

Surround the chicken with peach halves, cut sides down. Sprinkle the peaches (not the chicken) with cinnamon sugar. Bake for 20 minutes, or until the breasts are just cooked through but not dry.

Clafouti aux Pêches (Peach Flan)

Makes 6 servings.

A traditional French farmer's sweet, something like a big fruit pancake, that makes a nice brunch dish as well as a homey dessert.

1¼ cups milk (can be low-fat)

⅔ cup unbleached all-purpose flour

3 eggs or ¾ cup prepared egg substitute

⅓ cup sugar

½ teaspoon almond extract

¼ teaspoon cinnamon

⅛ teaspoon salt

*½ tablespoon butter or low-cholesterol
margarine*

3 large ripe peaches, peeled and sliced

cinnamon sugar (see Basics)

Preheat the oven to 350° F. In a blender or food processor, blend the milk, flour, eggs, sugar, and flavorings. Alternatively, whisk the ingredients together in a bowl until they are light and well-blended.

On the range top, melt the butter in a 10-inch cast-iron skillet or fireproof 2-inch-deep baking dish. Pour in ½ cup of the batter and place the skillet over low heat until the batter has set like a crêpe, about 5 minutes.

Remove the pan from the heat and lay the peach slices on the layer of batter. Pour the rest of the batter on top, and bake on the middle shelf of the oven for 50 minutes, or until the *clafouti* is puffed and brown and a cake tester inserted in the middle comes out clean.

Sprinkle with cinnamon sugar and serve warm (but not hot). It will fall slightly, but that's to be expected.

Peach and Raspberry Cranachan

Makes 4 servings.

Cranachan is a traditional Scottish dessert made with toasted oats. This version is made with low-fat pastry cream instead of whipped heavy cream.

You'll probably have some toasted oats left over, for which there are so many delicious uses that I keep a jar of them on hand. My favorite is to sprinkle them on ricotta cheese for a different breakfast dish (sort of like oatmeal with milk in reverse). Try them on any fruit or pudding.

1 cup uncooked
"old-fashioned" oats

2 tablespoons brown sugar

¼ teaspoon cinnamon

one 1-pound can cling peach slices, packed without sugar, or 3 large, fresh peaches, peeled and thinly sliced

1¼ cups pastry cream flavored with 1 tablespoon rum or, if you want to be really authentic, Scotch whisky (see Basics)

1 cup frozen raspberries, packed without sugar, unthawed but separated

Layer the oats in a baking pan and toast them in a 350° F. oven until they are golden, 8 to 10 minutes. Watch carefully that they don't become brown. Put them in a bowl, and stir in the brown sugar and cinnamon. Blend the mixture by rubbing it between your fingers.

Drain the peaches well.

Make the pastry cream. Put a heaping tablespoon of the pudding in each of 4 dessert bowls. Divide the drained peaches among the bowls. Top with the remaining pudding. Sprinkle with the frozen raspberries (which will thaw before serving). Press them down lightly. Chill until set, about 1 hour.

Just before serving, sprinkle the desserts with the toasted oat mixture.

Preheat the oven to 400° F. Roll out the pastry, fit it into a 9-inch tart shell, and trim. Prick the pastry with a fork all over. Bake about 15 minutes on the top shelf of the oven, or until golden. (If the pastry rises while cooking, prick it again with a fork.) Cool it completely on a rack.

Put the snipped apricots in a deep saucepan. Cover with water to about 1½ inches above the fruit. Bring the liquid to a boil, reduce the heat, and simmer for 20 minutes. Drain, reserving the juice.

Measure the juice. If necessary, add water to make 1 cup. Return the juice to the saucepan, adding the sugar and cinnamon. Mix the cornstarch in ½ cup water until there are no lumps. Bring the juice to a boil, add the cornstarch mixture, stirring constantly until thick. Reduce the heat; simmer 1 minute. Add the apricots. Cool to lukewarm.

Spoon the filling into the tart shell. Chill until firm. Remove the rack rim and place the tart on a serving plate or cake pedestal.

Apricot Tart

Makes 8 servings.

My version of *vlaai*, a favorite Dutch tart.

pastry for 1 tart shell (see Basics)
1½ cups dried apricots, snipped into small
pieces (about ¾ pound)
½ cup sugar
dash of cinnamon
⅓ cup cornstarch
½ cup water

Fresh Apricot "Cannoli"

Makes 4 servings.

Fruit replaces pastry in these cannoli. For this easy, luscious dessert, you'll need large, ripe apricots that are almost the size of peaches. Look for them in July.

4 large, perfectly ripe apricots
1 cup low-fat ricotta cheese
2 tablespoons honey, plus 2 teaspoons
2 tablespoons grated sweet
baking chocolate
dash of cinnamon
2 tablespoons chopped pistachio nuts

Halve the apricots and remove the pits. (It's not necessary to peel them.)

Whip the ricotta until it is quite creamy, beating in 2 tablespoons of the honey. Stir in the chocolate and cinnamon.

Place 4 apricot halves in dessert dishes. Spoon ¼ cup of ricotta filling on each. Top with the remaining apricot halves. Gently press pistachios around the sides of the filling. Drizzle the apricots with the remaining honey, ½ teaspoon each.

Refrigerate until serving time.

Nectarines Baked with Brandied Mincemeat

Makes 4 servings.

An effortless and elegant dessert. Serve it in glass bowls.

2 large ripe nectarines
⅓ cup prepared mincemeat
1½ tablespoons brandy (optional)
4 scoops frozen vanilla yogurt (optional)

Preheat the oven to 350° F. Peel the nectarines and cut them in half; remove the pits by cutting around them carefully with the point of a knife. Place the fruit, cut side up, in a baking dish. Mix the mincemeat and brandy, if you are using it. Stuff each nectarine half with mincemeat (about 1 full tablespoon each) and bake them for 25 to 30 minutes, until just tender. Serve warm—with scoops of frozen yogurt, if desired.

Gingered Peaches

Makes 2 servings.

There's no substitute for the peppery taste of the Fresh Ginger Syrup called for in this recipe, which must be started the day before—but it's easy enough to prepare, and you'll find many uses for the extra.

Ginger has a number of therapeutic uses. It prevents motion sickness *better than* the leading over-the-counter drug for that affliction, it's an anticoagulant, and some studies have indicated that ginger may help to block the cell changes that lead to cancer.

> *2 fresh ripe peaches*
> *¼ cup Fresh Ginger Syrup (see Basics)*
> *mint sprigs*

Peel and slice the peaches. Pour the syrup over them and chill in the refrigerator at least an hour, stirring once. Spoon them into dessert dishes and garnish with mint sprigs.

Note: Sliced fresh apricots or chunks of fresh cantaloupe can be substituted for the peaches.

For other apricot and peach recipes, see the following: Banana-Apricot Bread Pudding; Banana-Peach Frozen Yogurt; Quick-Mix Barley Spice Cake Loaf with Peaches; Rosy Raspberry-Peach Pie; Yogurt *Coeurs à la Crème*

5-Minute Praline Peaches

Makes 4 servings.

A last-minute microwave dessert that's special enough for last-minute company!

> *4 fresh ripe peaches*
> *4 tablespoons dark brown sugar*
> *cinnamon*
> *12 pecan halves*

Peel and slice the peaches; divide them among 4 microwave-safe dessert dishes. Sprinkle each portion with a tablespoon of brown sugar. Add a dash of cinnamon. Arrange 3 pecan halves on each serving.

Cook 2 dishes at a time in the microwave for 4 to 5 minutes, or until the peaches are tender. Let them cool to room temperature.

BANANAS AND PLANTAINS

POTASSIUM PUNCH . . . PLUS! The neatly packaged, easy-to-open, low-calorie, unassuming banana is a powerhouse of nutrition, especially notable these days for its high potassium content.

Potassium has been getting increasing attention for its role in cardiovascular health. This essential mineral works with sodium to regulate the heartbeat and nourish the muscular system. The body's supply of potassium can be depleted, however, by the use of some blood-pressure medicines, diuretics, or an excessive intake of salt. Any condition that lowers the body's fluid level, such as diarrhea or excessive sweating, will also reduce the body's potassium.

A banana a day will ensure that you get a plentiful supply of potassium. And that's not all! Although soft and creamy, a banana has as much bulk fiber for intestinal health as a half-slice of whole-wheat bread. It also has as much pectin (a soluble fiber and a cholesterol fighter) as a medium apple.

Besides being a low-fat, low-sodium delicious sweet, a banana is a soothing breakfast food for those who feel the stress of mornings most keenly. Bananas contain tryptophan, an essential amino acid that reduces stress. They're so digestible and nutritious that they're often recommended as the first solid food for infants—perfect for adults, too, who feel the need of a little babying. A banana also tucks tidily into a brown-bag lunch.

Bananas can be introduced into one's repertoire of entrées, and, of course, they are thoroughly at home in the dessert course—all of which is evidenced by the recipes included in this chapter.

The plantain, which looks like a large banana, is indeed its ancestor, the first known species in this fruit family. Because it's starchier and tougher than the banana, a plantain should be cooked before serving, which is why it's sometimes called the "cooking banana." An important source of food in West Indian and Latin American cultures, not for dessert but to replace more usual starchy foods like potatoes. Plantains may be baked, steamed, or sautéed while green or when ripe, thus adding an exotic note to the dinner menu.

All varieties of this fruit are gastrointestinal soothers and have showed promise in the treatment of ulcers. Like ulcer medicines, bananas and plantains help to neutralize stomach acid. But they do even more than that, according to research in Britain and India with banana-snacking rats. These little subjects were given some powerful ulcerogens, including aspirin. One group was fed plantain-banana powder, however, and it was found that these rats were protected by a strengthening of the stomach's mucosal resistance. Unlike acid-suppressing drugs, bananas and plantains actually help to thicken the stomach wall by stimulating cell growth and coating this surface with mucus.

In the Market

Happily, bananas are available all year round. They are picked green because they continue to ripen after harvesting. Buy slightly green bananas with no bruised spots.

Plantains are found in larger markets that cater to the adventurous cook, as well as in some ethnic markets. Buy them green but unblemished.

In the Kitchen

Store bananas and plantains at room temperature until they reach the ripeness you prefer, then use them as soon as possible.

Some recipes specify firm, green plantains, in which case you can skip the ripening process. But if you are ripening them, look for this primeval fruit to turn a mottled yellow rather than golden. You'll find that plantains don't peel as easily as the obliging banana; a paring knife may be needed.

Allow bananas to ripen until yellow or yellow flecked with brown, whichever degree of ripeness you prefer. At that point, if you still have quite a few left, refrigerate them. Although their skins will turn dark, the bananas will still be good eating for a few days longer. Ripe bananas may also be frozen in their skins, unwrapped, for longer storage. When thawed, they will lose their firm texture but may be used as an ingredient in baked goods.

If you're feeling deprived of the fat-laden dessert ingredients that are best avoided, savoring the creaminess of bananas can be a real comfort. I especially like a kind of mock ice cream that can be made from puréed frozen bananas laced with rum-soaked raisins. Another favorite is a dish of sliced bananas, low-fat ricotta cheese, and toasted old-fashioned oats flavored with a little brown sugar and cinnamon—sinfully rich taste but highly nutritious!

Pork Chops, Plantains, and Vinegar Peppers

Makes 2 servings.

Vinegar peppers are sold in jars in the Italian section of the supermarket. Don't confuse them with *peperoncini*, which are much smaller, or with roasted peppers, which are packed in oil. In Italian households, vinegar peppers (often homemade) are de rigueur with pork chops or sausages. Adding plantains makes this an interesting mix of cultures.

2 tablespoons oil
2 pork chops, ¾- to 1-inch thick
2 ripe plantains, peeled and sliced ½ inch thick
2 vinegar peppers, halved

Heat 1 tablespoon of oil in a large skillet. Over medium heat, fry the pork chops 5 to 7 minutes per side, or until just cooked through but not dry. Remove the chops from the pan and keep them warm.

If needed, add a second tablespoon of oil to the skillet. Fry the plantains until the centers are soft, just as you would potatoes. When the plantains are cooked, add the vinegar peppers long enough to warm them. Combine with the chops and serve.

Thyme-Scented Chicken with Plantains and Shallots

Makes 4 servings.

A versatile tropical fruit takes the place of potatoes in this savory dish.

2 large ripe plantains (about 2 pounds)
1½ to 2 pounds skinned, boneless chicken breasts
1 tablespoon butter or low-cholesterol margarine
2 tablespoons oil plus more if needed
¼ cup minced shallots (3 to 4)
¼ teaspoon dried thyme leaves
salt and pepper to taste
¼ cup dry vermouth or dry sherry

Peel the plantains and cut them into ½-inch slices on the diagonal. Cut the chicken into 1-inch-thick chunks.

Heat the butter and oil in a large skillet, and sauté the shallots until they are sizzling. Add the plantains in one layer and fry them until golden on both sides.

Push the plantains to one side and add the chicken in one layer. Over medium-high heat, brown the chicken on one side, turn, and sprinkle with thyme, salt, and pepper.

When the pieces are almost brown on the second side, add the wine, cover tightly, and lower the heat. Cook about 10 minutes, or until the chicken is cooked through but not dry.

yum!

Just Plain Baked Plantains

Choose ripe plantains and rub the skins with vegetable oil. Cut long slits in them lengthwise, plus a few cross slits. Put them in a preheated 400° F. oven and bake them for 20 to 30 minutes, or until the flesh puffs out of the slits. Dress them as you would baked potatoes. A dollop of nonfat yogurt mixed with fresh snipped chives is a tasty topping.

Baked plantains go well with baked fish fillets and cook at the same temperature in about the same amount of time.

Banana-Date Muffins

Makes 12 muffins.

These muffins freeze well and can be thawed in the microwave very quickly (about 2 minutes for 1 muffin on defrost setting). A quick and easy breakfast.

2 cups sifted unbleached all-purpose flour
1 tablespoon baking powder
½ teaspoon salt
2 medium ripe bananas
1 egg or ¼ cup prepared egg substitute

⅓ cup sugar
½ cup milk (can be skim)
⅓ cup vegetable oil
2 tablespoons toasted wheat germ
¼ teaspoon nutmeg
¼ teaspoon ground cardamom
½ cup chopped, pitted dates

Line a 12-cup muffin pan with paper liners. Preheat the oven to 400° F.

Sift the flour, baking powder, and salt into a large bowl.

In a food processor, purée the bananas (or mash them by hand). Blend in the eggs and sugar. Blend in the milk, oil, wheat germ, and spices; process until smooth.

Pour the mixture into the dry ingredients. Mix just enough to blend. Fold in the dates. Divide the batter among the muffin cups.

As soon as the muffins are in the oven, reduce the heat to 350° F. Bake in the top third of the oven for 25 minutes, or until the muffins are lightly browned on top and dry inside. Serve warm or at room temperature.

Light Banana Rum-Raisin "Ice Cream"

Makes 4 servings.

A creamy frozen banana purée with rum-soaked golden raisins. Maybe it's not real ice cream, but it's so good—and so easy!

4 ripe bananas
¼ cup golden raisins
¼ cup dark rum

Peel the bananas. Slice each one crosswise in rounds almost all the way through, keeping the form of the banana together. Wrap each banana individually in plastic wrap and freeze them solid.

About 1 hour before serving, soak the raisins in the rum.

Separate the frozen banana slices and purée them in a food processor. Add the raisins and the rum, and process for about 30 seconds more. Serve the ice cream immediately in stemmed sherbet glasses.

Banana-Apricot Bread Pudding

Makes 6 servings.

Herbs and spices have a chemical effect on the brain and body just as foods do. Nutmeg is one of the spice shelf's stimulants, along with all the mints.

3 whole eggs or ¾ cup prepared
egg substitute
1 cup whole milk
⅓ cup sugar
2 tablespoons banana liqueur or
1 teaspoon vanilla extract
¼ teaspoon nutmeg
4 slices whole-wheat bread

4 medium ripe bananas
½ cup snipped dried apricots
nutmeg for garnish
frozen vanilla yogurt for topping
(optional)

Preheat the oven to 350° F. Beat together the eggs, milk, sugar, liqueur (or vanilla), and nutmeg until well-blended.

Cut the bread into 1-inch squares (3 times each way). Put them into a 1½-quart casserole. Pour the egg-milk mixture over the casserole and let it stand for 10 minutes, pressing the bread down occasionally.

Purée the bananas in a food processor or blender (or mash by hand). Stir the bananas and apricots into the casserole, gently but thoroughly. Sprinkle more nutmeg on top.

Put the casserole into a larger pan; fill the second pan with hot water almost to the height of the pudding. Bake for 40 to 50 minutes, or until the pudding is set; a knife inserted in the center should come out clean.

Serve warm with a dollop of frozen yogurt.

Banana Cake with Peanuts

Makes 12 servings.

The flavor of this cake reminds me of one of my favorite sandwiches as a youngster—sliced bananas on peanut butter toast. (As a matter of fact, it's still a great combination!)

This is a moist cake that needs no icing,

as most of my cakes tend to be. If you put really healthful ingredients in a cake and skip the extra sugar of an icing, it takes the guilt out of dessert.

1 teaspoon lemon juice

⅓ cup milk (can be low-fat)

2¼ cups sifted unbleached all-purpose flour

1 teaspoon baking soda

¼ teaspoon each baking powder, salt, and nutmeg

1 cup peanuts, coarsely chopped (not too small)

1 teaspoon grated lemon peel

3 medium ripe bananas (about 1 pound)

½ cup (1 stick) butter or low-cholesterol margarine, softened

1¼ cups dark brown sugar, firmly packed

2 eggs, beaten, or ½ cup prepared egg substitute

This cake can be made in the food processor, but alternative directions are also given.

Preheat the oven to 350° F. Butter and flour an angel food cake pan.

Put the lemon juice in the milk and let it stand until needed.

Sift together the flour, baking soda, baking powder, salt, and nutmeg.

Processor method: Chop the peanuts in the food processor and remove them.

Combine the lemon peel, bananas, and butter in the work bowl, and process them un-

til puréed and mixed. Blend in the brown sugar, then the eggs.

When these ingredients are well-mixed, add the dry ingredients and milk in 3 additions: half the flour, all the milk, the remaining flour. Process after each with quick on/off turns just until blended.

Add the peanuts and mix with one or two on/off turns.

Note: This recipe is for a standard, full-size processor. If yours is smaller, use the alternative method.

Alternative Method: Chop the peanuts. In a medium-size bowl, mash the bananas. In another bowl, combine the milk and eggs.

In a large bowl, cream together the butter, sugar, and grated peel until light and fluffy. Blend in the bananas.

Beat in the flour and milk-egg mixture in several additions, beginning and ending with flour. Stir in the peanuts.

Spoon the batter into the prepared pan, smooth the top, and bake on the middle shelf for 45 to 50 minutes. To test, wait until the cake has risen and split, and the split appears dry. A cake tester inserted in the center should come out dry.

For other banana recipes, see: Banana-Cinnamon Yogurt; Banana-Peach Frozen Yogurt; Frozen Mango-Banana Mousse; Jamaican Chicken with Sweet Potatoes

BARLEY

A CINDERELLA HEALTH FOOD. Among the filling, staple foods that round out our contemporary menus, unfashionable barley receives little attention compared with potatoes, pasta, and rice. Although it's an important grain in the Middle East, barley is rarely encountered on the North American continent in restaurant dishes or in the ordinary home bill of fare, except as an ingredient in soups. But barley is a simply super grain that deserves the limelight and with a bit of thought and invention can take its rightful place on our dinner plates—as a savory risotto, a crunchy salad, or a hearty muffin.

Barley, like oat bran, contains a soluble gum fiber that promotes a healthy heart. But while oat bran has been receiving wide press coverage for its efficacy in lowering cholesterol, hardly any notice has been given to barley—an oversight that may be attributed to cooks not being exactly sure what to do with this humble grain. Oatmeal, we know, makes a nifty hot cereal, which, in my generation, was a must for a schoolchild's winter breakfast (and for after school, oatmeal cookies, of course). So without all this nostalgia and tradition to draw on, we're going to have to open new culinary vistas for barley.

Barley also contains a chemical substance that actually interferes with the liver's manufacture of LDL-type cholesterol, the bad kind of cholesterol that does all the damage in blood vessels. This makes barley one of the top grains of choice for a healthy diet.

As a seed food, barley also contains protease inhibitors, which are thought to inhibit cancer formation by suppressing the action of carcinogens.

Both these good effects can be obtained from pearl barley, which tastes better than unrefined barley. It's nice to reflect, too, that cooked barley has only 170 calories a cup.

Barley is also useful as an aid to regularity, but for this remedy the unhulled grain is needed. The best source of unhulled barley is barley flour, which is made from the whole grain. Barley flour can be substituted for all or part of the wheat flour in many recipes, and for a whole grain, it produces surprisingly light, tender baked goods.

In the Market

The refined grain, pearl barley, is generally available in supermarkets. You can buy whole-grain barley flour in health food stores.

Pearl barley is packaged in plastic bags; these ought to appear fresh and clean. Because barley keeps well, the store may have had it on the shelves for ages, so avoid packaging that looks dull, wrinkled, and dusty.

In the Kitchen

When shelved in a cool, dry place, pearl barley may be stored for months.

Keep barley flour in a canister or jar, like any other flour. For longer storage or in hot weather, keep it in the freezer. Because I often have several kinds of flour in stock, I routinely keep all flours in the freezer, except for about five pounds of unbleached white flour, which is constantly being used and replaced.

As with dried legumes, examine pearl barley for foreign particles. Then scoop the barley into a strainer and rinse it before using it in recipes. In general, barley is cleaner than dried legumes; this step is merely a precaution, no different from washing greens.

Although a much wider use of barley is desirable, this is not to disparage its use in soups. I like a good, thick, comforting soup, and barley is a great thickener. So great, in fact, that a little goes a long way; a half-cup is plenty to thicken two quarts of soup.

Between meltingly tender soup barley and chewy salad barley, there's a whole range of textures possible, depending on the length of cooking time. Do experiment with barley and discover its super potential! ▬

Mushroom and Barley Soup with Escarole

Makes 6 to 8 servings.

Whether to wash or brush mushrooms is matter for debate among cooks, but personally, I wash everything. Mushrooms are porous and hold water, but they dry well in a salad spinner.

3 tablespoons vegetable oil

one 10- or 12-ounce package fresh mushrooms, washed and sliced

1 onion, diced

1 sweet red pepper, diced

1 clove garlic, minced

¼ cup flour

2 cups boiling water

6 cups beef broth (or 3 cans broth)

½ cup pearl barley, rinsed and drained

1 tablespoon dry sherry or 2 tablespoons dry vermouth

1 teaspoon Worcestershire sauce

¼ teaspoon dried thyme leaves

1 bay leaf

4 cups well-washed, loosely packed chopped escarole

black pepper to taste

Heat the oil in a large saucepan. Add the mushrooms, onion, red pepper, and garlic, and cook over high heat, stirring, until the vegetable juices evaporate and the mixture begins to fry. Because of the high heat, watch that the vegetables do not burn.

Change the heat setting to low. Add the flour and cook, stirring constantly, until the flour is lightly browned. Add boiling water, whisking until smooth; with a metal spoon, scrape the bottom of the pot to free any browned bits. Add all the remaining ingredients except the escarole and black pepper.

Bring to a boil and simmer the soup, uncovered, stirring occasionally, for 40 to 45 minutes, until the barley is tender.

The soup can be prepared ahead to this point. Reheat over low heat and watch carefully that it does not stick. If the soup gets too thick, add a little water.

Add the escarole and simmer 10 minutes longer. Just before serving, remove the bay leaf and stir in the black pepper.

A Big, Thick Beef Barley Soup

Makes about 2 quarts.

Winter tip: After a snowstorm, put this soup on to simmer before going outdoors to shovel the walk or make a snowman. It's thick and hearty enough to be a one-pot meal. Serve lots of good rye bread on the side.

*1 thick slice of lean beef shin with
marrowbone, about 2 pounds, or
one 2-pound piece of fresh beef brisket*

2 tablespoons olive oil

1 large onion, chopped

2 cloves garlic, minced

*2 large carrots, peeled and
cut into diagonal chunks*

1½ quarts water

1 cup tomato purée

1 teaspoon celery salt

¾ cup barley, rinsed

2 cups loosely packed chopped cabbage

½ teaspoon ground black pepper

*one 10-ounce package frozen Italian green
beans, thawed just enough to separate, or
½ pound fresh green beans, sliced and
steamed until tender-crisp, 5 to 7 minutes*

Trim the shin meat or brisket of any visible
fat. Heat the oil in a very large pot and brown
the meat very well on both sides. When the
second side is brown, add the onion and garlic, and fry until the vegetables are soft.

Add the carrots, water, tomato purée, and
celery salt. Bring to a boil, reduce the heat,
and simmer, covered, for about 1½ hours, until the meat is nearly tender.

Add the barley and cabbage. Simmer another 45 minutes, covered, stirring occasionally. *The soup can be prepared ahead to this
point. Reheat over low heat and watch carefully that it does not stick. If the soup gets too
thick, add a little water.*

Remove the meat with a slotted spoon.
Add the black pepper and green beans. Bring

to a boil, turn off the heat, cover, and let stand
5 minutes. The remaining heat will cook the
unthawed green beans.

Dice the meat, discarding the bone and
gristle, and stir the beef into the soup.

Cockaleekie

Makes 4 servings.

Traditionally, this Scottish stew is made with
a tough old fowl that needs hours of cooking.
This version, however, made with skinless
chicken breasts, is quick-cooking and practically fatless. Prunes are a traditional addition,
but you may omit them, if you wish—the stew
is tasty either way.

2 whole skinned, boneless chicken breasts

2 tablespoons vegetable oil

4 leeks, white part only

2 cups water

½ cup pearl barley, rinsed and drained

1 bay leaf

½ teaspoon salt

*¼ teaspoon each dried thyme and
white pepper*

*8 whole pitted prunes (optional,
but traditional)*

2 tablespoons minced fresh parsley

Preheat the oven to 400° F. Cut each chicken breast into 4 pieces lengthwise. In a Dutch oven, brown the chicken pieces, a few at a time, in the oil. Remove the chicken.

Cut the leeks in half lengthwise and wash them well; chop them. Sauté the leeks in the Dutch oven until they are limp and lightly browned. Return the chicken to the pan and add the remaining ingredients, except the prunes and parsley.

Bring to a boil, cover, and place in oven. Bake 30 minutes. Add the optional prunes. Bake an additional 15 minutes, or until the barley is tender but still al dente. The chicken should be cooked through.

The stew can be prepared ahead and reheated in a microwave in a glass casserole for a few minutes (time varies depending on oven wattage and coldness of the dish) or in a conventional oven for about 30 minutes at 350° F.

Remove the bay leaf, sprinkle with parsley, and serve.

Lobster and Barley Salad

Makes 4 servings.

Barley al dente is the base for this piquant salad, complemented by the slightly bitter flavor of chicory.

1 cup barley, rinsed and drained
½ cup olive oil
¼ cup lemon juice
½ teaspoon salt
¼ teaspoon each dried tarragon, cayenne pepper, and paprika
2 tablespoons minced fresh flat-leafed parsley
4 scallions, including green tops, chopped
2 cups diced lobster meat (8 large claws)
about 6 leaves of chicory

Cook the barley in 2 quarts of boiling salted water until the grains are tender but not mushy, about 35 minutes. Drain and rinse in cold water.

Stir together the oil, lemon juice, salt, tarragon, cayenne pepper, and paprika. Mix well with the barley. Cool. Stir in the parsley and scallions, then the lobster. Chill the salad for 2 or 3 hours to allow the flavors to blend before serving. Let stand at room temperature 20 minutes (no longer) before serving.

Line 4 salad plates with chicory torn into bite-size pieces and divide the salad among the plates.

Microwave Barley Pilaf

Makes 4 servings.

If you think barley has to be mushy, here's a dish that will change your mind.

2 tablespoons olive oil

1 onion, chopped

1 sweet red pepper, seeded and finely diced

¾ cup pearl barley, rinsed and drained

1½ cups beef broth or prepared bouillon

Heat the oil in a medium skillet, and sauté the onion and pepper until softened. Add the barley and sauté 1 minute more.

Spoon the mixture into a 2-quart casserole. In a saucepan, bring the broth to the boiling point and then add it to the barley. Cover the casserole and microwave on high for about 8 minutes, until bubbly. Continue cooking on medium for about 30 minutes, or until all the broth is absorbed and the barley is tender but still crunchy. *The pilaf can be made ahead and reheated in the microwave for about 5 minutes.*

Barley with Green Beans Parmesan

Makes 4 servings.

Besides being a good source of fiber and potassium, green beans are rich in iron, about 1 milligram per ½ cup of beans. Unfortunately, the market availability of good fresh green beans is uncertain. When the produce section offers only limp, spotted "fresh" green beans, it's better to buy the frozen product.

Frozen green beans can be used in place of fresh for almost any recipe *except* that crunchy favorite: basil-scented Summertime Green Bean and Onion Salad *(page 205).*

½ cup pearl barley, rinsed and drained

1 tablespoon olive oil

1 small onion, chopped

one 10-ounce package frozen Italian green beans or ½ pound fresh green beans, sliced and steamed until tender-crisp, 5 to 7 minutes

¼ teaspoon each dried oregano, dried basil, and freshly ground black pepper

2 tablespoons grated Parmesan cheese

1 tablespoon minced fresh flat-leafed parsley

2 tablespoons pine nuts, toasted

Cook the barley in 1 quart of boiling salted water until the grains are tender but not mushy, about 35 minutes. Drain.

Heat the oil in a saucepan; sauté the onion until it is softened. Add the green beans and cook according to the package directions. When the beans are done, stir in the oregano, basil, and pepper.

Combine the barley and green beans. Stir in the cheese and parsley.

Just before serving, toast the pine nuts and sprinkle them over the dish.

Note: Take the pine nuts from the toaster oven or broiler when they have barely turned color; they will continue to brown after you have removed them from the heat.

Barley Scones with Currants

Makes 6 servings.

These scones are equally delicious with morning coffee or afternoon tea. Barley flour has a subtly distinctive flavor, sweet and pleasant.

2 teaspoons white or cider vinegar

⅔ cup milk

¼ cup dried currants

2 cups barley flour (available in health food and "whole food" stores)

2 tablespoons sugar

2½ teaspoons baking powder

½ teaspoon salt

¼ teaspoon baking soda

¼ cup butter or low-cholesterol margarine

1 egg, beaten, or ¼ cup prepared egg substitute

Preheat the oven to 400° F. Butter well a 9-inch pie plate.

Stir the vinegar into the milk to sour it, and let the mixture stand for 10 minutes.

Plump the currants up by covering them with hot water for a few minutes. Drain.

Mix the dry ingredients together and cut the butter in with a pastry blender until the mixture resembles coarse crumbs. Stir in the drained currants.

Mix the egg with the milk and pour it all at once into a well in the dry ingredients. Stir to form a dough. If it seems too soft to handle, add a bit more flour.

Gently pat the dough into the prepared pan and bake on the top shelf for 20 minutes, or until the center is dry when tested with a cake tester. Do not overcook!

Let the cake stand a few minutes; then use a spatula to loosen it completely from the pan and slide it onto a dish.

Serve warm, cut into wedges, with a nice selection of jams on the side.

Quick-Mix Barley Spice Cake Loaf with Peaches

Makes 1 loaf.

No need to frost this sweet cake with its hidden bonus of barley fiber. Serve the loaf as a dessert or a snack.

1¾ cups barley flour

1 cup sugar

1 teaspoon each cinnamon and baking powder

½ teaspoon each ground ginger and salt

¼ teaspoon each ground nutmeg and ground cloves

2 egg whites

pinch of cream of tartar

2 egg yolks plus ½ cup milk or ¼ cup prepared egg substitute plus ⅓ cup milk

½ cup (1 stick) butter or low-cholesterol margarine, melted and cooled

½ cup snipped dried peaches

cinnamon sugar (see Basics)

Preheat the oven to 350° F. Butter and flour a loaf pan, approximately 8½ by 4½ by 3 inches. Line the bottom with buttered wax paper.

Sift together the barley flour, sugar, spices, baking powder, and salt into the large bowl of an electric mixer (or any large bowl, if beating by hand).

In the small bowl of an electric mixer (or any small, deep bowl), beat the egg whites until they are foamy. Add the cream of tartar and continue beating until stiff peaks form. Set these aside.

Make a well in the dry ingredients; add the egg yolks, milk, and melted butter. Beat for 4 minutes on medium speed or by hand 400 strokes. Fold in the egg whites. Stir in the peaches.

Spoon the batter into the prepared pan and sprinkle with cinnamon sugar. Bake on the middle shelf for 50 minutes or until a cake tester inserted at the center comes out dry. Don't test until the cake has risen and split and the split appears dry.

Cool in the pan for 5 minutes. Remove and finish cooling on the rack; peel off and discard the wax paper.

BERRIES

GOOD NUTRITION COMES IN SMALL PACKAGES. A short season makes each variety of fresh berry such an absolute luxury that it's hard to believe they're so good for you. Not only do berries help to prevent a number of illnesses, they're "nutrition dense"—as foods are called that give you more nutrients for fewer calories. A dieter's dream, berries taste rich but are low in calories. Blueberries have the most, but that's only 87 per cup.

As an overall benefit, berries are chock-full of the fiber pectin, which reduces cholesterol and thus helps to prevent damage to the blood vessels. In addition, each berry has its own special niche in preventive medicine.

The therapeutic value of cranberries may be the most well known; cranberry juice has been a folk remedy for infections of the bladder and urinary tract for many years. Some scientists have decided that the amount of quinic acid and vitamin C in cranberry juice, although mildly effective, isn't enough to thwart a urinary infection unless you drink gallons of it. But recent studies suggest that cranberries work in a different way; they seem to prevent bacteria from clinging to the inside of the bladder and urinary tract. More recently still, some studies have indicated that blueberries may also have this effect. Cranberries and blueberries should be thought of as possible preventive measures in warding off urinary problems, not as a substitute for antibiotics once an infection has begun.

Cranberries, as well as strawberries and raspberries, are a great source of vitamin C to build immunity and speed wound healing. American sailors used to take barrels of cranberries to sea with them to ward off scurvy, just as English sailors stocked limes.

Blueberries, along with black currants,

are best known as a folk remedy for diarrhea. These two berries also contain high amounts of chemicals that act against bacteria and viruses and that help to counteract the damage caused by a high-cholesterol diet. (Black currants should not be confused with dried currants; the latter are similar to raisins, only smaller, made from tiny seedless grapes.) Fresh black currants are hardly ever found in the supermarket, but black currant preserve is a thick berry jam that's delicious on muffins, stirred into plain yogurt, or as an ingredient in sauces.

An animal study published in Britain in the 1940s concluded that raspberries contain a uterine relaxant, and this finding was confirmed by follow-up studies. A tea made from the leaves of raspberries and sold with other herbal teas is used to relieve morning sickness or uterine cramps.

A study of more than 1,000 elderly residents of New Jersey turned up an interesting fact about strawberries. The analysis of eating habits showed that people who consumed the most strawberries were least likely to die of cancer. Other superfoods were also linked to a low incidence of cancer, but strawberries and tomatoes topped the list. In a separate study, strawberries were found to block the formation of cancer-causing nitrosamines in the intestinal tract.

In the Market

In buying any kind of berry, look for a good bright color and the characteristic odor indicating ripeness. Stained cardboard containers are a warning of possible overripeness in soft berries, such as raspberries and strawberries. Of course, none of the berries in the carton you select should show traces of mold.

Strawberries, a cheering sign of spring, are usually in the market by Easter. I always plan an Easter dessert around strawberries to celebrate the season. Since they don't continue to ripen after picking, those greenish white strawberries often hidden beneath the pretty ones will never become red and sweet. Peer through the holes at the bottoms of cartons to spot those that have been stuffed with the underripe and useless berries. Strawberries should still have their caps when you buy them.

But raspberries should not have caps; when raspberries are picked at full ripeness, the caps detach. Midsummer is their prime season. Because they're expensive and easily crushed, raspberries are sold in tiny half-pint containers. If you love raspberries and have room for a couple of bushes in the backyard, they are easy to grow. The only problem is that they're quite invasive and will strive to take over the world. The raspberry bushes I planted along a fence have had to be rooted out of my vegetable patch and have come up in my neighbors' yard as well; fortunately, they enjoy raspberries, too.

Blueberries are the late-summer berry. Cultivated varieties can be rather large (and often cost more), but small wild blueberries, sometimes available in August, have the best flavor and make superior muffins and pies.

Cranberries come to market in September and November. They're hardy berries that will keep two weeks or more in the refrigerator and for months in the freezer. For years cranberries were sold in one-pound packages. Consequently, many older recipes call for a pound of cranberries. Recently, however, the package has shrunk to 10 or 12 ounces, so adjustments must be made. (This is the same marketing technique that coffee manufacturers have used with great success: Rather than raise the price, make the package smaller. Later, of course, the price does go up. Consumers are not supposed to notice that they're now paying more for less.)

In the Kitchen

Ideally, berries shouldn't be washed until you're ready to use them. But if you want to wash strawberries before refrigerating them (so that they'll be ready for snackers) the best way to store them is in plastic open-weave baskets saved from other berry purchases or in perforated berry cartons, not too many layers deep so that the berries won't be crushed. Place the containers on a flat dish or tray in the refrigerator to catch any draining (and staining) moisture. Unblemished strawberries should keep three days in the refrigerator.

Fresh blueberries will keep a week in the refrigerator or frozen at zero degrees for a year. Frozen blueberries can be added to muffin or griddle cake batter without thawing.

All berries can be frozen in loose pack (without sugar) and will usually keep their fresh flavor for many months. Once thawed, they will lose their shape and firmness, but they'll still be fine for pies and sauces. Since each berry's season is a limited one, freezing is a good way to enjoy them for a longer time, if you have the freezer space. To freeze berries, allow them to dry on paper towels after washing, then freeze them in one layer on a tray. After they are solidly frozen, scoop them into plastic bags, gently squeeze out the excess air, and seal. Two cups per batch is a useful size for storage.

Bagged cranberries can be frozen right in the bag; wash them before using in recipes.

Frozen whole unsweetened strawberries, blueberries, and raspberries are also available in the frozen foods section of the supermarket. These excellent products help to extend the short periods of availability.

Use extreme care in washing raspberries; they can fall apart under water pressure or rough handling. Raspberries must be used as soon as possible after purchase.

All varieties of berries need to be picked over carefully. The easiest way to do this is to spill them onto a large tray *before* washing them and discard any that are spoiled or seriously underripe.

Fresh berries, when they are perfectly ripe, are wonderful just as they are. Strawberries, with their hulls still on, can be served for dessert with a little dish of vanilla sugar *(see Basics)* for dipping. A wedge of Brie cheese surrounded by red strawberries is an eye-catching appetizer. A little Chambord poured over plain raspberries in a stemmed goblet makes an elegant dessert. Chopped raw cranberries with orange and sugar is the basis of a tangy quick relish. And dry cereal, of course, is considerably enlivened by a few spoonfuls of blueberries.

But berries also can contribute their sweet acidic flavors to a number of other dishes, such as Homey Chicken Stew with Blueberry Dumplings. Enjoy them all— they're berry good for you!

Cranberry-and-Orange-Stuffed Rock Cornish Hens

Makes 4 servings.

*4 Rock Cornish hens, small enough to be
1 serving each, or 2 large hens to split*

*½ seedless orange with peel, preferably
organically grown*

1 cup raw cranberries, picked over

1 tablespoon sugar

*1 cup herb stuffing mix (not the
stovetop variety)*

*about 1 teaspoon each thyme leaves
and paprika*

*1 orange sliced into thin rounds
for garnishing*

Preheat the oven to 375° F. Wash the hens in cold salted water and drain. Remove and reserve any fat in the cavity.

In a food processor, grind the half-orange, peel and all, very fine. Add the cranberries and sugar, and process until the cranberries are chopped. Remove the fruit to a bowl and mix it with the herb stuffing. (There is no need to add any butter.)

Divide the stuffing between the hens, tie the legs together with twine, and place the birds in a baking dish. Sprinkle them liberally with the thyme and paprika. Fix the fat from the cavities on top of the hens, using toothpicks or skewers.

Place the baking dish on the middle shelf of the oven. As the fat melts, brush it over the birds during cooking, basting them about 3 times. Roast the smaller birds for 1 hour and 15 minutes, the larger for 1 hour and 30 minutes, or until juices run clear when the thigh is pierced.

Garnish with orange slices before serving. If you're using the larger birds, they will split cleanly with a sharp carving knife. Serve them cut sides down.

Homey Chicken Stew with Blueberry Dumplings

*Makes 4 generous servings
with extra dumplings.*

Using chicken breasts, instead of a cut-up fryer, brings this delectable low-fat stew to the table in short order.

*2 tablespoons olive oil
2 whole skinned chicken breasts cut
into 4 pieces each
1 large onion, chopped
one 13-ounce can chicken broth
4 potatoes, peeled and halved
3 large carrots, cut into 4 pieces each
1 bay leaf
1 teaspoon dried marjoram leaves
½ cup cold water
2 tablespoons flour
paprika*

For the dumplings:

*1½ cups sifted unbleached
all-purpose flour
2 teaspoons baking powder
½ teaspoon each baking soda and salt
¼ teaspoon nutmeg
½ cup milk
1 egg or ¼ cup prepared egg substitute
2 tablespoons vegetable oil
1 tablespoon lemon juice*

*¾ cup blueberries, fresh or frozen
(need not be thawed)*

Heat the olive oil in a 12-inch skillet and brown the chicken pieces over medium-high heat. When the second side is brown, add the onion and fry until the pieces of onion are wilted.

Add the broth, potatoes, carrots, bay leaf, and marjoram. Simmer the stew, covered, for 15 minutes, or until the vegetables are just tender. *The stew can be prepared ahead to this point and reheated to a simmer in the skillet.*

Meanwhile, sift the dry ingredients for the dumplings into a medium-size bowl. In another bowl, beat together the liquid ingredients. Measure the blueberries. Reserve these ingredients unmixed until you're ready to finish the dumplings.

In a small jar, combine the cold water and 2 tablespoons of flour, cover, and shake briskly until there are no lumps. Pour all at once into the simmering stew, and stir well until the gravy bubbles and thickens.

Mix the liquid ingredients for the dumplings into the dry, stirring until just blended. Fold in the blueberries.

Spoon the dumpling batter by tablespoons over the stew. Sprinkle with paprika. Bring the gravy to a boil and reduce heat until it is just simmering. Immediately cover and cook without lifting the cover for 15 minutes. The dumplings should be dry inside when tested with a cake tester.

Oven-Fried Chicken with Hot Cranberry-Dijon Sauce

Makes 4 servings.

Fried chicken is a real "comfort food" after a rough day. This low-fat way of "frying" leg quarters is just as crusty and tasty as traditional fried chicken.

olive oil

4 chicken legs with thighs attached, skinned

2 peeled, crushed cloves garlic

For the chicken coating:

½ cup fine dry breadcrumbs

2 tablespoons toasted wheat germ

2 tablespoons grated Parmesan cheese

½ teaspoon paprika

¼ teaspoon each dried oregano, rosemary, and thyme

salt and pepper to taste

For the sauce:

one 9-ounce can jellied cranberry sauce

2 tablespoons Dijon mustard

juice of 2 limes

Preheat the oven to 375° F. Mix together the coating ingredients. Put them in a plastic bag.

One at a time, put each quarter in the bag, close it tightly, and shake well to coat the chicken on all sides. Discard any leftover crumbs.

Coat a baking sheet with olive oil. Lay the chicken, rounded side down, and the garlic on it. Bake for 25 minutes on the top shelf. Carefully loosen the chicken with a spatula, keeping the crust intact, and turn it over. Bake for an additional 20 minutes or more, until cooked through. Cooking time depends on the size of the leg quarters, which can vary considerably.

Meanwhile, make the sauce. Heat the cranberry sauce in a saucepan (or in a microwave-safe quart measure in the microwave) until it's liquefied and boiling. Whisk in the mustard and lime juice. Serve the sauce hot in a gravy boat with the chicken.

Cran-Raspberry Sauce with Merlot

Makes 4 to 4½ cups.

Merlot is a dry red wine with a pleasantly fruity taste that goes perfectly with these two tart berries. Serve the sauce as an accompaniment to any roasted meat.

Note: When wine is cooked, it loses its alcoholic content, but water can be substituted.

*one 12- to 13-ounce bag of
fresh cranberries*

*2 cups frozen, unsweetened whole
raspberries (about ⅔ of a 12-ounce bag—
save the rest for a fruit cup)*

1 cup Merlot wine

¾ cup sugar

Pick over the cranberries, removing any soft
or spoiled berries; wash and drain the cranberries.

Combine all the ingredients in a saucepan
and bring the sauce to a boil, stirring until the
sugar has dissolved.

Simmer the sauce for 20 minutes, uncovered, stirring occasionally—more often toward the close of the cooking time, when the
sauce should be quite thick. If it's too thick to
simmer without sticking, it's done even if the
sauce hasn't simmered for quite 20 minutes.

Spoon the sauce into a bowl, and after it's
cooled a bit, refrigerate it for several hours.

Although it's a bit too soft for a fancy
mold, this sauce can be unmolded from a
plain bowl and will hold its shape. Run a knife
around the edge of the bowl, and dip the bowl
in hot water for a few seconds. Put a serving
plate on top and invert to unmold.

Strawberry Griddle Cakes

Makes 8 to 12 cakes.

If you invest a few minutes in making your
own griddle cake mix, you'll have all the convenience of the store-bought variety with the
super nutrition of fresh fruit and whole wheat.

*1¼ cups whole-grain griddle cake mix
(see Basics)*

¾ cup water

1 egg or ¼ cup prepared egg substitute

1 tablespoon melted butter

*1 cup strawberries (fresh or frozen
blueberries can be substituted)*

pure maple syrup

Stir the mix well and measure it into a
medium-size bowl.

Combine the water, egg, and butter; beat
until blended. Pour all at once into the mix,
stirring until smooth.

Heat nonstick griddle to 375° F. (or use a
cast-iron frying pan lightly coated with butter).

Quarter the berries lengthwise, unless
they are very large—in which case, slice
them. Fold the berries into the batter. Stir additional water, up to ¼ cup, into the batter if it
seems too thick; pancake batter should pour
thickly but readily off a spoon.

Cook the cakes until bubbles form on top.
Turn and brown on the second side.

Serve with maple syrup.

Open-Faced Strawberry Sandwiches

Makes about 24 sandwiches.

A very pretty addition to a sandwich buffet. They will disappear like magic!

2 Boston brown breads, preferably without raisins (buy canned brown breads or see page 283 and make your own, omitting raisins)

one 12-ounce package cream cheese (can be the "lite" variety) at room temperature

1 quart strawberries, washed and hulled

Thinly slice off the heels of the breads. Cut each bread into about 12 slices. Lay the slices on a large tray in one layer.

Spread cream cheese on the slices. Cover the cheese with strawberries sliced lengthwise. Press them down slightly. Cover the tray loosely with wax paper and chill the sandwiches until ready to serve.

Blueberry Corn Muffins

Makes 12 muffins.

All muffins can be baked ahead of time, frozen, and thawed in the microwave for a quick, convenient breakfast.

1½ cups sifted unbleached all-purpose flour

1¼ cups stone-ground cornmeal, fine grade, preferably not degerminated

½ cup sugar

1 tablespoon baking powder

½ teaspoon each cinnamon and salt

1¼ cups milk (low-fat can be used)

2 eggs, beaten, or ½ cup prepared egg substitute

⅓ cup vegetable oil

1 cup blueberries

cinnamon sugar (see Basics)

Line a 12-cup muffin pan with paper liners. Preheat the oven to 400° F.

Sift dry ingredients together twice, ending in a large bowl.

Mix together the milk, eggs, and oil.

Pour the liquid mixture into the dry ingredients. Mix just enough to blend. Fold in the blueberries. Divide the batter among the muffin cups; this will fill them to the top. Sprinkle with cinnamon sugar.

Bake in the top third of the oven for 20 minutes, or until they are lightly browned on top and dry inside.

Serve warm or at room temperature.

Finnish Berry Squares

Makes 8 servings.

Any mix of small berries can be used for this pastry, but fresh raspberries, when available, are particularly nice.

⅓ cup sugar (½ if berries are tart)
2 tablespoons cornstarch
2 cups fresh raspberries
1 cup fresh blueberries
pastry for 2-crust
pie (see Basics)
cinnamon sugar (see Basics)

Preheat the oven to 375° F. Mix together the sugar and cornstarch until well-blended. Sprinkle the mixture over the berries and toss them lightly with two forks to coat the berries without crushing them.

Divide the pastry in thirds. Roll out two-thirds of the pastry and fit it into a 10-by-7-by-1-inch baking pan, nonstick if possible, so that it overlaps the sides a bit. Spoon the berries into a layer over the pastry.

Roll out the remaining third of pastry into an oblong shape. Cut into strips to form a lattice top over the berries. Fold the edge of the bottom pastry over the ends of the lattice and pinch them together with the tines of a fork. Sprinkle the top with cinnamon sugar.

Bake in the middle of the oven for 45 to 50 minutes, or until the pastry is lightly browned and the filling is bubbling, not just at the edges of the pan but all the way to the center.

Cool in the pan on a wire rack. If you've used a nonstick pan, this pastry can be coaxed out whole onto a serving plate where it will look very pretty. Otherwise, cut it into squares in the pan.

Strawberry-Watermelon Sorbet

Makes about 1¾ quarts.

Replacing ice cream with fruit sorbet or frozen low-fat yogurt means you're *adding* good nutrition as well as *subtracting* cholesterol from your diet.

1 envelope unflavored gelatin
½ cup water
½ cup sugar
1 quart strawberries, hulled
3 cups loosely packed watermelon cubes,
seeded

In a small saucepan, sprinkle the gelatin over the water and let it soften for 5 minutes. Add the sugar, and stir over very low heat until the gelatin and sugar are dissolved.

Purée the strawberries in a food processor. Purée the watermelon. Combine the two and strain the mixture through a mesh strainer. Discard the remaining solids (which should be no more than ½ cup) and pour the fruit into the container of an ice-cream maker. Stir in the gelatin mixture.

Freeze the sorbet according to the manufacturer's instructions.

Poached Pears with Fresh Raspberry Purée

Makes 6 servings.

A vanilla bean (cooked in syrup, not a milk pudding) can be rinsed, dried, and reused a number of times before it loses its essence. I store the beans in a pint jar of sugar *(see Basics)*, flavoring the sugar for use in custards and puddings.

3 cups water

1 cup sugar

1 vanilla bean

strips of orange peel and/or cinnamon stick (both optional)

6 pears

one 10-ounce package frozen, sweetened raspberries, thawed

Choose a deep pot in which the pears will fit in one layer, and make the syrup by combining the water and sugar and bringing the mixture to a boil; stir until the sugar dissolves. Add the vanilla bean, orange peel, and/or cinnamon stick, if using.

Peel the pears, keeping the stems intact. Add the pears to the syrup. If the pears are not covered, add water until they are. Simmer for 20 to 40 minutes (depending on ripeness) until tender. Cool in syrup.

Gently core the pears from the bottom, removing the seeds with a grapefruit spoon. Purée or mash the raspberries in their syrup. Divide the purée among dessert dishes and top each dish with a whole pear.

Spiced Blueberry and Apple Pie

Makes 6 to 8 servings.

A tasty combination, rich in fiber pectin!

¾ cup sugar (if the fruit is quite tart, use 1 cup)

¼ cup flour

½ teaspoon cinnamon

¼ teaspoon nutmeg

⅛ teaspoon each ground cloves and allspice

3 cooking apples, peeled and diced (not McIntosh)

1 pint fresh blueberries

pastry for a 2-crust pie (see Basics)

cinnamon sugar (see Basics)

Preheat the oven to 375° F.

Mix the sugar, flour, and spices until

blended. Stir in the apples and blueberries.

Divide the pastry dough in half, roll out the bottom crust, and fit it into a 9-inch pie pan. Spoon in the fruit filling. Roll out the top crust and lay it over. Trim and fold ½ inch of the top crust over the edge of the bottom crust. Crimp the edges with the tines of a fork. Cut vents in the middle of the pie to let steam escape. Sprinkle with cinnamon sugar.

Bake in the middle of the oven for 45 minutes to 1 hour. When the blueberry juice bubbles up all around (and probably runs over into the oven), allow the pie to cook 5 minutes more. Cool completely before cutting.

Strawberry-Almond Soufflé

Makes 6 servings.

This light soufflé is a cinch to make. The tricky part is timing it so that the soufflé is perfectly puffed and a thing of beauty just when you're ready to serve dessert.

*1 pint of strawberries, hulled and puréed
(about 1½ cups purée)*
⅓ cup sugar
3 tablespoons Amaretto (almond liqueur)
5 egg whites
⅛ teaspoon cream of tartar

Butter a 2-quart soufflé dish and dust it with sugar. Put the strawberry purée and sugar in a saucepan, and heat until the sugar is just dissolved. Stir in the liqueur.

In a large mixing bowl, beat the egg whites until foamy. Add the cream of tartar and continue to beat until the egg whites will hold stiff peaks. *At this point, you can cover and refrigerate the egg whites for an hour or so.*

Preheat the oven to 375° F.

Heat the purée in the saucepan to the simmering point. Pour the hot purée into the egg whites while beating at high speed until it's all incorporated. (The volume will expand, which is why a large bowl is needed.)

Spoon the mixture into the prepared soufflé dish and bake for 25 to 30 minutes, or until the soufflé is well puffed and browned on top. It will rise about 2 inches above the dish. Serve immediately!

Rosy Raspberry-Peach Pie

Makes 6 to 8 servings.

If you use frozen and canned fruit, this pie can be made when the snow flies!

When baking juicy pies, put them in the bottom third of the oven so that the bottom crust will be crisped before it gets soggy (pizza is baked the same way).

*two 1-pound cans peaches, packed
without sugar*
¼ cup sugar
1 tablespoon cornstarch
¼ cup water
1 cup frozen unsweetened whole raspberries
½ teaspoon almond extract
pastry for a 2-crust pie (see Basics)
*about 1 tablespoon unbeaten egg white or
prepared egg substitute*

Drain the peaches, reserving ½ cup of juice. Put the juice and the sugar in a medium saucepan, and heat it. Stir the cornstarch into the cold water until there are no lumps, and add it, all at once, to the juice, stirring constantly until the mixture bubbles and thickens. Remove it from the heat, and stir in the raspberries and almond extract. Gently stir in the peaches and then chill the filling while preparing the pastry.

Preheat the oven to 375° F. Roll out the bottom crust and fit it into a 9-inch pie pan. Paint the bottom crust with egg white or prepared egg substitute. Spoon in the filling. Roll out the top crust and lay it over. Trim and fold ½ inch of the top crust over the edge of the bottom crust. Pinch the edges together with the tines of a fork. Cut decorative vents in the middle of the pie to allow steam to escape. If using the egg substitute, paint it over the top crust, too; it makes a lovely glaze.

Bake the pie in the bottom third of the oven for 45 minutes, or until it is golden brown and the filling is bubbly.

Fresh Strawberries and Raspberries in Port

Makes 6 servings.

A perfectly simple and beautiful ending to a summer meal!

1 pint fresh strawberries
½ pint fresh raspberries
about 1 cup port

Cut the strawberries in half lengthwise (or in quarters if they're huge). Leave the raspberries whole. Combine the berries in a deep bowl. Pour the port over them, and marinate in the refrigerator for not less than 2 hours and not more than 4 hours. Stir occasionally.

Serve in stemmed wine glasses. Crisp chocolate cookies make an ideal accompaniment.

For other berry recipes, see the following: Beet Greens with Blueberries; Cantaloupe with Warm Blueberry Sauce; Cranberry Yogurt; Peach and Raspberry Cranachan; Pink Grapefruit with Raspberry Sauce; Strawberry Chambord Yogurt Parfaits; Steamed Sweet Potatoes with Poached Cranberries; Yogurt *Coeurs à la Crème*

BROCCOLI

A BUNCH OF HEALTH BEN-EFITS. Today it's America's favorite vegetable. Statistics show that broccoli consumption increased 800 percent between 1970 and 1989. Yet only a few decades ago, broccoli was found chiefly in the gardens and kitchens of Italian immigrants. When my husband and I were traveling by train in Italy, looking at the back gardens along the way, we always saw roses and broccoli, sometimes in the same row, the decorative green heads tucked into available spaces between the flower bushes. Although it's sometimes called "the poor man's asparagus," broccoli was the king of vegetables at Roman banquets. It was served up in many guises, the most popular being simply sautéed with cumin, coriander, onions, oil, and wine.

Broccoli has at least five important health benefits—and who knows how many more that we haven't discovered yet! First, as a cruciferous vegetable, it fights against stomach and colon cancer. Second, as a dark green vegetable loaded with carotenoids, it helps to prevent lung and related cancers, even among smokers. In fact, statistically, people who eat broccoli often have lower rates of all cancers. In animal experiments, broccoli has even protected guinea pigs against the effects of radiation. Third, a cup of cooked broccoli contains twice as much vitamin C, for all-around healing, as the recommended dietary allowance. Fourth, it's one of the best vegetable sources of calcium, which may help to prevent bone deterioration in older women as well as to promote healthy bones and teeth for everyone. And unlike the many dairy products that we may think of first in relation to calcium, there's practically no fat in broccoli. And fifth, broccoli packs in plenty of heart-protecting potassium, too.

Broccoli's reputation as a cancer fighter was first noted through statistical studies that compared what people ate with their rates of developing cancer. But recently, we have learned *why* this is so. Researchers at the Johns Hopkins University School of Medicine have isolated a substance in vegetables that increases the activity of enzymes in the cell that protect against tumors. This chemical, called sulforaphane, is found most abundantly in broccoli and other cruciferous vegetables, as well as in carrots and green onions.

Luckily, we can enjoy broccoli in appetizers, soups, stir-frys, pasta dishes, salads, pizzas, and breads—yes, even in sandwiches such as the vegetable pita pocket being seen on more and more restaurant lunch menus as an alternative to the fat-drenched burger.

In the Market

Good fresh broccoli is available in the fall and spring. Broccoli heads should be bright green, perhaps with a purplish haze, the buds tightly closed—never buy broccoli that shows a trace of yellow, a sure sign that the bunch is past its prime. Examine the stalks, too; porous and woody stalks mean the vegetable will be tough and tasteless. Avoid any broccoli that has a pronounced odor.

When broccoli is out of season, the frozen vegetable is a good product, although it will lack that desirable crunch. Frozen broccoli comes in four forms. *Short spears* offer the best quality, florets with a small portion of stalk. *Whole spears* are next best, with just about the same proportion of stalk to floret as you would get in a fresh bunch. *Broccoli cuts* contain larger pieces of both, but with a higher proportion of stalks, and *chopped broccoli* is largely stalks.

In the Kitchen

For storage, remove any wire twisted around the broccoli, wrap the bunch in a cloth (not terry) dishtowel, and put a plastic bag over that. Don't tie the bag shut. You can store broccoli this way for three days in the bottom of your refrigerator. If you have the refrigerator space, an even better way (which I always use for asparagus) is to treat it like a bunch of flowers. Slice off the ends of the stalks and stand them in a pitcher with about two inches of water, loosely cover the head with a plastic bag, and refrigerate.

For best taste, cooked broccoli should still be crunchy, not overcooked until it's limp and pale. Peeling the stalks helps them to cook in the same short time as the florets, thus eliminating the usual cause of overcooking. Fresh broccoli properly cooked will not be strongly flavored.

Eating broccoli four to five times a week is just right from a health standpoint, but it would be rather boring if we didn't vary the presentation. Serve broccoli in different forms and combinations, in different courses, taking advantage of its capacity for infinite variety. It's truly a five-star superfood! ■

To Steam or Blanch Fresh Broccoli

Cooked fresh broccoli is an ingredient in several of the recipes that follow. It can be steamed or blanched, but steaming is the best choice because it preserves more of broccoli's important potassium.

Wash the broccoli and peel the stalks. Cut off the florets. Cut the stalks into ½-inch pieces. If the florets are large, cut them in half lengthwise.

To steam: Bring an inch of water to boil in a steamer. Put the broccoli in the steamer basket, with the stalks on the bottom and the florets on top. Cover and steam until tender-crisp, about 6 minutes. Rinse in cold water to stop cooking action.

To blanch: Fill a large pot halfway with water and bring it to a boil. Cook the broccoli in the boiling water until tender-crisp, 2 to 3 minutes. Drain and rinse in cold water to stop cooking action.

It's important not to overcook broccoli that will be subject to additional cooking in these recipes.

Cream of Broccoli Soup with Smoked Turkey and Shiitake Mushrooms

Makes 4 servings.

Rich flavors lift this above ordinary broccoli soup (especially the canned variety with its too-salty flavor and anemic bits of vegetable).

> *two 13-ounce cans chicken broth, preferably low-salt*
> *2 cups cooked broccoli or frozen broccoli cuts, thawed to separate*
> *¼ cup dry white wine*
> *¼ teaspoon each dried basil, marjoram, and freshly ground black pepper*
> *2 tablespoons olive oil*
> *2 large shallots, minced*
> *4 fresh shiitake mushrooms, diced fine*
> *¼ cup flour*
> *one 12-ounce can evaporated skim milk*
> *3 ounces smoked turkey, slivered*

Combine the broth, broccoli, wine, and seasonings in a large saucepan. Bring to a boil, reduce the heat, and simmer for 5 minutes. With a slotted spoon, scoop out 12 broccoli florets and reserve them.

In a small skillet, heat the oil, and sauté the shallots and mushrooms until the mushrooms are tender.

In a food processor or blender, purée the mixture. If you're using a blender, do this step in two batches. Hot soup will foam up double while being puréed. *The soup can be made ahead to this point.*

Return the purée to the saucepan and bring it to a simmer. Combine the flour and milk in a pint jar, cover the jar, and shake it briskly until there are no lumps. If necessary, strain it through a tea strainer. Pour the flour mixture into the soup while stirring constantly. When the soup bubbles and thickens, simmer it for 5 minutes, stirring occasionally, to cook the flour.

Stir in the shallots, mushrooms, reserved florets, and smoked turkey. Simmer 2 more minutes before serving.

Broccoli Tetrazzini

Makes 6 servings.

This dish is particularly delectable made with prosciutto, but a half-pound of the more traditional slivered cooked turkey or chicken can be substituted. Sautéed mushrooms are another possibility. Whichever you use, a bright, acidic salad, such as one of the tomato salads *(pages 270-273)* or Orange and Onion Salad *(page 97)*, makes a harmonious accompaniment.

When preparing this dish, make the sauce first, so that you won't find yourself trying to finish the sauce and drain the linguine at the same time.

2½ tablespoons low-cholesterol margarine

2 large shallots, minced

3 tablespoons flour

2 cups milk (can be low-fat)

¼ teaspoon each tarragon, salt, and white pepper

¼ pound prosciutto (or ½ pound cooked turkey or chicken), slivered

½ pound thin linguine, cooked according to package directions

1½ pounds fresh broccoli, cooked according to the directions on page 56 (about 4 cups cooked)

1 cup fresh breadcrumbs

2 tablespoons grated Parmesan cheese

paprika

In a medium saucepan, melt the margarine and sauté the shallots until they have softened. Stir in the flour and cook the roux over low heat for 3 minutes, but don't brown it.

Heat the milk to scalding separately; this can be done most easily in the microwave in a microwaveable measuring pitcher, 4 to 5 minutes on high.

Pour the hot milk all at once into the roux, stirring constantly over medium heat until the sauce is bubbling. Lower heat and simmer 2 minutes. Stir in the tarragon, salt, and pepper; whisk until smooth. *The sauce can be cooked up to this point and held at room temperature, but no longer than 1 hour.*

Preheat the oven to 350° F.

Stir the prosciutto (or turkey or chicken) into the sauce.

Cook the linguine. Stir 1 cup of the sauce

into the linguine. Layer half the linguine into an oblong baking dish, 2-quart capacity. Top with all the broccoli, then the rest of the linguine. Smooth the mixture with a spatula, pressing down lightly. Pour over the remaining sauce.

Sprinkle with fresh breadcrumbs, cheese, and paprika. Bake 30 minutes, until brown and bubbly.

Let stand 10 minutes. To serve, cut into squares, like lasagna.

Skillet Cacciatore for Two, with Broccoli

Makes 2 hearty servings.

Italian cacciatore, a hunter's stew, and Japanese sukiyaki, which means "broiled on the blade of a plow," are similar in origin—they both were meant to be cooked outdoors, quickly and simply, with the foods at hand, including vegetables. An American version of cacciatore, in which a cut-up chicken is drowned in tomato sauce and stewed rather than braised, loses the spirit of the original.

I have to admit, though, that adding broccoli is a new twist. This version of cacciatore makes a complete meal in one skillet that needs only the addition of a good fresh bread to dip in the juices.

2 chicken legs and 2 thighs, skinned
2 tablespoons olive oil
1 green pepper, seeded and chunked
1 medium onion, sliced
1 clove garlic, minced (not pressed)
1 dried whole hot red pepper (cayenne; available in specialty stores and some supermarkets)
⅓ cup dry white wine
4 to 5 drained canned Italian-style tomatoes (about the contents of a 16-ounce can)
½ teaspoon each dried oregano and basil
salt and freshly ground black pepper to taste
one 10-ounce package frozen broccoli spears, thawed to separate
2 tablespoons chopped fresh flat-leafed parsley

Pat the chicken pieces dry to avoid splattering the range top when you fry them. Heat the oil in a large skillet and brown the chicken pieces on both sides over medium-high heat.

When the meat is well-browned, lower the heat, add the green pepper, onion, garlic, and hot red pepper to the pan, and sauté, stirring for a minute or two, until the vegetables are sizzling.

Add the wine, which will boil up and deglaze the pan, and continue cooking, stirring occasionally until it has almost evaporated.

Add the tomatoes, cutting each in half, oregano, basil, salt, and pepper. Cook over medium heat, stirring frequently and turning the chicken at least once, until the pieces are very well cooked, about 20 minutes longer.

Add the broccoli to the skillet, tucking the spears around the chicken pieces, and simmer until the vegetable is just tender-crisp.

Remove the dried red pepper, sprinkle with parsley, and serve.

Note: If you forget to let the broccoli thaw to separate, you can do so quickly under running cool water. Drain well.

Lemon-Scented Broccoli Risotto

Makes 4 servings.

One of the nice things about a microwave is the way it takes the mystique—and the constant stirring—out of preparing a perfect risotto. But if you don't have a microwave, follow the alternative directions.

one 10-ounce package frozen broccoli spears or 2 cups fresh broccoli, florets and ½-inch-thick sliced stalks

3 tablespoons olive oil

1 clove garlic, pressed

1 large onion, chopped

1 cup Arborio rice

one 13-ounce can chicken broth

1 tablespoon lemon juice

½ teaspoon grated lemon zest

⅓ cup freshly grated Parmesan cheese

Cook the frozen broccoli according to package directions, adding 1 tablespoon of the olive oil and the garlic to the cooking water. Cut the broccoli stalks into 4 pieces each. Or cook fresh broccoli with oil, garlic, and ¼ cup water, covered, until tender-crisp, 3 to 5 minutes.

In a saucepan, heat the broth and have it ready at a low simmer.

In a 3-quart casserole, microwave the onion in 2 tablespoons of olive oil on high for 3 minutes, or until it's soft. Add the rice, and stir well to coat it with the flavored oil. Add the hot broth, lemon juice, and grated rind. Cover and microwave on high for 6 to 7 minutes, until boiling. Change the setting to medium and continue to cook for about 10 minutes, until the rice is just tender and the liquid has been absorbed.

Stir in the broccoli with its juices. Blend in the cheese. Cover and let stand a few minutes before serving.

Alternative method: Sauté the onion in a medium-size saucepan and stir in the rice. Add about 1 cup of the hot broth and cook at a low boil (but not as low as a simmer), uncovered, stirring frequently, until the liquid is almost all absorbed. Add half the remaining broth and repeat the procedure. Pour in the last of the broth and cook until the rice is tender. Total cooking time should be 12 to 14 minutes. Add the broccoli and cheese.

Broccoli and Ziti Casserole

Makes 6 servings.

My favorite kind of dish—it can be prepared ahead of time and has all the nutritional components needed for a complete one-dish meal. This colorful casserole also makes an easy addition to a buffet. Served as the main course of a dinner, it may be accompanied with a tossed green salad and fresh Italian bread.

¼ cup olive oil

1 clove garlic, minced

1½ pounds fresh broccoli, cooked according to the directions on page 56 (about 4 cups cooked)

2 cups Italian tomato sauce (from a jar or either of the two tomato sauces given in Basics)

½ pound ziti, cooked according to package directions

¼ cup Parmesan cheese

1 pound low-fat ricotta cheese

¼ cup seasoned breadcrumbs

2 tablespoons toasted wheat germ

Heat the olive oil in a skillet; sauté the garlic until softened but not brown. Stir the broccoli into the garlic oil and set it aside.

In a large oblong casserole, layer half the tomato sauce, half the ziti, half the Parmesan cheese, all the broccoli, all the ricotta, the remaining ziti, the remaining sauce, crumbs, wheat germ, and the remaining Parmesan.

Cover and bake for 35 minutes in a preheated 350° F. oven (10 minutes longer if the dish has been refrigerated before cooking). Uncover during the last 15 minutes of cooking. The sauce should be bubbly and the top lightly browned.

Broccoli and Wild Rice Casserole

Makes 4 servings as an entrée, 6 as a side dish.

Wild rice, the seed of a North American aquatic grass, was first harvested by Native Americans. The complementary flavors and fiber content of wild and brown rice make them good additions to a healthy diet.

½ cup wild rice

½ cup brown rice

2 teaspoons olive oil

½ teaspoon salt

2 cups mornay sauce (see Basics)

1½ pounds fresh broccoli, cooked according to the directions on page 56 (about 4 cups cooked)

Bring 3 quarts water to a boil in a 4-quart pan. Add both kinds of rice, olive oil, and salt. Maintain a steady low boil (higher than a simmer) for 40 to 45 minutes, stirring occasionally, until rice is al dente. Drain the rice.

Pour ⅔ cup mornay sauce into a 3-quart baking pan or casserole. Layer all the rice over it and top with the broccoli. Drizzle the remaining mornay sauce over the casserole so that all the broccoli is coated. *The casserole can be prepared ahead and refrigerated for 1 to 2 hours.*

Preheat the oven to 350° F. Bake the casserole for 30 minutes (10 minutes longer if prepared ahead and chilled).

Note: A layer of sautéed mushrooms between the rice and the broccoli is a nice touch.

Broccoli with Mushrooms and Lemon-Pepper

Makes 6 or more servings.

Lemon is wonderful on broccoli (as it is on all vegetables), but unfortunately, lemon juice fades broccoli's beautiful bright green color, so this dish uses the grated zest instead. It's so flavorful, no salt is called for in the recipe.

about 12 ounces brown mushrooms, such as portobello
1 large yellow onion, chopped
¼ cup olive oil
2 cloves pressed garlic
1½ pounds fresh broccoli, cooked according to the directions on page 56 (about 4 cups cooked)
1 teaspoon grated lemon zest
¼ teaspoon (or more, to taste) freshly ground black pepper
¼ teaspoon oregano
lemon wedges for garnish

Wash the mushrooms, shake them dry (a salad spinner works well for this), and cut them in half or in slices if they are large. In a large skillet, fry the mushrooms and onion in the oil over medium-high heat, stirring often, until the mushrooms begin to brown. Stir in the pressed garlic and turn off the heat.

Stir the broccoli into the mushrooms. Sprinkle with grated lemon zest, separating the strands with your fingers so that there are no lumps. Add the pepper and oregano and stir well so that the seasonings are mixed throughout.

Garnish each serving with a lemon wedge. I like this dish best served at room temperature, but it can also be served hot or cold. Try any leftovers in a pita pocket for lunch.

Broccoli Corn Bread

Makes 8 servings.

Especially good with chicken! I like to make this bread in a cast-iron frying pan, which gives it a nice crusty bottom. To have the best of both worlds, flavor the crust by greasing the pan with a little butter and then use no-cholesterol vegetable oil in the batter.

1 cup stone-ground cornmeal, preferably not degerminated

1 cup unbleached all-purpose flour

1 tablespoon baking powder

1 teaspoon salt

1 cup milk

1 egg or ¼ cup prepared egg substitute

¼ cup vegetable oil

1 tablespoon butter

2½ cups frozen broccoli cuts, thawed, uncooked

½ cup chopped onion (1 medium)

Preheat the oven to 400° F. Sift the cornmeal, flour, baking powder, and salt into a large bowl. In another bowl, beat the milk, egg, or egg substitute, and oil.

Put the butter in a 10-inch cast-iron frying pan over low heat until it is sizzling.

Pour the liquid mixture into the dry ingredients; stir just enough to blend. Fold in the vegetables.

Spoon the batter into the hot pan. Bake in the top third of the oven for 35 minutes, or until lightly browned on top and dry inside.

Two-Crust Whole-Wheat Broccoli Pizza

Makes 6 servings.

Pizza means "pie," and the crusty exterior of this two-crust pie conceals a melting heart of cheese, tomatoes, and broccoli! The recipe may seem complicated, but once you get used to making pizza dough in a food processor, it's really a cinch and takes no more than 10 minutes to mix and knead.

1 sweet red pepper, seeded, cut into rings

olive oil

For the dough:

1 package yeast

1 teaspoon sugar

1 cup plus 2 tablespoons very warm water

2 cups whole-wheat flour

1½ cups unbleached all-purpose flour
¾ teaspoon salt
2 tablespoons olive oil

For the filling:

½ pound deli-sliced mozzarella
1½ pounds fresh broccoli, cooked according to the directions on page 56 (about 4 cups)
1½ cups tomato sauce (from a jar or either of the two tomato sauces given in Basics)
2 tablespoons grated Parmesan cheese

Stir the yeast and sugar into the warm water. Let the mixture stand for 5 minutes; the yeast should bubble up to show that it's active.

Combine the flours and salt in the work bowl of a food processor fitted with a steel blade. Process just enough to blend. Coat a medium-size bowl with a little of the olive oil; pour the rest into the flour mixture. Process to blend. With the motor running, pour the yeast mixture down the feed tube. Process 10 to 15 seconds until the mixture forms a ball that cleans the sides of the work bowl. (If the flour does not adhere in a ball, add a little water, 1 teaspoon at a time.) Continue to process, counting 30 seconds, or until the dough is elastic and springy. Knead by hand just enough to smooth the surface.

Alternatively, the ingredients can be combined in a bowl, and the dough can be kneaded by an electric-mixer dough hook for 5 minutes or by hand for 10 minutes. The important signal is that the dough should spring back when pressed.

Place the dough ball in the oiled bowl and cover it with plastic wrap. Let it stand in a warm place until double in bulk, about 1 hour and 15 minutes.

Punch down the dough and divide it, making one half a little bigger. Oil a 10-inch-wide, 2-inch-deep baking pan (I use a 10-inch cast-iron frying pan). Roll out the larger piece to fit so that the dough comes up the sides with a ½ inch overhang.

Layer half the mozzarella on the bottom of the pie. Add all the broccoli; top with tomato sauce and Parmesan cheese. Finish with the remaining mozzarella.

Roll out the remaining dough to fit on top of the pie with an overhang. Pinch the dough together all around the edges and flute it. Brush the top with olive oil. Lay the red pepper rings on top, pressing them down slightly. Let the pizza stand for 30 minutes at room temperature.

Preheat the oven to 400° F.

Bake the pizza in the middle of the oven for 45 minutes, or until the top and bottom (lift with a spatula to check) are well-browned. Let the pizza rest 5 minutes; gently slice it with a serrated knife, and remove the slices with a spatula.

For other broccoli recipes, see the following: Fusilli with Broccoli, Sun-Dried Tomatoes, and Black Olives; Stir-Fry Pork with Supervegetables

CABBAGE AND BRUSSELS SPROUTS

BIG AND LITTLE DEFENDERS OF GOOD HEALTH. Kings of the cruciferous family, cabbage and Brussels sprouts help to defend the human body against illnesses in several ways.

First, as potent cancer fighters. Surveys of eating habits have revealed that those who eat the most cabbage (and its tiny cousin the Brussels sprout) have the least incidence of colon cancer, and in fact, the lowest rates of death from all diseases. In animal studies, cruciferous vegetables have been shown to ward off cancer formation, and more recent studies have suggested why this is so. Sulforaphane, a chemical found in high concentrations in cabbage and

Brussels sprouts, has been discovered to be an active ingredient in stimulating enzymes that guard against tumors.

And then there's the cabbage paradox. Although its sulfur content can cause gas distress in some people, fresh cabbage juice has proved to be effective in the prevention and treatment of ulcers.

In addition, cabbage is as rich as citrus fruits in vitamin C with all its protective and healing properties. Just one cup of shredded cabbage will give you two-thirds of the recommended dietary allowance of this important vitamin, which you need to consume on a daily basis because the human body is not able to store it.

Taking all this into consideration, an ordinary dish of coleslaw, with the great beta carotene in those shredded carrots, is a powerful preventive medicine—especially a home-made slaw with plenty of carrots to sweeten it instead of sugar and with an olive oil vinaigrette instead of gobs of mayonnaise. With the advent of the food processor, you can shred a whole head of cabbage plus three or four carrots in just a few minutes. This is one salad that tastes even better after it marinates and wilts a bit in the refrigerator. I consider coleslaw the quintessential sandwich companion and an absolute must with a baked bean supper.

Cabbage has always been considered a food of the common folk, but a dish of Brussels sprouts is the fare of royalty—the British royal family could hardly have a Christmas dinner without buttered sprouts, which although native to Belgium, have by adoption become as British as Yorkshire pudding. But don't wait for holidays to enjoy these tiny green cabbagy vegetables. They are chock-full of compounds that detoxify cancer-causing chemicals like aflatoxin (a fungal mold sometimes present on grains and nuts) and even guard against precancerous growths in the colon called polyps.

In the Market

If your idea of cabbage is a sodden slice of vegetable perched on a corned beef dinner, consider that there are several kinds of cabbage from which to choose. Besides the readily available, large, compact, light green head, there is also the slightly sweeter yet peppery red cabbage; the crinkly-leafed, mild-flavored Savoy from France; and cool, crunchy, elongated bok choy, a celery look-alike, also known as Chinese cabbage. And each of those can be multiplied to infinity by the number of ways they can be prepared.

The more delicate Savoy is at its best during the fall, but the bred-for-storage common green and red cabbages can be enjoyed all winter. Even bok choy, if it looks crisp and fresh, can be bought through January. In all varieties, look for bright, crisp leaves, and steer clear of wilted, yellowed leaves and signs of mold or worm damage.

Brussels sprouts, unlike the versatile cabbages, are always and only themselves. Fall and winter are their seasons; the rest of the year, frozen Brussels sprouts fill in nicely.

In the Kitchen

Green and red cabbages will keep quite well in your refrigerator for two weeks or more. Wrap the whole head of cabbage in paper towels and store it in a plastic bag, not tightly closed, in the crisper section, if it fits. Savoy and Chinese cabbage will keep about a week, given the same treatment.

There are innumerable ways to introduce more cabbage into your diet. Combine shredded Savoy with various kinds of lettuce in tossed green salads. Red cabbage, too, makes a nice color accent when tomatoes are scarce. Bok choy, of course, is a natural for stir-frys. Green cabbage is delightful in a quick sauté, but both green and red cabbage are also delicious in gentle, slow braises. Above all, enjoy different varieties of delightful coleslaws. Cabbage may be common, but it's uncommonly good for you. As some anonymous poet mused on cabbage's lowly state:

I wonder if the cabbage knows
He is less lovely than the rose;
Or does he squat in smug content,
A source of noble nourishment;
Or if he pities for her sins
The rose who has no vitamins.

Stir-Fry Pork with Cabbage and Other Supervegetables

Makes 4 servings.

Although the emphasis in this dish is on some terrific vegetables, I've found it appeals to the most finicky-about-vegetables people. Serve with plain hot rice, white or brown, and Hot Mustard Sauce *(see Basics).*

*4 boneless pork chops
(about 1¼ to 1½ pounds)*

*2 cups broccoli florets,
blanched for 3 minutes*

2 stalks celery, thinly sliced

1 large onion, thinly sliced

*2 sweet red peppers, seeded and cut into
triangle-shaped chunks*

*1 head of bok choy, thinly sliced
(about 4 cups)*

2 cups fresh bean sprouts, rinsed

about 3 tablespoons vegetable oil

1 clove garlic, minced

1 slice fresh ginger, minced

1 cup beef broth or prepared bouillon

¼ cup soy sauce

¼ cup brown sugar

*1 teaspoon sesame oil (available in
the Asian section of the supermarket)*

*2 teaspoons oyster sauce (available
in the Asian section of the supermarket)*

*¼ teaspoon (or more, to taste) hot red
pepper sauce (optional)*

1½ tablespoons cornstarch

¼ cup cold water

Remove all fat from the pork and cut it into thin slices. Have the vegetables ready in separate piles on a platter.

Prepare the sauce. Heat 1 tablespoon of oil in a small saucepan. Sauté the garlic and ginger until sizzling. Add the broth, soy sauce, brown sugar, sesame oil, oyster sauce, and hot red pepper sauce, if using. Simmer 5 minutes. Stir the cornstarch into cold water until there are no lumps. Add it to the sauce, stirring constantly until thickened. Simmer a few minutes longer.

Heat 1 tablespoon of oil in a 12-inch skillet or wok. Over high heat, stir-fry the pork until it's just cooked through. Remove and reserve the pork. Add another tablespoon of oil to the skillet. Over medium-high heat, stir-fry the celery and onion 1 minute. Add the red pepper and broccoli; stir-fry 1 minute. (Add more oil if needed.) Add the cabbage; stir-fry 1 minute. Add the sprouts and cooked pork. Stir in the sauce and heat through, stirring well to blend the flavors.

Cabbage Stir-Fry with Shiitake Mushrooms

Makes 4 servings.

This crisp vegetable stir-fry can be a side dish, or it can be enriched with slivered cooked meat and served as an entrée with hot rice. It's great with the last of the Thanksgiving turkey!

1 to 2 tablespoons vegetable oil

4 ounces fresh shiitake mushrooms, slivered

1 large onion, thinly sliced

1 cup thinly sliced celery

1 sweet red pepper, seeded and thinly sliced

1 head of bok choy, thinly sliced (about 4 cups)

¼ cup or more soy sauce

Heat 1 tablespoon of oil in a skillet or wok until it's hot but not smoking. Fry the mushrooms and onion over medium-high heat until the mushrooms begin to brown. Add the celery, red pepper, and cabbage, stirring constantly, until the cabbage just begins to wilt and the other vegetables are still crisp. Season with soy sauce and serve immediately.

Braised Curried Savoy Cabbage with Toasted Peanuts

Makes 6 servings.

If you think cooked cabbage has too strong a flavor, try this quick braising method.

3 tablespoons vegetable oil

1½ teaspoons curry powder

1 large or 2 small onions, finely sliced

3 tablespoons chicken broth or water

1 head Savoy cabbage (about 2 pounds), finely shredded

⅓ cup toasted peanuts

In a 12-inch skillet, heat the oil and stir in the curry powder until blended. Add the onion; when it's sizzling, add the broth and cabbage. Cook over medium heat, stirring, until slightly wilted, about 2 minutes. Add more liquid if needed. Cover and cook, stirring occasionally, an additional 6 minutes, until tender-crisp.

Sprinkle with peanuts and serve.

Brussels Sprouts Dijon

Makes 4 servings.

Good fresh Brussels sprouts are not always available, so here's a frozen vegetable quickie. The mushrooms should be about the same size as the Brussels sprouts.

1 tablespoon olive oil
1 cup whole button mushrooms, cleaned
1 clove garlic, minced
one 10-ounce package of frozen Brussels sprouts
½ cup water
1 tablespoon Dijon mustard

Heat the oil in a saucepan and cook the mushrooms until they are browned. Remove the mushrooms and add the garlic to the pan. Sauté until the garlic begins to sizzle.

Add the sprouts and water, bring to a boil, and cover. Lower the heat and simmer the sprouts for 5 to 6 minutes, until tender. Remove the sprouts.

Stir the mustard into the remaining pan juices (which should be 2 to 3 tablespoons). Return the mushrooms and sprouts to the pan, and heat through.

Braised Brussels Sprouts and Pears

Makes 4 servings.

A pleasing combination that brightens the flavor of sprouts.

½ pound medium (1¼ to 1½ inch) Brussels sprouts
2 tablespoons butter or low-cholesterol margarine
¼ cup apple cider or apple juice
2 pears
pinch of cinnamon

Pull off any loose outer leaves of the sprouts and trim the stems; cut an X in the bottom of each to allow for even cooking of core and leaves. Put the sprouts in a saucepan with the butter and cider or juice, bring to a boil, and simmer, covered, for 5 minutes.

Meanwhile, peel and core the pears. Cut them into chunks roughly the size of the sprouts. Add them to the saucepan with a pinch of cinnamon and continue simmering another 5 to 7 minutes, until the sprouts and pears are both tender.

Watch that the cider doesn't evaporate; if necessary, add a *little* more.

Note: This dish can be made with frozen sprouts, in which case add the pears and cinnamon at the beginning and cook only 5 to 7 minutes total time.

Red Cabbage Slaw with Dilled Yogurt Dressing

Makes 6 or more servings.

In salad dressings that are usually made with mayonnaise, low-fat yogurt can be substituted for part of the mayonnaise. The slightly sharper flavor goes especially well with cabbage salads. Besides reducing the fat and calories of the standard dressing, you have the added nutritional benefits of yogurt.

1 small head red cabbage
(about 1½ pounds)

For the dressing:

½ cup low-fat yogurt
¼ cup mayonnaise
2 tablespoons rice vinegar or cider vinegar
2 tablespoons minced sweet onion
½ teaspoon each dried dill, celery salt,
and white pepper

Remove the outer leaves, and rinse and dry the cabbage. Remove the core and finely grate the cabbage (which can be done in a food processor).

Mix the dressing ingredients until well-blended. Combine with the cabbage. Chill an hour or more before serving.

Pineapple Slaw

Makes 8 servings.

Kids love this sweet slaw!

1 small head cabbage (1½ to 2 pounds)
one 8-ounce can crushed pineapple packed
in its own juice, undrained
2 carrots, grated
¼ cup golden raisins
⅓ cup mild-flavored vegetable oil
¼ cup rice vinegar
½ teaspoon salt
¼ teaspoon white pepper

Remove the outer leaves of the cabbage, and rinse and dry it. Remove the core and grate the cabbage fine (which can be done in a food processor).

In a large bowl, mix the cabbage with all the remaining ingredients. Chill an hour or so. Toss well before serving.

Shredded Cabbage Salad with Anchovy Dressing

Makes 4 servings.

No one seems to be indifferent to anchovies—they inspire equally fervent love or hate. If you're an anchovy *lover*, this salad is a zestful change from ordinary coleslaw.

4 cups very finely shredded cabbage, loosely packed (about ½ of a 2-pound head)
½ cup chopped scallions with the green tops

For the dressing:

½ cup olive oil
3 tablespoons red wine vinegar
¼ teaspoon celery salt
¼ teaspoon freshly ground black pepper
4 flat anchovies, rinsed with vinegar, chopped

Combine the cabbage and scallions in a salad bowl.

Put the dressing ingredients in a jar, cover it, and shake to blend. Pour it over the salad and toss well.

Let the salad sit at room temperature for 30 minutes, tossing occasionally, before serving.

For other cabbage recipes, see the following: Big, Thick Beef Barley Soup; Cantonese Egg Foo Yung; Eggplant with Red Cabbage; Japanese-Style Noodle Soup; Rice-Stuffed Cabbage Leaves with Pineapple-Tomato Sauce

CANTALOUPE

SWEET AS SUGAR AND GOOD FOR YOU, TOO! What a surprise that something as sweet and delicious as cantaloupe is a superfood that can protect you against disease! Cantaloupes are rich in substances that ward off cancer and strokes. They're surprisingly low in calories, in addition, which makes them "nutrition dense," meaning their nutrient content is high in proportion to calorie content—just the opposite of the "empty calories" in sugar itself. Half of a two-pound cantaloupe contains 100 percent of an adult's required dietary allowance of vitamin A and vitamin C plus 825 milligrams of heart-protecting potassium, but only about 90 calories—a dieter's delight!

The attractive orange color of cantaloupe comes from beta carotene, the plant version of vitamin A. Recent studies have shown that people who eat a diet rich in carotenoids (found in yellow and green vegetables and fruits) have a lower incidence of cancer, especially lung cancer, than those who don't. Even among smokers, a diet rich in beta carotene appears to offer some protection against lung cancer—although quitting, of course, is by far the best prevention!

Those who eat large amounts of vitamin-rich fruits, including cantaloupe, have a lower incidence of cancer of the esophagus.

The chemical adenosine, which is found in cantaloupe (as well as in onion and garlic), inhibits human platelet aggregation—in other words, it may be helpful in preventing the formation of blood clots that lead to strokes.

With the fast, modern transport of produce from far places, melons are generally available all year, but the best-tasting melons come from the heaps of locally grown cantaloupes you'll find at the grocer's during the summer months.

In the Market

There's always a bit of a mystery about selecting a good melon. The Spanish have a proverb that choosing a good melon is as difficult as choosing a life's companion.

Cantaloupe, being part of the muskmelon family, is noted for its pronounced fragrance, so begin your search for the perfect melon by smelling them. If picked at its peak, a melon will exude that pleasant "cantaloupey" scent. The riper the cantaloupe, the more intense the aroma will be.

A ripe cantaloupe should have a thick, raised webbing with a yellow (not a green) background. The round, depressed stem hollow should be smooth, not rough, indicating that the melon was slipped off the vine when truly ripe. The rind will give slightly when pressed at the end opposite the stem hollow.

In the Kitchen

Cantaloupes will not sweeten further once picked, but one or two days on the kitchen counter will add to a melon's juiciness. After that, refrigerate cantaloupes until you're ready to use them—up to three to four days.

An easy way to encourage snackers to reach for cantaloupe, instead of less nutritious treats, is to turn it into finger food. When melons are in season, peel and seed two or three, cut them into small wedges, and store them under clear plastic wrap in a prominent place in the refrigerator. Those sweet, juicy segments won't be there long!

A quarter of a cantaloupe is a natural serving size. A nice presentation is to cut the melon into bite-size squares and then reassemble them in the rind. Fruit salads can be attractively served in small cantaloupe shells.

Cantaloupe is a pleasant addition to a summer appetizer course. It's always been served with thinly sliced prosciutto as a starter, but try it instead with smoked salmon or with Bel Paese cheese and a drizzle of raspberry vinaigrette. Havarti or fontina will also complement cantaloupe. Not just as an appetizer, melon and cheese might be part of a light luncheon or served as the finale to dinner. In fact, cantaloupe can be featured in any course, from soup to dessert!

Shrimp and Cantaloupe Salad with Lemon Mayonnaise

Makes 2 servings.

Yes, this is a homemade mayonnaise, but you can whip it up in a blender in 5 minutes!

½ pound cooked, shelled, deveined medium-size shrimp or frozen cooked shrimp, thawed
2 cups diced cantaloupe, loosely packed
1 tablespoon minced fresh cilantro leaves

For the mayonnaise:

1 egg or ¼ cup prepared egg substitute
2½ tablespoons lemon juice
½ teaspoon grated lemon zest
about ¾ cup light vegetable oil, such as canola
¼ teaspoon salt
several grindings of black pepper

Combine the shrimp and cantaloupe; chill.

Put the egg, lemon juice, and lemon zest in a blender container, and whip until the mixture is frothy. Pour the oil into a pitcher. With the motor running, pour the oil *in a very thin stream* through the feed hole into the egg mixture until the mayonnaise is thick and will incorporate no more oil. It's okay to stop and check at any point.

Spoon the mayonnaise into a bowl. Whisk in the salt and pepper. Refrigerate.

Just before serving, mix the shrimp and melon mixture with ½ cup of mayonnaise. (If you do it earlier, the melon will make the dressing watery.) Sprinkle with cilantro.

The remaining mayonnaise will keep a week in the refrigerator.

Shrimp and Cantaloupe Salad with Champagne Vinaigrette

Instead of using mayonnaise and cilantro, dress the salad with a mixture of ¼ cup of champagne and ¼ cup of virgin olive oil. Freshly grind black pepper on top. Garnish with watercress. (Serve the rest of the champagne with the luncheon.)

Chicken and Cantaloupe Salad with Lime Vinaigrette

Makes 4 servings.

Lime has a way of enhancing the flavor of melons. This makes a lovely summer supper dish.

*2 cups cooked, diced chicken
(poached breasts or leftover
roasted chicken, or you can substitute
turkey—see Basics for basic
cooked chicken)*

2 cups cantaloupe balls

*tender inner leaves of chicory,
well-washed*

lime wedges

For the vinaigrette:

⅓ cup olive oil

¼ cup fresh lime juice

1 tablespoon rice vinegar

½ teaspoon grated lime zest

¼ teaspoon salt

¼ teaspoon white pepper

Combine the chicken and cantaloupe balls in a medium-size bowl.

Line 4 salad plates with chicory leaves torn into bite-size pieces.

In a small bowl, whisk together the vinaigrette ingredients and taste to correct the seasoning. Pour the dressing over the chicken and melon. Toss gently and divide among the 4 plates. Garnish with lime wedges.

Cantaloupe Mousse

Makes 8 servings.

For this chilled (and very low calorie) dessert, you want an absolutely ripe melon.

*2 tablespoons (2 packages)
unflavored gelatin*

⅓ cup apricot or orange juice

¼ cup curaçao (orange liqueur), optional

*one 2½- to 3-pound cantaloupe,
peeled and chunked*

3 tablespoons sugar

2 tablespoons lemon juice

⅓ cup unflavored yogurt

In a small saucepan, sprinkle the gelatin over the juice, and let it stand a few minutes to soften. Add the curaçao, if using, or increase the juice by ¼ cup. Stir over low heat until the gelatin is completely dissolved.

In a blender or food processor, purée the melon with sugar and lemon juice. Pour in the gelatin mixture through the feed tube while the motor is running. Blend in the yogurt. Spoon the mousse into a bowl and refrigerate several hours or overnight, until well set. Serve in sherbet glasses.

Cantaloupe with Warm Blueberry Sauce

Makes 4 servings.

If any blueberry sauce is left over, it's delicious stirred into plain yogurt.

1 small ripe cantaloupe

For the blueberry sauce:

2 cups blueberries
¼ cup sugar
1 tablespoon cornstarch
dash of cinnamon

Peel and dice the cantaloupe; divide it among 4 dessert dishes.

The easiest way to make this blueberry sauce is in the microwave. Put the berries in a 4-cup microwaveable measuring pitcher. Mix together the sugar, cornstarch, and cinnamon. Stir into the berries. Microwave on high for 6 to 8 minutes, stirring every 2 minutes. The sauce is done when a liquid base is formed that's thick and bubbly but the berries still retain their shape.

Alternatively, make the sauce in a saucepan. Combine the berries, sugar, cinnamon, and ¼ cup of water in the pan; bring to a simmer, stirring. In a cup, stir the cornstarch into ¼ cup of cold water until dissolved. Add the cornstarch mixture all at once to the berries and stir constantly until the sauce thickens.

Allow the sauce to cool until it is warm but not hot. Spoon some over each portion.

Cantaloupe Balls with Honey-Lime Sauce and Mint

Makes 4 servings.

For this cooling summer dessert, fresh mint is an absolute must!

⅓ *cup honey*

juice of 2 large limes

4 cups melon balls (honeydew can be substituted for some of the cantaloupe, if desired)

8 fresh mint leaves, snipped, plus 4 sprigs

Warm the honey slightly until it thins. Whisk in the lime juice. Gently stir the sauce into the melon balls. Sprinkle with snipped mint leaves and stir again. Chill well.

To serve, divide the melon among 4 glass bowls; garnish with mint sprigs.

Cantaloupe Cocktail

Makes about 1 quart, undiluted.

A summertime smoothie, only to be made with a musky, locally grown summer melon.

one 2- to 2½-pound cantaloupe

1 cup orange juice

¼ *cup honey*

¼ *cup curaçao (orange liqueur), optional*

Seed, peel, and dice the melon. Purée it in a food processor; when the texture is very fine, add the remaining ingredients. Chill.

There are three ways to serve this delicious drink: undiluted, over ice in "old-fashioned" cocktail glasses; in tall glasses, mixed half-and-half with chilled soda water; or, if there's some cause for celebration, in stemmed goblets, topped off with Asti spumante (an Italian sparkling wine).

For another cantaloupe recipe, see:
Peach-Melon Soup with Fresh Mint

CARROTS

AN ORDINARY ROOT OF EXTRAORDINARY VALUE. There is hardly a soup, stew, or ragout worthy of the name that doesn't contain some golden orange nuggets of carrot to give it added color and flavor! Truly a vegetable for all seasons, the carrot will still be fresh in winter when all the good tomatoes have disappeared and also perky in summer when pumpkins and butternut squash have faded from the scene—and maybe that's the secret of the carrot's success. Whatever other vegetables may be hard to get, a cook can always count on carrots. So isn't it nice to know that such a common vegetable is now getting the recognition it deserves as a superstar of disease prevention!

It's not hard to catch the "root" connection between *carrots* and words like *beta carotene* and *carotenoids* that have been popping up lately in nutrition news. The rich, deep orange color that's synonymous with carrots is also a clue to the presence of beta carotene, a plant form of vitamin A that is particularly efficacious in helping to prevent cancer. Even the modest serving of a half-cup of carrots a day may be enough to keep an antidotal supply of beta carotene in one's blood. Of course, other vegetables besides carrots also contain carotenoids, so plenty of variation is possible.

One of the ways studies are designed to assess the value of a particular nutrient in preventing certain diseases is to correlate blood levels of that nutrient with the incidence of disease. A recent study revealed that people with high levels of beta carotene are less likely to have a type of cancer that is common to smokers, called squamous-cell carcinoma of the lung. (In this same study, high levels of vitamin E and selenium were consistent with a low incidence of all types of lung cancer.) These results shouldn't be taken to mean that smokers who consume great amounts of beta carotene are safe from lung cancer, since it may be that smoking reduces the level of beta carotene in the blood no matter how many carrots, tomatoes, and dark leafy greens the smoker consumes. But there now have been so many studies pointing up a promising relationship between beta carotene and a reduction of the risk of cancer that the National Cancer Institute especially recommends foods rich in this important nutrient.

Beta carotene has also been linked to prevention of cancers of the mouth, throat, esophagus, stomach, and intestines, as well as the lungs.

It's also been found that older people with high levels of carotenoids in their blood are less likely to have their vision obscured by cataracts than those with low levels.

Raw carrots also reduce blood cholesterol, but cooked (and not overcooked) carrots release more carotenes. So you might as well enjoy them both ways!

Carrots first came on the culinary scene in ancient Afghanistan, among sun worshipers who saw a holy significance in their sunny color. A cultivated crop since the beginning of the Christian era, this world-traveling root vegetable has been adapted to a variety of cuisines and is equally at home in every course from carrot soup to carrot cake. Carrots have made their way into the dessert course because they're basically sweet. Because of its sweetness, grated carrot is also sometimes added to tomato sauce to cut its acidic taste.

In the Market

You'll find them in the market all year long, but not all carrots are created equal. Well-formed, firm carrots with a deep, rich orange color and green tops still attached are the freshest and sweetest. But carrots are so well suited to storage that winter carrots can be tasty, too, if you avoid the pale or flabby ones. It may be hard to check the color of carrots that are packaged in orange cellophane, but you *can* check for flabbiness by bending one a bit. Don't buy carrots that have moldy or sprouting tops, or lots of thready roots hanging off their sides; they will be old, strong, and ready to self-destruct.

Overlarge carrots probably have big, woody cores. At the other end of the scale, what are sold as "baby carrots" in plastic bags taste nothing like lovely new little carrots pulled from the garden, which hardly need to be scraped. Rather than buying bogus baby carrots, choose carrots of a small to medium size for best taste.

It's not all that much work to scrape a carrot, so those limp, whitish sticks of carrots prescraped "for your convenience" are certainly not worth the extra money. Frozen scraped carrots are a slightly more palatable product, but they are so watery and lacking in true carrot flavor that there is no reason to bother with them when good fresh carrots are usually available.

In the Kitchen

Carrots, depending on how old they are, may stay firm as long as two weeks in a plastic bag stored in the refrigerator crisper. And any well-stocked refrigerator ought to hold a couple of pounds of carrots at all times, they're so good for you and so versatile! ▬

Carrot and Ginger Soup

Makes 4 servings.

The flavor of fresh ginger makes this soup so peppery that no other seasoning is needed.

Besides preventing motion sickness, ginger has been used as a digestive aid since ancient Roman times. Modern herbalists prescribe it for morning sickness. And after a heavy meal, a cup of tea laced with ginger is very soothing.

2 tablespoons butter or
low-cholesterol margarine

4 slices fresh ginger, peeled and finely
minced (1 to 1½ tablespoons)

4 medium carrots, scraped and sliced
(about ¾ pound)

two 13-ounce cans chicken broth,
preferably low-salt

1 cup milk (can be low-fat)

In a saucepan, melt the butter and sauté the ginger until it's sizzling. Add the carrots and stir-fry them for about 3 minutes. Pour in the broth and simmer uncovered until the carrots are quite tender, 10 to 15 minutes.

In a food processor or blender, purée the soup in 2 or more batches (hot foods expand when beaten). *The recipe may be prepared to this point and refrigerated for later use.*

Whisk in the milk and reheat the soup, but don't boil it or it will separate.

Carrot and Sweet Potato Tzimmes

Makes 4 servings.

Old-world tzimmes was a long-cooked dish usually made with a good-size piece of beef as the base; there have been as many variations to the recipe as there have been cooks. Although this is a shortcut version, the basic flavors of the dish are all here.

one 13-ounce can of beef broth

4 large carrots

2 large sweet potatoes or yams

8 pitted prunes

⅓ cup raisins

Pour the broth into a large skillet. Peel the carrots and sweet potatoes, and cut them into 2-inch chunks. Add them and the prunes and raisins to the skillet. Cook over medium-high heat, with the cover ajar, until most of the liquid has evaporated and the vegetables are tender, about 20 minutes. Watch carefully during the last few minutes! *The recipe may be prepared to this point and reheated.*

The dish is ready to eat, but to meld the flavors further (as older recipes specify), spoon the mixture into a casserole and bake, covered, in a 350° F. oven for 30 minutes.

Bean Sprout and Carrot Stir-Fry

Makes 4 servings.

The Chinese don't drown this dish in heavy seasonings; you'll find that the flavors of the vegetables alone are a wonderful medley. For a quick dinner, serve the stir-fry with grilled or broiled pork cutlets (5 minutes a side) basted with soy sauce.

For dishes to make with the unused bok choy, see the chapter on cabbage.

2 cups bean sprouts
2 carrots, scraped
1 sweet red pepper, seeded
1 onion, peeled
12 white mushrooms or
4 shiitake mushrooms
2 ribs of bok choy with leaves
2 peeled slices fresh ginger, ¼ inch thick
1 tablespoon vegetable oil
2 tablespoons dry white wine

Prepare the vegetables. Pour boiling water over the sprouts, wait 20 seconds, then drain them and refresh in cold water. Julienne the carrots and sweet red pepper. Parboil the carrot sticks for 30 seconds; drain. Slice the onion and mushrooms thin. Julienne the bok choy stalks; chop the leaves and keep them separate. Mince the ginger.

In a wok or large skillet, heat the oil and fry the ginger until sizzling. Add the carrots, onions, and mushrooms, and stir-fry for 1 minute. Add the bok choy stalks and sweet red pepper; stir-fry 1 minute. Add the bok choy leaves and bean sprouts; stir-fry until the leaves are just wilted, about 30 seconds. Pour on the wine; as soon as it boils up, remove the pan from the heat.

Carrot Slaw with Vidalia Onion and Lemon Dressing

Makes 4 servings.

This little salad packs a mighty nutritious punch with its combination of superfoods!

4 large carrots (about 2 cups grated)
1 medium Vidalia onion (or any sweet onion, about ½ cup)
1 teaspoon grated lemon zest
2 tablespoons olive oil
1 tablespoon lemon juice
freshly ground black pepper to taste
salt to taste (optional)

Scrape and grate the carrots. Mince or grate the onion. (Using a food processor is the easy way to prepare both vegetables at once.) Add the remaining ingredients and toss to blend. (A lot of pepper goes well with this salad.) If omitting salt, you may wish to add extra lemon juice. Chill to allow the flavors to blend before serving.

Pickled Carrot Sticks

Makes 8 servings.

Make this colorful, crunchy accompaniment to sandwiches when you've finished a jar of store-bought pickles.

3 large carrots
juice left over from 1-pint jar of gherkins or dill pickles

Scrape and slice the carrots lengthwise. Cut them into 2-inch sticks, about ¼ inch thick. Put them into the jar of juice, and refrigerate the carrots overnight or longer.

Orange-Glazed Ginger Carrots

Makes 4 servings.

This is a delicious way to serve carrots to those who might ordinarily be a bit indifferent to this supervegetable!

2 cups scraped, diagonally sliced fresh carrots

2 teaspoons butter

1 cup orange juice

1 teaspoon cornstarch

½ teaspoon ground ginger

½ cup water

Combine the carrots, butter, and orange juice in a saucepan. Bring the liquid to a boil, reduce the heat, and simmer, covered, for 5 to 8 minutes, until the carrots are tender. The juice should be reduced to about half.

Combine the cornstarch, ginger, and water in a cup; stir until smooth. Add the mixture all at once to the simmering carrots, stirring constantly, until thickened and glazed. Cook 1 minute longer, stirring.

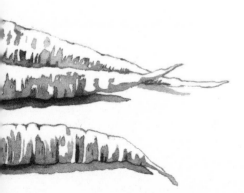

Casbah Carrots

Makes 4 servings.

This spicy dish involves some high-skill stirring and careful watching at the finish.

4 large carrots, scraped and cut into diagonal slices

1 clove garlic, pressed

1 tablespoon olive oil

1 cup water

1 teaspoon sugar

½ teaspoon cinnamon

¼ teaspoon each ground cumin and dried thyme leaves

⅛ teaspoon ground cloves

2 tablespoons lemon juice

2 tablespoons golden raisins

Put the sliced carrots into a heavy, medium-size saucepan. Add the garlic, olive oil, and water. Bring to a boil and then simmer until the carrots are tender, about 8 minutes.

Mix the sugar and spices, and stir them into the carrots.

Over high heat, stirring constantly, reduce the pan juices to a glaze. Immediately remove the pan from the heat. Stir in the lemon juice and raisins.

Carrots with Tomatoes and Elbows

Makes 4 servings.

A 10-minute dish that raises ordinary carrots to a new dimension!

1 tablespoon olive oil
1 small onion, chopped
4 canned tomatoes, chopped,
with ½ cup juice
6 large carrots, scraped and sliced
¼ teaspoon each salt, pepper, and sugar
2 tablespoons chopped fresh
flat-leafed parsley
1 teaspoon butter
1 cup elbow macaroni, cooked according
to package directions

In a saucepan, sauté the onion in oil until it's soft but not brown. Add the tomatoes, carrots, salt, pepper, and sugar. Cover and simmer 5 minutes. Remove the cover and simmer, stirring often, for another 5 minutes, or until the carrots are tender and the tomatoes are reduced to a sauce. Stir in the parsley.

Mix the butter with the cooked elbows. Stir in the carrot mixture.

Maple-Walnut Carrots

Makes 4 servings.

Who could resist the crunch and sweetness of these carrots?

2 cups scraped, sliced fresh carrots
1 cup water
¼ cup maple syrup
½ teaspoon dry mustard
¼ cup walnut halves

Combine the carrots and water in a saucepan, bring the liquid to a boil, and cook, covered, until the carrots are tender, 5 to 8 minutes. Remove the carrots with a slotted spoon.

Over high heat, reduce the pan juices to about ¼ cup. Whisk in the syrup and dry mustard, and continue to cook over lowered heat, stirring constantly, for 3 minutes. Add the walnuts. Return the carrots to the pan until they are heated through and well glazed.

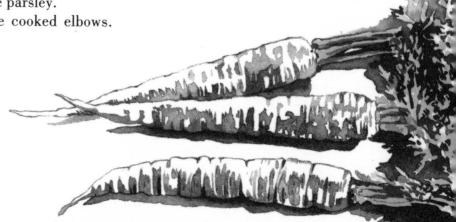

Carrot-Pineapple Snacking Cake

Makes 9 or more servings.

Here's a rich, moist cake that can be mixed up in a few minutes, doesn't need frosting, and is actually nutritious.

1½ cups sifted all-purpose unbleached flour

1 teaspoon each baking soda and cinnamon

½ teaspoon each nutmeg and salt

2 eggs or ½ cup prepared egg substitute

½ cup vegetable oil

½ cup each brown sugar and granulated sugar

1½ cups finely grated carrots (about 4 large)

one 8-ounce can of crushed pineapple, packed in its own juice, undrained

½ cup chopped walnuts (optional)

Preheat the oven to 350° F. Butter a 9-inch square or 7-by-11-inch oblong cake pan.

Sift together the flour, baking soda, cinnamon, nutmeg, and salt into a large bowl.

In another bowl, beat the eggs with the oil, then blend in the brown and white sugars.

In a third bowl, combine the carrots, pineapple with its juice, and walnuts, if you're using them.

Beat the egg-oil mixture into the dry ingredients. When well-blended, stir in the carrot-pineapple mixture. Spoon the batter into the prepared pan and bake on the middle shelf of the oven for 25 to 30 minutes, or until the cake is risen and a cake tester inserted at the center comes out dry.

For other carrot recipes, see: Big, Thick Beef Barley Soup; Braised Veal Breast with White Beans; Gratin of White Turnip, Carrots, and Rice; Homey Chicken Stew with Blueberry Dumplings; Molded Cauliflower with Spicy Carrot-Tomato Sauce; Old-Fashioned Pork Stew with Whole Garlic Cloves; Papaya Salad with Raspberry Vinaigrette; Pineapple Slaw; Ragout of Lamb with Turnips and Carrots; Scallops with Vegetable Sauce; Take-It-Easy Minestrone

CAULIFLOWER

THE "FLOWER OF THE CABBAGE" IS A NUTRITIOUS BOUQUET. In the midst of all the golden orange and dark green vegetables that defend us against disease, there's one that's pure white, yet a superstar in its own snowy way. As soon as the green bud of a cauliflower is the size of a golf ball, farmers tie the leaves together over the head to keep it blanched.

The cauliflower, whose name literally means "flower of the cabbage," is indeed a member of the cabbage family. This group of cruciferous vegetables is especially recommended by the National Cancer Institute. Eating more cruciferous vegetables, which are rich in the cancer-fighting chemical sulforaphane, may reduce the risk of some cancers, particularly of the colon, rectum, and stomach.

Animal studies find that cauliflower-eating rats have a greater resistance to carcinogens, which usually produce tumors. This may be cauliflower's greatest benefit—but far from the only one. A cup of cauliflower contains 100 percent of the recommended dietary allowance of vitamin C—for only 25 to 30 calories, depending on whether it's raw or cooked. It's a source of potassium and fiber for a healthy heart. And cauliflower also gives you B vitamins to calm you against the stresses of everyday life.

In the Market

September through November is the peak season for cauliflower. The highest quality is white or cream-colored, compact, crisp-textured, and free from blackish speckles. A floret should not crumble readily when scraped. The green leaves surrounding the head should not be moldy yellow. A good cauliflower may have a faint cabbagy scent but never a strong odor.

There's also an unblanched cauliflower on the market (actually a cross with broccoli called broccoflower) that is purplish green. It's milder in flavor and can be used in any recipe calling for cauliflower—just keep in mind that the new variety cooks a bit faster.

In the Kitchen

A perfectly fresh cauliflower is deliciously mild-flavored served raw, as an appetizer with a flavorful dip, or in salads with dark greens and sweet red pepper to add color.

To store, wrap the head in a dishtowel and put it into a large plastic bag. It may be kept this way up to five days on the bottom shelf of the refrigerator.

When cauliflower is out of season, frozen cauliflower is available. It lacks the crisp texture of the fresh vegetable, of course, and can be watery, but it will do for a sauced dish.

Whenever I work with cauliflower, I always remember M. F. K. Fisher's lyrical account of preparing cauliflower au gratin (in *The Gastronomical Me)*. "There in Dijon, the cauliflowers were small and very succulent, grown in that ancient soil," she begins and goes on to nap barely cooked florets with grated Gruyère, heavy cream, and a sprinkling of black pepper. After the cheese was melted and browned "in a little tin oven," the casserole was immediately devoured—with bread to clean the plate and red wine brought by a friend. Anyone who feels a bit snobbish about the commonness of cauliflower ought to read this evocative account.

Our version of this elemental dish *(pages 90-91)* forgoes the cream but adds pasta in the shape of shells to wrap themselves around the sauced florets. This delectable entrée needs only a showy salad of vivid colors and fresh bread as accompaniments.

To Steam Fresh Cauliflower

Cooked fresh cauliflower is an ingredient in several of the recipes that follow. Steaming is the best cooking method, not only to protect the delicate florets but also because it preserves more of the vegetable's nutrients.

Good news! If you include a bay leaf when cooking cauliflower, the vegetable will not fill the house with its characteristic odor. The bay leaf adds a nice flavor, also.

Wash the cauliflower. With a sharp knife, cut out the core to free the florets. If some florets are larger than the rest, cut them in two lengthwise, to keep the floret shape.

Bring an inch of water to boil in a steamer. Put the florets in the steamer basket. Cover and steam until tender-crisp, about 6 minutes. Rinse briefly in cold water to stop the cooking action.

It's important not to overcook cauliflower that will be subjected to additional cooking in these recipes.

Cauliflower with Sun-Dried Tomatoes and Garlic Vinaigrette Appetizer

Makes 8 servings.

Try lightly cooked, well-seasoned vegetables at room temperature as an appetizer—for a change from the ubiquitous crudités. Dishes like this appetizer are particularly nice as part of an antipasto selection.

1 cup olive oil
½ cup red wine vinegar
⅓ cup snipped sun-dried tomatoes
*3 tablespoons minced fresh
flat-leafed parsley*
1 large clove garlic, pressed
¼ teaspoon cayenne pepper
¼ teaspoon salt, or more to taste
*1 large head (about 2 pounds) cauliflower,
trimmed, cut into florets, and
steamed*

Combine the olive oil, vinegar, tomatoes, parsley, garlic, cayenne, and salt in a jar. Cover and shake well. Marinate at room temperature for an hour or more.

Shake the vinaigrette again and pour it over the cauliflower. Marinate in the refrigerator for a few hours or overnight, stirring once or twice.

Serve as an appetizer with cocktail forks —or as a salad for an autumn dinner.

Molded Cauliflower with Spicy Carrot-Tomato Sauce

Makes 6 servings.

A fancy presentation that you can serve hot, cold, or at room temperature—"at the chef's pleasure."

1 large head (about 2 pounds) cauliflower, trimmed, cut into florets, and steamed (page 88)

For the sauce:

2 tablespoons olive oil

1 onion, chopped

1½ cups tomato purée

2 large carrots, grated

½ teaspoon salt

¼ teaspoon each ground ginger, cardamom, cumin, coriander, and cayenne pepper

2 peperoncini (mildly hot Italian chilies), seeded and chopped

Choose a bowl *(see note below)* that's the same shape but smaller than the original head of cauliflower, and arrange the florets with the stems facing the center. Fill the center with remaining pieces of floret or stem. Put a weighted plate on top of the bowl and let it stand for 15 minutes. Gently tip the bowl to pour out any accumulated liquid.

Refrigerate the bowl, with the weighted plate in place, for 2 hours. Remove the weighted plate. Invert a serving plate over the bowl. Then invert the plate and bowl together. Lift the bowl, leaving the molded cauliflower on the serving plate.

Meanwhile, make the sauce. In a medium-size saucepan, sauté the onion in the oil until it is golden. Add all the remaining sauce ingredients and simmer for 20 minutes. If the sauce gets too thick to fall gracefully from a spoon, add a little water.

To serve warm: before unmolding, set the covered bowl in 2 inches of simmering water for 10 minutes—or heat it in the microwave for 5 minutes on high. In either case, check to be sure the desired temperature is reached.

Note: If you're planning to heat the cauliflower on the range top, choose a metal bowl for the mold. If using the microwave, choose a plastic or glass bowl for the mold.

Put the sauce in a gravy boat and serve it with the molded cauliflower.

Cauliflower with Hot Peanut Sauce

Makes 4 servings.

This hot and spicy sauce is equally good over broccoli.

½ large head (about 1 pound) cauliflower, trimmed, cut into florets, and steamed (page 88)

For the sauce:

⅓ cup smooth peanut butter

3 tablespoons soy sauce

2 tablespoons rice vinegar

1 tablespoon chili sauce

½ teaspoon cayenne pepper, or more to taste

⅓ to ½ cup water

¼ cup coarsely chopped unsalted peanuts

Arrange the cauliflower in a vegetable dish and keep it warm.

Combine the sauce ingredients, except the water, in a small saucepan and whisk the mixture over low heat until well-blended. Add water, a tablespoon at a time, until a sauce consistency is reached and simmer the sauce for 3 minutes. The sauce will thicken the moment it's off the heat, so make it a bit thinner than you want it to be.

Pour the sauce over the cauliflower and sprinkle the chopped peanuts over the top.

Serve immediately.

Cauliflower Casserole with Shell Pasta

Makes 6 servings.

Parmesan cheese is one of the lowest of the hard cheeses in fat and cholesterol and one of the highest in calcium.

½ large head (about 1 pound) cauliflower, trimmed, cut into florets, and steamed (page 88)

2 tablespoons butter or low-cholesterol margarine

2 tablespoons flour

2 cups milk (can be low-fat)

¼ teaspoon salt (optional)

¼ teaspoon white pepper

¼ cup grated Parmesan cheese

½ pound shredded mozzarella (can be low-fat)

½ pound shell pasta cooked according to package directions

seasoned breadcrumbs

paprika

Put the cauliflower in a 2-quart gratin dish.

Preheat the oven to 350° F. In a medium saucepan, melt the butter and add the flour. Cook the roux over low heat for 3 minutes, stirring often, but don't brown it.

Heat the milk to scalding separately; this can be done most easily in the microwave in a microwaveable measuring pitcher, 4 to 5 minutes on high. Pour the hot milk all at once into the roux, stirring constantly over medium heat until the sauce is bubbling.

Add the seasonings and Parmesan cheese; whisk until smooth. Remove from the heat and stir in the mozzarella.

Combine the shell pasta with the cauliflower. Pour the sauce over the mixture. Melted mozzarella strings out like melted Swiss cheese, but you can gently incorporate it into the cauliflower and shells. Top the casserole with seasoned crumbs and paprika. Bake for 30 to 40 minutes, until browned and bubbly.

Cauliflower in the Spanish Style

Makes 6 servings.

A composed salad that's pretty to look at and fun to make.

1 large head (about 2 pounds) cauliflower, trimmed, cut into florets, and steamed (page 88)

1 cup or more olive oil mayonnaise with garlic (page 197)

stuffed green olives

pitted black olives

strips of pimento

anchovies, rinsed in wine vinegar

4 hard-boiled eggs, peeled (optional)

When the cauliflower has cooled, stand the florets, stems down, in a flat-bottomed vegetable dish that will hold them upright.

With a spatula, smooth the mayonnaise over the top.

Decorate the cauliflower with olives tucked between the florets and a crisscross pattern of pimento and anchovies. Surround the florets with hard-boiled eggs, sliced or quartered.

Refrigerate the salad until ready to serve.

CITRUS FRUITS

A PANOPLY OF VITA-MIN C—AND MUCH MORE! Thanks to imagination and cultivation, we have so many citrus fruits today that you could fill a fruit bowl using just one specimen of each. The fragrant lemon, the world's most sour natural food and a salt substitute *extraordinaire*. The lime, a tangy close relation. The beautiful orange and its offspring: the temple orange (part tangerine) and the navel orange (which has no seeds). Then the obliging mandarins (actually Chinese oranges), which slip their skins so easily; we call them tangerines. Besides the regular tangerine, there are clementines (Algerian tangerines), which are often seedless and therefore useful in cooking, and tangelos, a cross between the tangerine and the grapefruit. Next, America's wake-up fruit, the eye-opening grapefruit, which may be either rosy-fleshed or white. Finally, the citron, whose candied skin enlivens fruitcakes, and the rarely seen pungent kumquat, which is poached in syrup and eaten skin and all.

Citrus fruits are so synonymous with vitamin C that they're used as the standard—other foods often are described as having more or less vitamin C than oranges. Citrus fruits do have *plenty* of vitamin C, and there's no more palatable way to get your recommended dietary allowance. One average orange fulfills the RDA for this important vitamin, but one should never stop there. With so many stresses on the body every day, it's wise to enjoy more than one vitamin C-rich food throughout the day. When citrus fruits are eaten raw, as they frequently are, none of the precious vitamin C is lost in cooking.

Through the decades, vitamin C has been in and out of favor as a cancer fighter—perhaps because some claims were extreme and unable to be duplicated in subsequent studies. But lately there's been a swing back. In experiments with mice, the substance that puts the sour in citrus has been found to block tumor formation. A recent Canadian study indicated that as little as three ounces of orange juice a day could lessen one's chances of developing stomach cancer. The actual juice, by the way, worked better than vitamin C supplements, although the supplement dose was greater. (It's frequently the case that whole foods are more potent than supplements, a fact that suggests there's an x factor or two we've yet to discover and understand.) In a Swiss analysis, it was found that people who ate citrus fruits daily were less likely than others to develop pancreatic cancer. (Carrots showed a similar value.)

The first function of vitamin C is to maintain collagen, a protein that's necessary for the formation of skin, ligaments, and bones. That's why vitamin C is also a healer of wounds and burns. Vitamin C assists in the metabolism of all cells, even brain cells. It helps to form red blood cells, to fight bacterial infections, and to promote healthy gums. Vitamin C is water-soluble, so the body doesn't store it up for a rainy day. That's why an extra daily helping or two of citrus fruits is so important.

For people who still smoke, one pack of cigarettes a day causes the body to use up more vitamin C than eight oranges provide.

Scientists are still debating whether vitamin C is effective against rhinovirus, otherwise known as the common cold. In laboratory experiments on human cell cultures infected with rhinovirus, the spread of the infection was checked to an impressive degree in those cultures treated with vitamin C.

Grapefruit, the whole fruit rather than the juice, confers a special benefit that other citrus fruits don't provide. It lowers the LDL cholesterol, which clogs blood vessels, and improves the ratio of "good" HDL cholesterol to "bad" LDL. Polysaccharide, a compound found in grapefruit but not in other citrus fruits, may be the therapeutic agent. The membranes that hold the fruit together are thought to be the source of the cholesterol-lowering substances, which is why grapefruit juice doesn't cause the same effect.

In the Market

Grapefruit is available all year but is at its peak from January to May. Grapefruit should be firm (but not hard), well-rounded, and heavy for its size.

Lemons and limes are also all-year fruits, but they're cheaper and more abundant at peak times of the year. The lemon peak is from March to September; slightly greenish lemons are fresher and have a better flavor.

The top months for limes are June through August; look for glossy green skins and heaviness for their size.

Oranges are a fall and winter fruit; they should be firm, heavy for their size, and have finely textured skins. A little greenish tinge doesn't mean the fruit isn't ripe; more likely, it means the fruit wasn't gassed or colored to turn it the glowing orange that shoppers expect. Tangerines are available from November through April. Look for deep orange skins that are puffy and loose, except in so-called honey tangerines, whose skins are tight; avoid tangerines with soft spots.

I've found the flavor of organically grown citrus fruits—though they may be smaller and have a few blemishes—to be far superior to that of conventionally grown fruit and well worth the cost. Perhaps conventionally grown fruit is picked when it's greener, then colored to look tree-ripened. Whatever the reason, compare the flavors yourself and see!

In the Kitchen

Grapefruit, oranges, tangerines, and their various offspring will keep two weeks or more in a refrigerator or a "cold room" (an unheated room that maintains a temperature of 40 °F. to 50° F.).

The best-keeping of all fruits, lemons can last a month or more in the refrigerator. Use limes within a couple of weeks, before they begin to turn yellow-brown.

The oils of citrus fruits, found in the skins, are some of nature's most aromatic flavoring agents. For best results, grate the peel (called the "zest," and no wonder!) before you cut or squeeze a citrus fruit. Soak citrus fruits in warm water before you squeeze them: They'll give up more juice.

For the best of health, revel in raw citrus fruits every day—both eaten out of hand and incorporated into tasty recipes. Their zesty flavors enliven every food they touch. ■■■■

Most-Lemon Hens

Makes 4 servings.

As in so many other good recipes, method is more important than precise measurements in making this dish, which yields a light, flavorful, moist meat. The same roasting method works as well on a large "oven stuffer" as it does on Rock Cornish hens, but the hens have much less fat.

2 large Rock Cornish hens (each big enough for 2 servings) or 4 small hens
2 small lemons
dried thyme leaves
paprika
2 chicken bouillon cubes
juice of 2 lemons (about ½ cup)
1½ tablespoons cornstarch
sprigs of fresh mint for garnish (optional)

Preheat the oven to 400° F. Remove the giblets and all fat from the interior cavities of the hens. Cut the lemons into quarters; divide the quarters and insert them into the cavities. Sprinkle the hens *liberally* on all sides with thyme and paprika.

Place the hens in a baking pan—no trussing necessary. Pour in enough water to make ½ to ¾ inches on the bottom of the pan; put the bouillon cubes in the water.

Roast the hens for 1 hour and 15 minutes, or until the juices run clear when the thigh is pricked with a fork. Baste the birds with pan juices 3 or 4 times during cooking.

Remove the hens. *They can be kept warm, covered loosely with foil, for 30 minutes.* Pour the pan juices into a 2-cup microwaveable measuring cup. Skim off any fat. You should have about 1½ cups. If you have too much, reduce the liquid by boiling rapidly. If you have too little, add chicken broth. Bring the liquid to a boil in a saucepan.

Mix the lemon juice with the cornstarch until there are no lumps. Pour the mixture all at once into the pan juices, stirring constantly until thickened. Reduce the heat and simmer 2 minutes. If necessary, strain the sauce.

If you are using the larger hens, cut them in half lengthwise. Place the hens, cut side down, on dinner plates or a platter. Pour sauce over them and garnish with mint leaves.

Veal Scallops with Tangerines

Makes 4 servings.

It's so deliciously easy, you can make this dish while carrying on a conversation with guests.

1¼ to 1½ pounds thin, small veal cutlets
cut from the leg
flour for dredging
2 tablespoons olive oil, or more if needed
pinch of rosemary
salt and pepper to taste
½ cup dry vermouth or dry sherry
2 seedless tangerines or clementines

Pound the veal cutlets with a mallet. This breaks the sinews and keeps the cutlets from curling up when cooked. Flour the veal and shake off the excess.

Heat 2 tablespoons of oil in a large skillet and stir in a pinch of rosemary. Brown the veal on both sides, in batches, in the hot oil, and season it with salt and pepper. When the scallops are cooked, remove them from the pan and keep them warm on a serving platter.

Meanwhile, peel the tangerines, separate the sections, and remove as much of the white pith as possible.

Deglaze the hot pan with the dry vermouth and let it boil until reduced by half. Add the tangerine sections and heat them through over low heat (so as not to reduce the sauce further). To serve, pour the sauce and tangerines over the scallops.

Grapefruit and Gorgonzola Salad

Makes 4 servings.

A tangy and delightful combination!

2 medium grapefruit
¼ cup olive oil
freshly ground black pepper to taste
4 cups chicory, loosely packed,
torn into bite-size pieces
¼ cup crumbled Gorgonzola cheese
(Italian blue cheese)

Peel the grapefruit down to the flesh, removing not only the peel but also the outer membrane. Use a fruit knife or grapefruit knife to remove the sections from the rest of the encasing membrane, letting the sections fall into a strainer. Remove any seeds. Save the juice.

Combine the grapefruit, juice, oil, and pepper in the bottom of a salad bowl. Add the chicory and top with the crumbled cheese. Chill the salad; don't toss it until ready to serve, to keep the greens from wilting.

Orange and Onion Salad

Makes 4 servings.

Oranges seem to give a special beauty and magic to winter dishes, but since winter onions are strong, they are sweetened in wine or vinegar for this colorful, fresh-flavored dish. If you make the salad in summer with sweet Vidalia onions, you can skip this step.

Oranges and onions together will not only perk up your taste buds but also arm you against those ubiquitous winter viruses.

8 thin slices Bermuda onion or red onion, ringed

½ cup dry vermouth, sherry, or mild vinegar such as rice vinegar

4 seedless oranges, peeled and sliced into rounds

12 Kalamata olives, pitted and halved

salt and white pepper to taste

4 tablespoons olive oil

2 cups loosely packed, chopped inner leaves of escarole, crisp and chilled

1 tablespoon minced parsley

Soak the onion rings in cold water for 10 minutes, drain them, and then marinate them in wine or vinegar for 1 hour or more. Drain the rings and discard the liquid.

Combine the onion rings, orange slices, olives, salt, pepper, and 3 tablespoons of the oil in a bowl. Let the salad stand at room temperature for 30 minutes and stir it occasionally.

Put the escarole on a platter. Arrange the oranges and onions over the escarole. Top with parsley and drizzle with the remaining tablespoon of oil.

Orange, Grapefruit, and Avocado Salad with Mint

Makes 4 servings.

Around the Mediterranean, the salad course is served after the entrée, not before, as is the American custom, which is probably fostered by restaurants wishing to keep their customers from becoming restless. This fragrant, tart-flavored salad makes a perfect refresher between the meat course and dessert.

2 navel oranges

1 large white grapefruit

1 small ripe avocado

3 tablespoons olive oil

about ⅛ teaspoon salt or to taste

8 fresh mint leaves, finely shredded

4 large leaves of romaine lettuce, shredded

Peel the oranges and slice them into half-rounds. Pare the grapefruit right down to the flesh, removing not only the peel but also the outer membrane, and slice the flesh into quarter-rounds; remove any seeds. Put the fruit into a shallow salad bowl.

Peel the avocado and slice it into half-rounds. Immediately toss it with the citrus fruit to keep it from turning color. Add the oil, salt, and shredded mint, and toss again.

Put the shredded romaine on top and refrigerate the salad, without tossing it again (so the lettuce will stay crisp) until ready to serve.

Fresh Orange Cream Pie

Makes 6 servings.

Actually, there's not a bit of cream in this "cream pie," but I don't think you'll miss it. A light, refreshing dessert with "real orange" taste and nutrition.

4 large oranges, preferably seedless
1¼ cups pastry cream (see Basics)
1 tablespoon curaçao (orange liqueur)
½ teaspoon grated orange zest
1 baked 9-inch pie shell (see Basics)

Set a strainer over a deep bowl. Using a knife, peel the oranges thick to remove the outer membrane. Use a fruit knife or grapefruit knife to remove the sections from the rest of the encasing membrane, letting them fall into the strainer. Remove any seeds.

Make the pastry cream and flavor it with the curaçao and orange zest. When the filling has cooled to lukewarm, stir in half of the drained orange sections. Spoon the mixture into the pie shell.

Garnish the pie with the remaining orange sections. (The juice that remains in the bowl might be a nice little treat for the cook.) Chill the pie until the filling is firm, about 2 hours.

Pink Grapefruit with Raspberry Sauce

Makes 4 servings.

This uncooked raspberry sauce is so easy that it is handy as a basic ingredient in other quick desserts, too.

½ cup raspberry jelly

one 12-ounce package unsweetened, frozen raspberries, slightly thawed

2 tablespoons Chambord (raspberry liqueur—optional)

2 large pink grapefruit

Melt the jelly in a microwaveable cup about 1 minute on high in the microwave or in a small saucepan over low heat. Stir in the raspberries and Chambord.

Use a knife to peel the grapefruit down to the flesh, removing not only the peel but also the outer membrane. Then remove the sections from the rest of the encasing membrane. Remove any seeds.

Divide the grapefruit among 4 bowls and top with the raspberry sauce.

Sparkling Limeade

Makes 1¼ quarts.

Don't bother with the powdered or reconstituted stuff when you can have the real thing!

*1 cup fresh lime juice
(from 8 or more limes soaked in hot water for 15 minutes or so)*

¾ cup sugar dissolved in 1 cup hot water, then cooled

3 cups chilled sparkling water

1 fresh lime, sliced into paper-thin rounds for garnishing

Combine the lime juice and sugar dissolved in water in a 1½-quart pitcher. Add the sparkling water. Check for desired sweetness; you can always stir in a little more sugar, although it will be more difficult to dissolve. But once you've made this beverage, you'll always know how much sugar to begin with.

Last of all, add some ice. Garnish each glass with a slice of lime.

Sparkling Lemonade

Substitute 1 cup of fresh lemon juice (from about 6 medium lemons) for the lime juice and thinly sliced lemon rounds for the garnish.

For other citrus recipes, see the following: Cantaloupe Cocktail; Chicken and Cantaloupe Salad with Lime Vinaigrette; Cranberry and Orange-Stuffed Rock Cornish Hens; Melon Balls with Honey-Lime Sauce; Orange and Brazil Nut Salad with Basil; Orange-Glazed Ginger Carrots; Poached Salmon Steaks with Grapefruit; Tangerine Yogurt

EGGPLANT

A PURPLE POWERHOUSE OF PREVENTION. The eggplant is really a big berry of the nightshade family, and is called *aubergine* by the French and *melanzana* by the Italians. The latter name is a corruption of the Latin for "mad apple." One well may wonder how this delicious vegetable, so beloved of cooks in the Mediterranean Basin and elsewhere, earned such a misnomer in ancient times. Perhaps someone ate a mess of raw eggplant; eggplant is one vegetable that should always be cooked. But like the tomato—also a member of the nightshade family and also considered to be poisonous in earlier centuries—the eggplant has lived down its unfavorable reputation and recently has been revealed as a superfood of good health.

Eggplant has some highly beneficial effects. Compounds in this glossy vegetable protect against the development of fatty plaque in the arteries and therefore help to prevent atherosclerosis. Eggplant also contains protease inhibitors—substances thought to inhibit cancer formation and the growth of some viruses. There's also evidence that eggplant may be an anticonvulsant.

A cup of cooked eggplant (before you add the cheese, olive oil, and so forth) weighs in at only 38 calories! And yet there's something positively "meaty" about eggplant, which is indeed used as a meat substitute in Mediterranean and Asian countries.

Eggplant has a rather bland flavor that acts as a "sponge" for the more flavorful companions it's usually teamed with—and should be. Plain boiled eggplant is dull stuff indeed, but eggplant sautéed in a little oil with garlic or onion and herbs, though a dish of peasant origins, is a food fit for the gods!

Speaking of that "spongy" characteristic, a frying eggplant will soak up a half-cup of oil if not salted and drained before cooking, the standard treatment called for in all of the following recipes in which it is not baked whole. After salting, the sliced eggplant can be sautéed in as little as two tablespoons of oil. Salting is also supposed to drain any "bitter juices" from an eggplant, but in truth, a properly selected, fresh, ripe eggplant should not have a bitter taste.

In the Market

Eggplants are available all year but are at their peak in June and July. They may be round or oblong, but choose smaller, younger eggplants that are firm, glossy, heavy for their size, rich in color, and free of blemishes. When the flesh of an eggplant is pressed, you should be able to cause an indentation that springs back to its original shape just as soon as the pressure of your finger is released. If you can't dent the eggplant, it's too green. If it doesn't spring back, it's too old.

A small, thin variety of eggplant is variously called Italian eggplant, Asian eggplant, or Japanese eggplant. By any name, these little fellows are delicious on the grill and may be eaten skin and all. Whether to peel the full-size variety is a matter of choice and the requirements of the dish you're making. The skin is perfectly edible. I never peel those I take from my garden but usually peel the larger ones I buy at the market, unless the eggplant is to be halved and baked. The skin on a big eggplant may remain tough.

In the Kitchen

The perfect storage temperature for an eggplant is 50° F., about 10° F. warmer than a refrigerator. That's why it's best to buy an eggplant shortly before you plan to use it. If your kitchen is warm, it's okay to refrigerate the vegetable for a day or two.

When planning a meatless meal, an eggplant dish is the natural choice as an entrée that will be completely satisfying. If the meal includes cheese, the eggplant will work to neutralize the dairy product's cholesterol—a nice thought if you happen to be as fond of eggplant parmigiana as I am!

Crunchy Eggplant-Walnut Pâté with Whole-Wheat Pita Bread

Makes about 2 cups.

This appetizer has proved to be so popular with my guests that I hardly ever have a teaspoon of it left over. The eggplant must be well-cooked to bring out its rich flavor.

1 medium eggplant (about 1 pound)
½ cup walnuts
1 clove garlic
1½ tablespoons red wine vinegar
2 tablespoons olive oil
½ teaspoon each ground cumin and salt
¼ teaspoon pepper
*2 tablespoons minced fresh
flat-leafed parsley*
whole-wheat pita bread or bagel chips

Preheat the oven to 375° F. Prick the eggplant with a fork, place it (whole and unpeeled) on a baking sheet, and bake for 45 minutes, or until it collapses when lightly pressed with the back of a spoon. Cool.

Toast the walnuts under the broiler (be careful not to burn!) or in a toaster oven set for medium toast. Coarsely chop the walnuts in a food processor; scoop them into a dish.

Without washing the work bowl, mince peeled garlic by dropping it down the feed tube while the motor is running. Scoop the roasted eggplant out of its skin; discard the skin. Purée the eggplant flesh with the garlic. Add the vinegar, oil, cumin, salt, and pepper. Taste to correct the seasoning and texture; you may want more oil, vinegar, or spice.

Alternatively, mash the eggplant by hand and crush the garlic in a garlic press.

Transfer the pâté to a bowl, and stir in the walnuts and parsley. Serve with pita bread cut into wedges and warmed, or bagel chips.

Imam Bayeldi

Makes 4 servings.

The literal translation of this traditional Turkish dish's name is "the priest fainted." There is much speculation on how the name might have originated, but the consensus is that the poor fellow was overwhelmed by pleasure when he tasted this dish.

*2 medium-to-small eggplants
(about ¾ pound each)*
3 tablespoons olive oil or more
1 large onion, chopped
2 cloves garlic, minced
*4 large ripe tomatoes, peeled and
chopped (about 2 cups)*
*½ teaspoon dried thyme
leaves plus 2 pinches*
salt and pepper to taste
juice of ½ lemon
1 teaspoon sugar
1 cinnamon stick

Cut the eggplants in half lengthwise. Cut off strips of peel lengthwise at 1-inch intervals, leaving strips of peel intact. On the flat side, make several deep slashes in the eggplant flesh but don't cut all the way through. Salt the cut eggplant and let it drain in a colander for 30 minutes. Rinse, squeeze out any excess moisture, and pat dry.

Heat the oil in a skillet. Brown the flat side of the eggplants in the hot oil and place the eggplant halves in a baking dish, flat side up.

Sauté the onion and garlic in the same oil (adding another tablespoon, if necessary) until they are softened but not brown. Add the tomatoes, ¼ teaspoon thyme, and salt and pepper to your taste. Cook over medium-high heat, stirring often, until the tomatoes are reduced to a sauce consistency. Spoon the sauce over the eggplant halves, pressing it into the slashes. Sprinkle each half with an additional pinch of dried thyme.

Preheat the oven to 400° F.

Put enough water in the pan to come halfway up the sides of the eggplant. Add the lemon juice, sugar, and cinnamon stick to the water. Cover tightly. If using foil as a cover, tent it so that the foil doesn't touch the eggplant. Bake for 1 hour. Let cool in the pan juices. With a large slotted spatula, remove the eggplant halves to a serving dish.

Serve in thick slices at room temperature as an appetizer or an accompaniment.

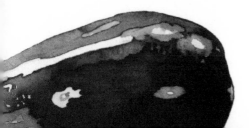

Meatless Moussaka

Makes 4 to 6 servings.

This delicate moussaka is similar to a soufflé and is best served right out of the oven.

2 medium eggplants (about 2 pounds)
olive oil
salt and pepper to taste
1 pound low-fat ricotta cheese
1 egg or ¼ cup prepared egg substitute
2 tablespoons minced fresh flat-leafed parsley
¼ teaspoon white pepper
2 egg whites
pinch of cream of tartar
2 tablespoons butter
2 tablespoons flour
1½ cups milk (can be low-fat)
½ teaspoon salt
¼ teaspoon nutmeg
¼ cup grated Parmesan cheese

Peel the eggplant and slice it into rounds. Salt both sides and stand the slices in a colander to drain for 30 minutes. Rinse the slices, squeeze out the moisture, and pat them dry. Preheat the oven to 375° F. Brush the slices on both sides with olive oil and lay them in a single layer on baking sheets. Salt and pepper them to your taste. Bake for 15 minutes, or until lightly browned and tender.

Mix the ricotta cheese with the egg, parsley, and white pepper.

Beat the egg whites with cream of tartar until they are stiff.

Melt the butter in a medium saucepan. Stir in the flour and cook over low heat for 2 minutes, stirring often. In another pan or in the microwave, heat the milk to a simmer, and add it all at once to the butter-flour mixture, stirring constantly over medium heat until thickened. Add the salt and nutmeg. Fold the beaten egg whites into the hot sauce.

Assemble the moussaka. In a nonreactive (glass or stainless steel) oblong baking dish or roasting pan, 2½-quart capacity, arrange one-third of the eggplant, then all the ricotta, another third of the eggplant, the tomato sauce, the remaining eggplant, and top with the white sauce. Sprinkle with Parmesan cheese.

The moussaka can be prepared an hour or so ahead of time to this point. Cover and refrigerate until ready to cook.

Bake in a preheated 375° F. oven for 45 minutes, or until golden brown on top and bubbly throughout.

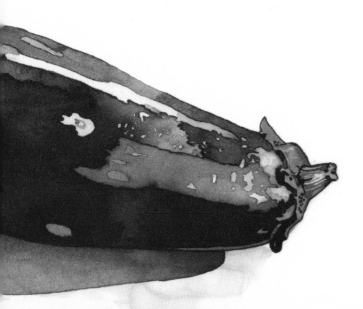

Ziti *alla Siracusa*

Makes 4 big servings as an entrée.
A green salad of bitter or peppery greens, such as dandelion or watercress, with plenty of raw onion and a vinaigrette dressing, would go well with the sweet, rich taste of this dish.

1 large eggplant (about 1½ pounds)
⅓ cup olive oil
1 green pepper, diced
2 cloves garlic, minced
one 28-ounce can Italian-style tomatoes with juice
½ cup pitted black olives
4 flat anchovies
1 tablespoon drained capers
1 dried hot red pepper
.1 teaspoon oregano
½ teaspoon salt
¼ teaspoon freshly ground black pepper
¼ cup chopped fresh flat-leafed parsley
1 pound ziti
grated Parmesan cheese as an accompaniment

Peel the eggplant and slice it into rounds. Salt both sides and stand the slices in a colander to drain for 30 minutes. Rinse the slices, squeeze out the moisture, and pat them dry. Dice the eggplant.

Heat the oil in a large skillet. Stir-fry the eggplant and green pepper over medium-high heat until the eggplant is softened and lightly browned; stir in the garlic and fry another minute. Don't brown the garlic.

Add all the remaining ingredients, except the parsley, and simmer, uncovered, over low heat for about 30 minutes, stirring often. The eggplant should be very soft but retain its shape, and the tomatoes should have cooked down to a sauce consistency. Remove the red pepper pod and stir in the parsley.

Meanwhile, cook the ziti according to the directions on the package. Toss with the egg-plant mixture and serve with grated cheese as an accompaniment.

Orange-Scented Stuffed Eggplant

Makes 6 servings.

An appetizer, a meatless entrée, or an accom-paniment, this versatile and undemanding dish is delicious hot, cold, or at room temper-ature. Leftovers make great pita sandwiches.

1 large eggplant (about 1½ pounds)
3 tablespoons olive oil, more if needed
1 clove garlic, minced
1 small onion, chopped
8 mushrooms, chopped
3 canned Italian plum tomatoes, drained
8 very thin strips of orange peel, no pith (use a potato parer to scrape off the peel)
10 Kalamata olives, pitted and halved
¼ teaspoon black pepper
¾ cup herb stuffing mix (not the stovetop variety) or seasoned breadcrumbs
1 whole clove garlic, crushed

Halve the eggplant lengthwise. To make the shells, cut a slit ¾ inch inside the peel. Cut the centers in a crisscross pattern at ½-inch intervals. Do not cut through the peel. Salt the halves, pressing them open so that the salt gets into the cuts. Let them drain in a colan-der for 30 minutes.

Rinse the eggplant thoroughly. Scoop out the cut part, which will come out diced, leav-ing the shells. Squeeze the juice out of the diced eggplant.

Preheat the oven to 375° F.

Heat 2 tablespoons of oil in a large skillet, and stir-fry the garlic, onion, diced eggplant, and mushrooms over high heat until their juice has evaporated and they begin to brown. Add more oil if needed. Add the tomatoes, breaking them up with a spoon, orange peel, olives, and pepper, and cook over medium heat, stirring often, for 8 to 10 minutes. Stir in the stuffing mix or seasoned crumbs.

Divide the stuffing among the eggplant shells and place them in a large baking pan. Pour 1 inch of water into the pan, add the remaining tablespoon of oil and the crushed garlic. Brush additional oil on the cut edges of the eggplant shells. Cover loosely with foil and bake on the middle shelf of the oven for 45 minutes. Remove the foil and bake 15 minutes longer. *The eggplant can be kept warm, covered, for 30 minutes.*

To serve, cut each half into 3 slices.

Heat about 1 tablespoon of the oil in a large skillet. Stir-fry the eggplant until it begins to wilt, about 5 minutes, adding another tablespoon of oil when needed. Add the garlic and cook 5 minutes longer, stirring often.

Add the cabbage, marjoram, another tablespoon of oil, and salt and pepper to your taste. Continue to stir-fry until the cabbage is tender but not mushy, about 10 minutes. If it is needed, use the last tablespoon of oil.

Serve warm or at room temperature.

Eggplant with Red Cabbage

Makes 4 big servings.

Two anticancer vegetables teamed up for a colorful, quick, and different ratatouille.

*1 medium-to-large eggplant
(about 1¼ pounds)*

4 tablespoons olive oil

2 cloves garlic, minced

2 cups finely sliced red cabbage

*1 tablespoon minced fresh marjoram or
1 teaspoon dried*

salt and pepper to taste

Peel the eggplant and slice it into rounds. Salt both sides and stand the slices in a colander to drain for 30 minutes. Rinse the slices, squeeze out the moisture, and pat them dry. Dice the eggplant.

Grilled Japanese Eggplant

Makes 4 servings.

Plan to make the garlic and herb oil ahead of time so that it can develop a full flavor. Leftover oil can be used in salad dressings or brushed on Italian toast for garlic bread.

*4 Japanese eggplants or small
Italian eggplants (less than ½ pound each)
garlic and herb oil (see Basics)*

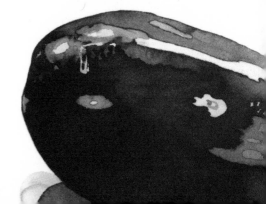

Slice the eggplants in half lengthwise. Make 4 to 5 slits crossways in the cut side. Salt the eggplant flesh and stand the halves in a colander to drain for 30 minutes. Rinse the halves, squeeze out the moisture, and pat them dry.

Brush the oil well into the slits and over the surface of the eggplant. Prick the peel on the rounded side of the eggplant with a fork. Grill on an oiled rack about 5 inches from the coals, cut side down, until brown, about 4 minutes. Turn the eggplant halves, move them to the side of the grill, and cook on the rounded side 4 to 6 more minutes, until tender, brushing the cut side with additional oil.

Alternatively, the eggplant can be broiled 4 to 5 inches from the broiler flame for 8 minutes. No need to turn the eggplant when using a broiler. Brush the cut side with oil again just before serving.

Eggplant and Green Bean Salad

Makes 6 servings.

A summer favorite combining several superfoods. Real anticholesterol medicine in an appetizing guise.

1 medium eggplant (about 1 pound)
1 pound fresh green beans
3 tablespoons olive oil
1 sweet red pepper, seeded and cut into strips
2 cloves garlic, minced
½ teaspoon dried oregano
salt and pepper to taste
¼ cup wine vinegar
1 tablespoon drained capers

Peel the eggplant and slice it into rounds. Salt both sides and stand the slices in a colander to drain for 30 minutes. Rinse the slices, squeeze out the moisture, and pat them dry. Cut the eggplant into strips.

After snipping off their ends, cut the green beans diagonally into 3-inch lengths. Steam the beans for 7 minutes, or until tender-crisp. Rinse the beans in cold water to stop the cooking action.

Heat the olive oil in a large skillet. Sauté the eggplant with the sweet red pepper over medium-high heat, stirring often, until the eggplant is just tender. Stir in the garlic and continue to cook for about 2 minutes. Season with oregano, and salt and pepper.

Combine the eggplant with its oil, the red pepper, and the green beans in a salad bowl. Toss with the vinegar and capers. Let the salad cool and serve it at room temperature. If it must be refrigerated, let it come to room temperature before serving.

For more eggplant recipes, see: Butternut Ratatouille; Tuna Provençal

FIGS

A SWEET TREAT WITH SURPRIS-ING BENEFITS. One of the earliest fruit trees to be cultivated, the fig spread throughout the area around the Aegean Sea and became a staple of the early Greeks. By the time it reached Rome, the fig had become sacred to the god Bacchus, lover of *la dolce vita*, and was employed in religious ceremonies. Among ancient peoples, the fig was always thought to promote good health and was used as a treatment for many ailments and diseases, including cancer. This faith in the restorative power of figs has found some surprising justification recently.

The fact that the fig was a traditional treatment for malignant tumors throughout the world interested a group of Japanese re-searchers in the late 1970s, and they studied the effect of fig juice on mice that had been implanted with tumors. The weight of the tumors in the treated mice was reduced by 39 percent compared with the tumor weight in a control group of un-treated mice. Subsequent studies isolated the active compound, which is called benzalde-hyde. When the compound was administered to human cancer patients, it was even more effective than it had been with mice; a few of the patients even went into complete remis-sion. Obviously, there is a carcinostatic agent of promise in figs, and the fruit deserves to join the list of foods that have demonstrated some ability to fight this disease.

Figs also qualify as an excellent source of

plant fiber, which is good for lowering cholesterol and for contributing a feeling of fullness that helps to prevent overeating.

It's nice to know that two large raw figs, even though they're an intensely sweet treat, have only 100 calories. A sweet fruit is a healthful way to satisfy the sugar craving that is often part of premenstrual syndrome. Both sweets and carbohydrates have been shown to relieve some of the angry and depressed moods that are associated with PMS.

Ounce for ounce, figs are higher in calcium than cow's milk and higher in potassium than bananas.

In the Market

The only known fruit that has the blossom on the *inside*, figs come in many different kinds and colors. In this country, we have golden Calimyrna figs and purplish black Mission figs (named for the Spanish mission gardens where they were first cultivated), which are sold both fresh and dried. Pale green Kadota figs are usually canned or made into fig paste. In dried figs, I prefer the Calimyrnas that are preserved so that they retain a soft, plump texture that's very much like that of the fresh fruit; this product is sold in bags, usually in the produce section of the supermarket.

In choosing fresh figs, look for firm ones that are free of blemishes and have a pleasing fragrance; a sour smell is the tip-off that the fruit is overripe. Fresh figs are available from June to November, but the supply is always small. The appearance of really good fresh figs in a local market is such a happy event that it ought to give rise to some impromptu dessert or other delicious fig dish on that night's menu.

In the Kitchen

Fresh figs don't keep well, which is a good excuse to use them immediately. If absolutely necessary, they can be kept a day or two in the refrigerator, no longer.

Dried figs, on the other hand, are readily available all year and will keep for a month or more on the shelf. After opening the bag or box, however, it's best to refrigerate dried figs.

The easy way to chop dried figs is to snip them with scissors, pausing from time to time to run the blades under hot water.

In a pinch, dried Calimyrnas can be substituted for fresh figs in many recipes. ∎

Fennel and Fig Antipasto

Makes 6 servings.

Fresh figs are preferable for this dish, but they aren't always available when fennel is in the market during the fall and winter.

*1 medium-size bulb of fennel
(about 1 pound)*

¼ cup olive oil

2 tablespoons red wine vinegar

salt and freshly ground pepper to taste

*12 fresh figs or 12 plump and soft,
dried Calimyrna figs—don't substitute
the hard imported figs*

Trim the stalks and "hair" from the fennel bulb. (They can be saved for salads.) Quarter the bulb; cut out and discard the core. Chop the fennel into bite-size pieces.

In a flat vegetable dish, combine the fennel with the oil, vinegar, salt, and pepper. Toss well to prevent browning.

Remove the hard stem ends from the figs and cut them in half. Gently toss them with the fennel. Chill until ready to serve.

This appetizer can be divided among 6 salad plates lined with inner leaves of leafy red lettuce, or it can be passed with other antipasti at the table.

Chicken Sauté with Figs and Almonds

Makes 4 servings.

A different and pleasing combination of flavors in an entrée that won't take more than 30 minutes to prepare from start to finish.

4 to 6 fresh plum tomatoes (about 1 pound)

1½ tablespoons olive oil

*2 whole skinned and boned chicken breasts,
cut in half lengthwise (4 pieces)*

1 large shallot, minced

*1 sweet red pepper, seeded and cut
into small dice*

salt and pepper to taste

8 dried Calimyrna figs

¼ cup shelled whole unblanched almonds

Pour boiling water over the tomatoes.

Heat the oil in a large skillet and brown the chicken on one side. Turn the pieces to brown them on the second side, adding the shallot and red pepper to the skillet.

Meanwhile, drain, peel, and chop the tomatoes in small dice. When the peppers begin to brown, add the tomatoes; their moisture will keep the peppers from overbrowning while the chicken finishes cooking. Add salt and pepper to the dish.

Add the figs and almonds and continue sautéing until the chicken is cooked through, 15 to 20 minutes total cooking time. If the tomatoes dry out during this time, add 2 tablespoons of water to the skillet.

The sauté can be cooked ahead, refrigerated, and rewarmed in a skillet over low heat.

"Couscous" with Figs and Raisins

Makes 4 servings.

This is not refined white couscous but a whole-grain type that can be served as an accompaniment to roasted or braised chicken.

2 tablespoons vegetable oil
1 large shallot, minced
2¼ cups low-salt chicken broth or water
¼ teaspoon each thyme, salt, and pepper
⅛ teaspoon cinnamon
4 dried Calimyrna figs, stems removed, snipped into small pieces
2 tablespoons dark raisins
1 cup fine-grained cracked wheat, found in whole food/health food stores (refined white couscous can be substituted)

In the top of a large double boiler, heat the vegetable oil and sauté the shallot over direct heat until it's sizzling. Add the broth or water, seasonings, and dried fruits, and bring the mixture to a boil. Add the wheat in a slow stream so that the water never stops boiling.

Meanwhile, bring 2 inches of water to a boil in the bottom of the double boiler. Cook the cracked wheat, covered, over simmering water for 15 to 20 minutes, until it tastes done. If substituting refined white couscous, cook only 5 minutes. Fluff well before serving.

Figs Poached in Marsala

Makes about 26 poached figs.

These succulent figs may be served in so many ways: as a brunch dish; as a garnish for roast veal or pork; as a dessert, atop a slice of plain cake with some of the juice, or in a stemmed glass with a scoop of lemon sherbet.

one 14-ounce package dried figs
1 cup Marsala wine (white grape juice may be substituted)
1 cup water
1 lemon, sliced, seeds removed

Combine the figs, the Marsala or grape juice, water, and lemon in a saucepan. Bring the mixture to a boil, reduce the heat, and simmer, covered, for 30 minutes. Let the figs cool in the liquid.

Coffee-Can Fig and Nut Bread

Makes 2 loaves.

Coffee-can breads are fun to make and easier than most yeast breads, because the dough requires little kneading, one rising will suffice, and there are no pans to wash. Save two empty coffee cans (about 13-ounce size) to make this recipe.

1½ tablespoons dry yeast (1½ packages)
½ cup warm water
1 teaspoon sugar
¼ cup melted butter or low-cholesterol margarine
1½ cups scalded milk
¼ cup honey
1 teaspoon each ground cardamom and salt
1½ cups whole-wheat flour
2½ cups unbleached all-purpose flour plus about ½ cup more
1 cup snipped figs
½ cup coarsely chopped walnuts

Sprinkle the yeast on the warm water and sugar. Allow the mixture to stand for 10 minutes; it should bubble up.

Use a pastry brush to paint the insides of two 13-ounce coffee cans lavishly with the melted butter. Do the same with the insides of the plastic covers.

In a large bowl, stir the remaining butter into the hot milk along with the honey, cardamom, and salt. Stir in the whole-wheat flour and the yeast; beat the mixture for 2 minutes (a hand-held mixer makes this easier).

Stir in the white flour, 1 cup at a time. After the first cup, stir in the figs and nuts while the dough is still soft enough to incorporate them.

Knead the dough right in the bowl, adding as much of the extra ½ cup of flour as is necessary, until a smooth ball is formed. Divide the dough into 2 even portions and pack them into the coffee cans. Put the covers on.

Let the cans stand in a warm place until the rising dough pops the covers. Don't let the dough overrise.

Put the cans uncovered in a cold oven and set the heat for 350° F. Bake on the middle rack for 45 minutes, or until the top is nicely browned and sounds hollow when tapped. Transfer the breads to a wire rack.

As soon as you can handle the cans, remove the bottoms with a hand-held can opener. (This is the only tricky part, since you don't want to damage the top crusts. Lay a coffee can on its side with about 1 inch over the sink, so that the hand-held can opener can have room to turn.) Use a spatula very gently to loosen the sides of the breads and the top crusts; then ease them out. Lay the breads on their sides to cool completely on the rack before cutting. After cooling, you can stand them up, where they will look like 2 robust brown mushrooms.

To serve, cut either into rounds or long wedges. I prefer the wedges, because each long slice then has a bit of the top crust.

One or both of the breads can be frozen for later use.

Broiled Fresh Figs with Brown Sugar

Makes 4 servings.

Fruits provide just as many health bonuses as vegetables. The nutritional goodness you add is just as important as the sugar and fat you subtract when you switch from heavy sweets to light fruit desserts.

> *sections from 2 seedless oranges,*
> *for garnishing*
> *8 fresh Calimyrna figs (golden*
> *skins, amber pulp)*
> *brown sugar*

Use a knife to peel the oranges thickly to remove both the peel and the outer membrane. Cut the sections out of the rest of the encasing membrane with a serrated fruit knife.

Slice the tough little stems off the figs, and cut the figs in half. Place them in a baking dish, cut sides up. Sprinkle each one with brown sugar and broil them in a preheated broiler until the sugar begins to caramelize.

Divide the figs among 4 dessert plates and garnish them with orange sections.

HEALTH SECRET OF THE INUIT REVEALED AT LAST! By the 1950s, scientists had it figured that fat in the diet was a leading cause of heart disease. Then researchers began to wonder why the North American Inuit, whose diet may be higher in fat than that of any other people in the world, had so little heart disease, arthritis, and ailments of the immune system. It took some nutritional detective work to find that the *amount* of fat in the Inuit diet didn't count, because the *kind* of fat conferred a unique protection. The Inuit customarily dine on fish rich in beneficial omega-3 fatty acids; the animal fat eaten by other groups, on the other hand, is laced with omega-6 fatty acids, and this makes all the difference.

Omega-3 fatty acids lower the artery-clogging LDL cholesterol, raise the helpful HDL cholesterol, lower the blood pressure, and protect against strokes by making the blood less prone to clotting.

Further research has demonstrated that omega-3 fatty acids behave like aspirin and other anti-inflammatory agents in curbing the formation of fatty acids known as prostaglandins. Overproduction of prostaglandins is implicated in asthma, arthritis, systemic lupus erythematosus, psoriasis, and multiple sclerosis. While omega-3 fatty acids are not a cure for these disorders once they are full-blown, a hearty helping of fish oil in the diet may help prevent them.

When I was a youngster, children were routinely forced to take cod-liver oil throughout the fall and winter months to prevent colds and flu. The lucky ones got pills (which nevertheless "repeated" all morning); the less fortunate had to drink up a tablespoon of the nauseating oil itself. What a way to start a school day! At the other end of the age scale, those little golden pills with the powerful smell were believed by old-time doctors to be good for arthritis. Cod-liver oil went out of fashion in later decades, but now we have discovered the wonderful benefits of fish oil—again. How much nicer, though, to enjoy delicious fish dinners instead of having to imbibe a spoonful of cod-liver oil! There is also less danger of overdosing on vitamins A and D when one's fish oil comes in the form of, say, Tuna Provençal.

Besides, there's more to a fish dinner, as opposed to a pill, than just the omega-3 fatty acids in fish oil. A study done in the Netherlands indicated that eating even *lean* fish was linked to a lower incidence of heart disease. Obviously, that surprising x factor in whole foods (encompassing all the nutritional benefits that we haven't got a handle on yet) has cropped up here! As few as two fish meals a week can lead to a healthier heart.

In other studies, fish oil also has demonstrated beneficial effects in the treatment of migraine headaches and certain kidney diseases in the early stages.

High on the list of fish rich in omega-3 fatty acids are mackerel, anchovies, salmon, herring, whitefish, tuna, bluefish, swordfish, and trout. Other fish, such as cod, perch, and haddock, have some of these important nutrients but not as many.

It wasn't too long ago that people on low-cholesterol diets were told to avoid shellfish, but researchers have found that shellfish (with the exception of shrimp) actually lower cholesterol. Oysters, crabs, and clams top the list of cholesterol fighters.

Whatever healing properties are offered by omega-3 fatty acids can be obtained from shellfish as well as fish. Mussels, oysters, and shrimp contain the most omega-3 fatty acids—not as much as oily mackerel, but more than a white fish such as haddock.

Oysters, herrings, and clams are among the richest sources of the mineral zinc, which is involved in making sperm and producing male hormones. A deficiency in zinc can lead to a low sperm count.

Swordfish, lobster, salmon, and tuna head the list of foods rich in selenium. Studies have shown that diets high in selenium have a negative effect on the development of atherosclerosis.

"Fish is good brain food," many of our parents told us, and they were right! A light, protein-rich fish lunch will fill your bloodstream with amino acids, including tyrosine. Tyrosine crosses a protective filter called the blood-brain barrier, where it's converted into the chemicals dopamine and norepinephrine. These chemicals help you to feel alert and sharp. And that's not all! Fish gives you another substance that affects the brain, choline, which improves the memory and is a natural relaxant. (Choline is also essential to proper liver function.)

So if you go easy on the alcohol, fat, and carbohydrates, but do have a cup of black coffee (caffeine being another alertness chemical), you should be ready to take that after-lunch meeting by storm, while less savvy lunchers are still foggy from manhattans and weighed down by beef fat.

In the Market

Good fresh fish does not smell "fishy"! If you press the flesh, it will spring back into place. Whole fish should have clear eyes and red gills. But the best insurance of fresh fish is to shop at a large fish market with a high turnover of merchandise, a place where the fish is kept on ice and not wrapped in plastic. If you notice that the stock is low on a particular day of the week—Monday perhaps—don't buy. There will be fresher fish later in the week.

Commercially frozen fish and shellfish are never as good as fresh. Shrimp's the best of the lot, however, and nice to have in your freezer. Most of the shrimp you'll see in the fish-market case have been frozen and thawed anyway. Some brands of frozen shrimp are superior to others, so when you find one with a sweet, not briny, flavor, stick with it.

Having said that, let me add that I often freeze fish myself. To save trips to the fish store, I buy enough fresh (never frozen) fish for two or three meals during the week, and freeze some of it for a few days. This short-term freezer storage doesn't seem to affect the flavor adversely.

The term "fresh" when seen on fish-market signs (such as "fresh swordfish") is not a comment on its quality but is supposed to indicate that the fish has never been frozen. Choose only fresh fish for home freezing. If in doubt, ask.

Fish is expensive, right up there with beef tenderloin and veal chops, but there is less waste and portions are often smaller. And it's so satisfying to know that the more you replace red meat with fish, the bigger the payoff in good health.

In the Kitchen

As soon as you get home, put the fish on ice; this means that you should arrange a layer of ice cubes in a glass baking dish, top the ice with foil, and lay the fish over the foil, covered with wax paper rather than plastic wrap. Store the fish this way in the coldest part of your refrigerator for no more than a day or two. If you find you can't use the fish within that amount of time after all, cook it; this will give you another day or two of storage. Before cooking any fish, rinse it in cold water and pat it dry with paper towels.

If you buy raw shrimp and plan to shell and devein them before cooking, keep in mind that some people suffer from an allergic reaction to handling raw shrimp. It's a little clumsier, but wearing rubber gloves will prevent this problem.

Fish is the original fast food. Nearly all kinds of fish steak can be baked in 20 minutes in a 400° F. oven or poached in even less time, which is a comfort to a busy working person. Steaming small shellfish takes less than 5 minutes. In fact, one of the cardinal rules of cooking is: Never overcook fish! It makes the dish taste fishy instead of delicate, as fish is meant to be.

Ma's *Minestra* with Mussels

Makes 4 to 6 servings.

This soup is so good when entirely home-made, it's worth the trouble of making a full-bodied chicken broth (*see Basics*), which would, as a side benefit, leave you with a whole boiled chicken for the second course.

1 to 1½ pounds mussels
6 to 7 cups well-flavored chicken broth
1 bunch escarole (about 1 pound)

While stored in the refrigerator, mussels should be kept on ice (but not in the freezer) and allowed to breathe; don't store them in airtight plastic.

If possible, buy cultivated mussels that have been cleaned of their "beards" (fibers growing on the outside of the shells) and are grit-free, requiring no soaking. They should be bagged and labeled with that information.

Otherwise, soak the mussels in cold water for an hour before cooking. Scrub the shells under running water with a stiff brush and pull off the beards.

Discard any mussels that have cracked shells. Use only mussels that are closed or that close up tightly when you tap them, indicating that they're still lively.

Wash the escarole very well and roughly cut the leaves into thirds.

In a large pot, bring the broth to a boil, add the escarole, and simmer until the greens are tender, about 10 minutes. *The soup can be prepared ahead to this point and reheated.*

Put the cleaned mussels into the pot on top of the greens. Cover and cook until the shells have opened, 3 to 5 minutes. If one or two haven't opened when the rest have, discard the closed ones.

Top each portion of the soup with some of the mussels in their shells.

Poached Salmon Steaks with Grapefruit

Makes 2 servings.

The fish that are best for a healthy heart are the oily ones, such as salmon and trout. I find that citrus fruits are especially complementary with the strong flavors of oil-rich fish.

1 grapefruit, red or white
1 tablespoon olive oil
2 salmon steaks, about ½ inch thick
1 teaspoon snipped fresh chives

Cut the grapefruit in half and remove each section with a grapefruit knife from the encasing membrane. Squeeze and reserve the remaining juice from the grapefruit halves.

Put the oil in a glass pie plate and turn the steaks over to oil both sides. Place the steaks so that the thickest parts are toward the edges of the pie plate. Pour 2 tablespoons of the grapefruit juice over the salmon.

Cover loosely with microwave-safe plastic wrap and microwave on medium for 7 minutes. Turn the steaks and spoon the grapefruit sections over them.

Cover loosely with plastic wrap and microwave for about 7 minutes on medium, or until the salmon flakes easily at the thickest part. Sprinkle the steaks with chives and serve.

Alternative method: The steaks can be poached on the range top over low heat in a skillet with a tight cover. Use ¼ cup grapefruit juice.

Baked Half Salmon with Vegetable-Dill Stuffing

Makes 4 or more servings.

Admittedly, boning a salmon is a tricky step, but it makes the finished dish a lot more enjoyable. Peas with Pesto *(pages 222-223)* is a perfect accompaniment.

half a fresh salmon in one piece
(2 to 3 pounds)
1 lemon
1 tablespoon olive oil

For the stuffing:

3 slices whole-wheat bread
3 scallions, finely chopped
¼ cup grated carrot
½ sweet red pepper, finely diced
2 tablespoons minced fresh dill or
1 teaspoon dried dill
pepper to taste

Rinse the fish inside and out. With a long, sharp knife, remove the *inner* membrane, bones, and spine. Cut horizontally just underneath the membrane (as if you were skinning a chicken breast). Then remove the spine with the point of a sharp knife, taking care not to cut off any more of the fish than necessary. Don't remove or pierce the *outer* skin.

Slice into thin rounds and seed the lemon.

Grease a baking dish with the olive oil. Cut 3 long pieces of kitchen twine and lay them crossways on the dish. Put the fish, skin side down, open for stuffing, over the twine.

Crumb the bread in a food processor or by hand. Mix together all the stuffing ingredients. Spoon the stuffing into the cavity; it will be quite full. Lift the ends of the twine and tie and knot them to close the fish completely over the stuffing. Carefully slide the fish over so that the cut side is underneath.

Lay the lemon slices over the top of the salmon, tucking them under the string as necessary. *The salmon can be prepared to this point a few hours early; chill in the coldest part of the refrigerator until ready to cook.*

Bake the fish in a preheated 350° F. oven

for 45 to 50 minutes, or until cooked through. Gently remove the twine. Let the fish stand for a few minutes before slicing. *The salmon can be kept warm for 15 to 20 minutes.*

Fresh Tuna Provençal

Makes 4 servings.

Salting won't really take the bitterness out of an old eggplant, so be sure to buy a fresh, firm, young eggplant. But salting does prevent the eggplant from sponging up too much oil while it fries, thus allowing you to make a much lighter dish.

1 small eggplant (about 1 pound)

2 tablespoons olive oil

1 green pepper, seeded and chunked

1 clove garlic, pressed or very finely minced

one 14- to 16-ounce can whole Italian tomatoes with juice

½ cup large brine-cured black olives, pitted

¼ teaspoon salt

¼ teaspoon pepper

1½ pounds fresh tuna (4 steaks)

2 tablespoons chopped fresh flat-leafed parsley

Peel and slice the eggplant into rounds. Salt both sides and stand the slices in a colander to drain for 30 minutes. Rinse the slices, squeeze out the moisture, and pat them dry. Dice the eggplant.

Heat the olive oil in a 12-inch skillet. Sauté the green pepper until it begins to soften; add the garlic and cook 1 minute longer. Add the eggplant and stir-fry until it is slightly softened. Add the tomatoes, olives, and seasonings. You won't need much salt, because the olives are salty. Simmer the mixture over medium heat, uncovered, stirring occasionally, for 15 minutes or until it is reduced to a sauce consistency. You can help this along by chopping and crushing the tomatoes with a spatula as they cook. *The sauce can be prepared ahead and reheated.*

Lay the tuna steaks in the sauce and spoon some of it over them. Cover and poach over very low heat until the tuna will flake apart at the center, 10 to 15 minutes. Don't overcook. Sprinkle with parsley and serve.

Pan-Fried Trout with Caper Sauce

Makes 4 servings.

Fish is my idea of the perfect fast food. Almost any fish dish cooks in 20 minutes or less.

*4 small trout, filleted (8 pieces), or
2 large (4 pieces)*

*stone-ground cornmeal,
preferably not degerminated*

salt and pepper to taste

¼ cup vegetable oil

*4 small bunches seedless green grapes for
garnish (optional)*

For the sauce:

1 tablespoon olive oil

2 flat anchovies, rinsed in vinegar

½ cup dry vermouth

½ cup bottled clam juice

2 tablespoons drained capers

2 tablespoons chopped green olives

2 tablespoons chopped black olives

Warm the olive oil in a small saucepan; add the anchovies and stir over low heat until they have dissolved into a paste.

Add the remaining sauce ingredients and simmer the mixture until it is reduced by one-third, about 10 minutes.

Meanwhile, dredge the fillets in cornmeal; salt and pepper them to your taste.

Heat the vegetable oil in a cast-iron or other heavy skillet, and pan-fry the fillets until they are golden brown on both sides. While the fish are frying, put the grapes in the freezer for 5 minutes.

To serve, divide the fillets among 4 warm plates and spoon the sauce over them. Garnish with icy grapes.

Baked Bluefish with Potatoes

Makes 4 servings.

Bluefish's definite flavor stands up well to plenty of garlic and herbs. The meltingly tender potatoes layered underneath the fish taste as if they've been cooked in a good strong chowder. Tomato salad or carrot slaw *(page 82)* would go well with this dish.

⅓ cup olive oil

2 cloves garlic, chopped

¼ teaspoon each dried basil and rosemary

4 potatoes, peeled and thinly sliced

salt and pepper to taste

1½ to 2 pounds bluefish fillets

1 tablespoon minced fresh parsley

lemon wedges

Preheat the oven to 400° F. Combine the olive oil, garlic, and herbs in the bottom of a baking dish. Add the potatoes and stir to coat them with the oil, pressing them into an even layer. Salt and pepper them to your taste. Bake the potatoes for 20 minutes on the top shelf, or until they are cooked halfway through.

Remove the dish from the oven and place the bluefish fillets over the potatoes, skin side down. Brush some of the oil-garlic mixture over the fish.

Bake the fish for 20 minutes, or until both fish and potatoes are cooked through. Sprinkle with parsley and garnish with lemon.

Baked Flounder Fillets with Fennel Crust

Makes 4 servings.

Another fast fish dish, ready in less than 30 minutes, including preparation time!

2 pounds flounder fillets
1 teaspoon fennel seed
1 teaspoon paprika
2 tablespoons toasted wheat germ
⅔ cup seasoned dry breadcrumbs
1 egg beaten with 3 tablespoons water or ¼ cup prepared egg substitute
3 tablespoons vegetable oil
4 scallions, chopped
1 cup chopped raw fennel
fennel hair for garnish (optional)
lemon wedges

Preheat the oven to 400° F. Rinse the fillets and pat them dry on paper towels.

Crush the fennel seed in a mortar. Mix the fennel seed, paprika, wheat germ, and crumbs on a sheet of wax paper. Dip the flounder first in the egg, then in the crumbs.

In a baking pan that will fit the fish in one layer, mix the oil, scallions, and raw fennel. Place the pan in the oven until the vegetables are sizzling but not brown.

Pushing the vegetables aside, turn the fillets once in the pan to oil both sides. Spoon the vegetables under the fillets. Bake for 15 to 20 minutes, until the fish flakes easily.

Garnish with sprigs of fennel hair, if desired, and serve with lemon wedges.

Golden Orange Smelts

Makes 4 servings.

This recipe uses a marinade that makes oily fish taste lighter and frozen fish taste fresh.

24 fresh or frozen dressed smelts (about 1 pound)
1½ cups orange juice
¼ cup rice vinegar
2 teaspoons grated orange zest
¼ cup cornmeal
¼ cup unbleached all-purpose flour
vegetable oil for frying
salt to taste
orange and lemon wedges for garnish

Put the smelts in a shallow dish. Mix the orange juice, vinegar, and orange zest, and pour the marinade over the fish. Refrigerate for at least 4 but no more than 6 hours before cooking, turning the fish once or twice.

Mix the cornmeal and flour on a sheet of wax paper. Pick up each smelt by the tail, leaving whatever zest clings to the fish, and dip it in the dry mixture, coating both sides.

Fry in hot oil until golden; salt to your taste. Garnish with orange and lemon wedges.

Lemon Sole with Lemon-Pepper Sauce and Egg Bows

Makes 4 servings.

The original Italian pasta *al limone* is made with heavy cream. This much lighter version uses milk and a very small amount of butter.

1½ to 2 pounds lemon sole fillets
1 tablespoon olive oil
½ teaspoon rosemary
½ lemon, very thinly sliced, seeded
½ pound egg bow pasta

Sauce:

2 tablespoons vegetable oil
1 tablespoon butter
3 tablespoons unbleached all-purpose flour
1½ cups milk
juice of ½ lemon
1 teaspoon grated lemon zest
½ teaspoon salt
½ teaspoon white pepper
several dashes of nutmeg

Preheat the oven to 400° F. Rinse and pat the fish dry. Pour the olive oil into the baking pan (choose an attractive one you can serve from). Place the fish fillets in the pan in 1 layer. Sprinkle with rosemary. Top with lemon slices. Bake 20 minutes, or until cooked through.

Meanwhile, cook the pasta according to the package directions and make the sauce.

Heat the vegetable oil and butter in a medium saucepan. Stir in the flour, and cook the roux, stirring occasionally, over low heat for 3 minutes, but don't let it brown. Heat the milk to the scalding point in the microwave or another saucepan. Pour the hot milk at once into the roux, stirring constantly over medium heat until the sauce bubbles and thickens. Whisk in the lemon juice, lemon zest, salt, white pepper, and a dash of nutmeg.

Gently transfer the fish to a platter. Mix the egg bows into the pan juices. Add 1 cup of sauce and stir. Slide the fish on top. Spoon on the remaining sauce and another dash of nutmeg. Serve from the pan.

Down-Home Oyster Pie à la Rockefeller

Makes 4 servings.

A super luncheon dish based on the ingredients of that classic oyster appetizer. You'll have a little leftover pastry dough, nice for making a very small jelly tart.

one 10-ounce package frozen leaf spinach, cooked according to package directions

2 tablespoons vegetable oil

2 shallots, chopped

1 stalk celery, finely diced

2½ tablespoons butter or low-cholesterol margarine

¼ cup flour

1½ cups very hot milk

1 teaspoon anisette (small but essential)

¼ teaspoon each dried tarragon, white pepper, and salt

1 pint of shucked oysters, well-drained

pastry for a 2-crust pie (see Basics—the oil pastry preferred)

beaten egg or prepared egg substitute to glaze the crust (optional)

Put the drained spinach in a 9-inch pie pan or a straight-sided glass dish of the same size. Use a knife and fork to chop it coarse.

In a medium-size saucepan, heat the oil and sauté the shallots and celery until they are softened. Remove them with a slotted spoon and sprinkle them over the spinach.

Melt the butter with the oil remaining in the same pan. Stir in the flour, and cook the roux over very low heat for 3 minutes. Add the hot milk all at once, stirring constantly over medium-high heat, until the sauce bubbles and thickens. It will be very thick. Blend in the anisette, tarragon, white pepper, and salt. Pour the sauce over the spinach, lifting the vegetable a bit so that the sauce will slide underneath. Let the mixture cool to room temperature. Do not chill the mixture.

With the back of a spoon, make little "nests" in the thickened sauce for the oysters. Place the drained oysters over the spinach.

Preheat the oven to 400° F.

Use about three-quarters of the pastry to roll out a thicker-than-usual top crust that overhangs the rim of the pan by a half-inch all around. Turn the overhang under, and secure the crust to the edge of the pan by pressing it down with the tines of a fork. If desired, glaze the pastry by brushing on beaten egg or prepared egg substitute. Cut vents in the crust to allow steam to escape.

Bake the pie in the top third of the oven for 30 minutes or until the top is golden and the sauce has been bubbling for 5 minutes (to cook the oysters). Let it stand 5 minutes before serving.

Fresh Codfish Cakes

Makes 6 servings.

Although the traditional recipe calls for salt cod, which is then freshened in many changes of water for two days, why not start with fresh fish instead? Actually, you don't even have to be restricted to cod (or scrod); you can make these cakes with any leftover flaked fish such as bluefish, for instance.

2 pounds potatoes
1 teaspoon white or cider vinegar
½ teaspoon salt
¼ cup minced shallots
2 tablespoons olive oil
about ½ cup bottled clam juice
¼ teaspoon white pepper
1 tablespoon fresh minced parsley or
1 teaspoon dried parsley
¼ teaspoon crushed tarragon leaves
1 pound cooked fresh cod, flaked
fine dry breadcrumbs
paprika
vegetable oil for frying

Peel and cube the potatoes. Boil them in water to cover, to which you've added the vinegar and salt, until they are quite tender.

Meanwhile, sauté the shallots in the oil until they are soft but not brown.

Drain the potatoes well and mash them, adding enough clam juice to make them fluffy but not runny (remember, you will form this mixture into cakes). Whip in the shallots with oil, pepper, parsley, and tarragon.

Add the fish and blend gently but well. Taste to correct the seasoning, adding more salt and white pepper as desired. Form the mixture into 12 cakes, flatten them slightly, and dip each cake in breadcrumbs on all sides.

Put enough vegetable oil in a large skillet (cast iron does this best) to coat the bottom, and fry the cakes in 2 batches, keeping the cooked ones warm, until they are golden on both sides. Sprinkle them with paprika as they cook. Add more oil to the pan as needed.

Grilled Fish Steaks

Makes 4 servings.

An easy summer favorite! Why not grill eggplant on the side *(pages 106-107)?*

4 fish steaks—swordfish, salmon, shark,
or tuna—about ½ pound each,
¾- to 1-inch thick
lime wedges for garnish

For the marinade:

⅓ cup vegetable oil
⅓ cup rice vinegar
3 tablespoons soy sauce
1 teaspoon sesame oil
1 large clove garlic, minced

Rinse the fish steaks and pat them dry. Mix together the marinade ingredients. On a deep platter, marinate the fish in this mixture for at least 2—but no more than 4—hours in the refrigerator, turning occasionally.

Oil the grill bars. Cook the fish steaks over ash gray coals or medium-high gas about 6 minutes per side.

If no grill is available, the fish may be broiled on an oiled broiling pan. Broil 6 minutes per side, or until cooked through.

Test the fish for doneness by separating at the center of a steak with a fork. The fish should be opaque all the way through and separate cleanly. Serve with lime wedges.

Scallops with Vegetable Sauce

Makes 4 servings.

This is a great vegetable sauce with any fish. The grated carrots add sweetness; the black and cayenne peppers add spice.

¼ cup olive oil
1 onion, finely chopped
1 large clove garlic, minced
1 green pepper, finely chopped
2 stalks celery, finely chopped
2 large carrots, finely grated
one 28-ounce can tomatoes, drained
½ teaspoon each salt, sugar, and dried basil
¼ teaspoon each dried thyme and black pepper
cayenne pepper to taste (the more the better in this dish!)
1½ pounds sea scallops

In a large skillet, heat the oil, and sauté the onion, garlic, and green pepper until slightly wilted. Add all the remaining ingredients except the scallops. Simmer uncovered until the vegetables are tender and the tomatoes are reduced to a sauce, about 20 minutes. *The sauce can be prepared ahead and reheated.*

Add the scallops, cover, and simmer for 5 minutes, or until the scallops are just cooked.

Serve with hot cooked rice on the side—or on a bed of ½ pound cooked corkscrew pasta, such as rotini or rotelle.

For other fish recipes, see: Baked Swordfish with Tarragon Yogurt; Lobster and Barley Salad; Greek-Style Shrimp with Shell Pasta; Paella with Brown Rice; Poached Swordfish with Grapes; Red Snapper with Rosemary-Scented Shallot Confit; Salmon Steaks with Cucumber-Mint Sauce; Scrod Baked with Onion, Lemon, and Rosemary; Shells with Tuna and Peperoncini; Shrimp with Apple and Celery; Smoked Salmon Pasta Salad with Peas and Scallions; Sole with Linguine; Sunshine Oat Bran Pizza; Tomato and Anchovy Salad; Tomato, White Bean, and Tuna Salad; *Tonno* and Brazil Nut Salad with Sweet Red Pepper Dressing; Tuna Tapenade

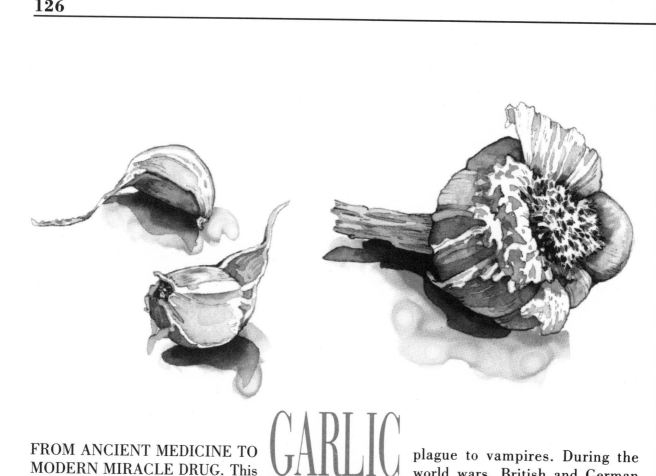

GARLIC

FROM ANCIENT MEDICINE TO MODERN MIRACLE DRUG. This pungent member of the lily family is hardly languishing from neglect. Literally hundreds of recently published studies have sorted through the cure-all claims that physicians through the ages have put forth for garlic, and in 1990, the "world's first congress on the health significance of garlic" was held in Washington, D.C., cosponsored by the U.S. Department of Agriculture and Pennsylvania State University.

In ancient and medieval times, garlic not only was valued as a cure for everything from consumption to snake bite, it was *carried* as a charm to ward off sundry evils, from the plague to vampires. During the world wars, British and German doctors found that garlic afforded some protection from sepsis and gangrene.

A good many of garlic's legendary and anecdotal powers to prevent and cure illnesses have been proved in modern trials. (The jury is still out on vampires.) Garlic contains an odorless constituent called allium, which, when crushed, is changed into dozens of sulfur-containing compounds and also releases that characteristic odor. Allium is an antibiotic, an intestinal antispasmodic, a decongestant, an expectorant, and much more.

In experiments on everything from bacteria in petri dishes to animals and humans, evidence has been found that demonstrates garlic's wide expanse of medicinal activity. Garlic lowers the levels of blood cholesterol and triglycerides (the main vehicle that carries fats in the blood). It lowers blood pressure and reduces the blood's tendency to clot, thus protecting against strokes. It stimulates the immune function and is an antioxidant. It detoxifies the effects of chemical pollutants and lessens the effects of radiation. It's a germicide, a fungicide, and an intestinal worm killer.

In a study done in China, it was found that people who consumed a high quantity of allium vegetables (garlic, onion, scallions) had a 60 percent lower incidence of stomach cancer than those who eschewed garlic. A study in Italy produced similar results. In laboratory experiments, various garlic derivatives have proved inimical to cancerous growth tissues of the lymph glands, colon, esophagus, and skin. Although this doesn't prove that garlic can be used to *heal* cancer, it does make a case for increasing garlic consumption as a preventive measure.

How much garlic? Recommendations run from one or two cloves a day to seven. Most of us will probably opt for a conservative dose. Luckily, garlic is an "in" food around culinary circles these days and is sometimes called "the ketchup of intellectuals."

Can you overdose on garlic? Some people will get stomach distress from too much garlic or from raw garlic. Excessive amounts can contribute to anemia. As in all things, it's wise to be moderate. Good sense should accompany good foods.

Considered from a medicinal point of view, garlic is most effective when it's eaten raw, especially for lowering cholesterol. Next best is barely cooked garlic. The well-cooked bulb, however, does retain *many* of its disease-fighting properties, including lowering blood pressure.

Sautéed or roasted garlic is more digestible than raw, and boiled garlic is most digestible of all. Never, never brown garlic, however, since this turns its pleasant flavor into a bitter one.

Unfortunately, people do worry about offending others with the strong odor of garlic. The quick remedy of chewing up a sprig of parsley, which fills your mouth with breath-freshening chlorophyll, is not, regrettably, a complete remedy. Stubborn garlic lingers on, emanating from the stomach and from perspiration. But if you've just minced a clove of garlic and you're off to an embassy party where someone may want to kiss your hand, wash those garlicky fingers thoroughly with a wedge of lemon followed by some salt, and the odor will dissipate.

The ideal solution to the garlic problem is to feed your friends garlic, too—and relax. As a matter of fact, it's also a good idea to feed garlic to your dog. Dogs love its flavor, and garlic (along with brewer's yeast) discourages fleas and worms.

Not only does garlic offer so many protective qualities, it's also a flavorful substitute for salt, curing the "bland blues" for those wishing to cut down on sodium.

In the Market

The most common garlic, an Italian type, has white papery bulbs containing over a dozen buds, or cloves. The Spanish type has a tinge of purple, smaller cloves, and a more pungent flavor. "Elephant garlic" has the largest cloves and the mildest flavor. In choosing any of these at the market, look for firm, dry heads with no darkish cloves or sprouts. The bulbs should have a pleasing rather than bitter odor.

Garlic powder, garlic salt, and dried minced garlic don't provide all the health benefits of fresh garlic, nor are they as pleasant-tasting as fresh garlic. In fact, they add an acrid and strong essence without the savoriness of the real stuff. Since fresh garlic is available all year, why bother with these products? If you think it's too much trouble to mince garlic, buy a good garlic press. To speedily peel a clove, smash it with a mallet or the flat of a chef's knife. Then pop it into a press and enjoy the great flavor you can get only from a fresh clove. Cooking really good-tasting, simple, fast food hinges on numerous little choices like this to go for the freshest and best. And if something must be skimped on, it should never be the flavoring ingredients.

In the Kitchen

Store garlic in a cool, dry, dark place, but not in the refrigerator. I store garlic, shallots, and onions in new clay flowerpots of successively larger sizes, away from heat and direct light; they keep well and look nice, too.

If despite your best efforts, a bulb of garlic begins to sprout, you can plant the cloves in a potting-soil-filled flowerpot, place it in a sunny window, and soon have garlic chives to snip onto salad or omelets.

Glorious garlic—how many dishes are lifted from bland ordinariness to a new distinction by its discreet use! It's especially magical when lightly sautéed in olive oil, in a combination of two of the most potent "heal-all" foods in nature's pharmacy!

Roasted Eggplant and Garlic Soup with Sweet Red Pepper

Makes 4 servings.

Each of these vegetables acquires a special flavor when roasted. The eggplant is richer, the pepper tastes grilled, and the garlic is milder.

1 medium eggplant (about 1 pound)
½ bulb garlic
1 sweet red pepper
2 cups chicken broth
1 cup beef broth
2 tablespoons olive oil
½ teaspoon oregano
¼ teaspoon freshly ground black pepper
1 cup herb croutons

Preheat the oven to 350° F. Pierce the eggplant with a fork in several places. Put it in a small roasting pan and cook for 15 minutes. Break a whole bulb of garlic in half and add a half bulb to the roasting pan with the red pepper. Bake the vegetables until they are *very* tender. The pepper and garlic will take about 30 minutes, the eggplant 45 minutes. To test, the pepper and eggplant should collapse when pressed with a fork. The garlic should be tender when pierced with a paring knife.

Put the pepper in a plastic bag until it's cool enough to handle (this loosens the skin). Peel, seed, and dice it.

Peel the garlic and eggplant. Purée them together in a food processor or blender. *The soup can be prepared ahead to this point.*

In a large saucepan, whisk together the eggplant and garlic purée, broth, olive oil, oregano, and black pepper. Bring the soup to a boil, reduce the heat, and simmer for about 5 minutes, stirring occasionally. Stir in the diced red pepper.

Just before serving, sprinkle each portion with croutons. Do this at the *last moment,* so that they won't be mushy.

Sopa de Ajo a la Castellana (Castilian Garlic Soup)

Makes 4 servings.

If you want to enjoy the easy, nutritious dishes in any country's cuisine, just seek out the food of the peasants, such as this simple soup.

3 tablespoons olive oil
4 thick slices Italian bread
2 cloves garlic, minced (or more, to your taste, up to 4)
1 quart beef broth (two 13-ounce cans)
2 tablespoons minced fresh flat-leafed parsley
freshly ground black pepper to taste

Put 1 tablespoon of the oil in a skillet and fry the bread until golden. Add another tablespoon of oil to the pan and fry the bread on the second side. When the bread is almost done, add the remaining tablespoon of oil and the minced garlic, putting it between the slices so that it will sauté.

When the garlic is pale gold, add the broth, and simmer it for 10 minutes. Sprinkle the soup with parsley and pepper, and serve.

Using a spatula to keep them intact, transfer the bread slices to individual bowls and then pour the remaining broth (most of it will be absorbed by the bread) around each slice.

Pa's Garlic and Parsley Steak

Makes 2 servings.

This is one of those perfectly simple dishes that has one trick to it that makes all the difference. It's vital that the pan be hot when you add the steak, and that you don't crowd the meat. If you put too much steak in a too-cool pan, the meat will steam and toughen instead of searing. So if you decide to double this recipe, be sure to do it in two batches.

¾ to 1 pound trimmed, lean steak, sirloin or round (don't use frozen, thawed steak; it will contain too much moisture)

2 tablespoons olive oil

1 to 2 cloves garlic, minced

2 tablespoons fresh minced flat-leafed parsley

salt and pepper to taste

Cut the steak into 1-inch cubes. Heat the oil in a 12-inch skillet. When it's quite hot, add the steak, quickly separating the pieces. When the steak begins to sizzle, add the garlic, and stir-fry the meat until it's seared on all sides (for medium rare).

Remove the meat to a warm platter. Add the parsley, salt, and pepper.

Garlic-Stuffed Veal Roast with Garlic Mirepoix

Makes 6 servings.

A mirepoix is a sauce of finely chopped vegetables, "sweated" in butter, used to flavor braised meats. A veal roast especially needs a moist mirepoix to keep it from being dry and flavorless. It's equally good for roast venison, for the same reason.

2 tablespoons olive oil

one 3-pound veal roast, boned, rolled, and tied

1 tablespoon butter or low-cholesterol margarine

2 cups finely chopped vegetables: a mixture of onion, shallot, carrot, celery, and/or peppers can be used

2 cloves minced garlic

1 cup finely chopped fresh or canned tomatoes

¼ teaspoon each dried thyme, salt, and pepper

2 cloves of garlic, slivered

½ cup white wine (optional)

½ cup chicken broth (optional)

Put the oil in a Dutch oven and brown the veal on all sides over medium-high heat. Remove the veal.

Add the butter to the oil that remains, and sauté the vegetables and minced garlic over low heat until they are very soft but not brown. Add the tomatoes and cook 5 minutes longer. Add the thyme, salt, and pepper.

Preheat the oven to 350° F. Cut small slits, 1 inch apart, in the veal roast, and insert a sliver of garlic in each. Put the veal in the pan, spooning some of the mirepoix over it. Cover and bake the veal on the middle shelf of the oven until quite tender, about 2 hours. Let it stand about 10 minutes before slicing.

The roast can be kept warm, covered, for 30 minutes.

If you desire, deglaze the pan with ½ cup each of white wine and broth, then purée the wine, broth, and vegetables to make a sauce.

Garlic Roasted Potatoes

Makes 4 servings.

You'll have to remind yourself that there are only 2 tablespoons of oil in this dish (most of which will remain in the roasting pan), because these potatoes have all the finger-licking goodness of French fries—and a nice fillip of garlic as well!

6 Idaho or russet potatoes

2 cloves garlic, thinly sliced

2 tablespoons olive oil

salt and freshly ground black pepper to taste

paprika

Preheat the oven to 450° F. Peel the potatoes; cut them into fourths lengthwise, about 1 inch thick. If the potatoes are round rather than long, cut them into eighths. Place them in one layer in a baking pan from which you can serve. Add the garlic and oil; turn the potatoes in the oil to coat all sides. Sprinkle them with salt and pepper to your taste and a liberal coating of paprika.

Bake for 30 minutes. Loosen the potatoes with a spatula and turn them over. Bake an additional 15 to 20 minutes, or until quite tender inside and crusty outside. Serve from the pan.

Old-Fashioned Pork Stew with Whole Garlic Cloves

Makes 4 servings.

Each diner is invited to mash the whole garlic cloves right into the gravy of this savory stew, which is a no-trouble-at-all oven-cooked dish. Beef can be substituted for the pork.

3 tablespoons olive oil

1½ to 2 pounds boneless pork cutlets, trimmed of all fat, and roughly cut into 2-by-2-inch pieces

1 onion, sliced

3 tablespoons flour

2 cups very hot water

2 tablespoons each red wine vinegar and tomato paste

½ teaspoon each dried tarragon and salt

¼ teaspoon each dried thyme leaves and freshly ground black pepper

1 bay leaf

4 large potatoes, quartered, or 8 small, halved

4 carrots, scraped and cut into 2 pieces each

8 whole garlic cloves, unpeeled, but with the rough ends opposite the roots cut off

Preheat the oven to 350° F. Heat 1 tablespoon of oil in a Dutch oven and sear the meat on all sides. Remove the meat and fry the onion slices until they are golden.

Add the remaining 2 tablespoons of oil and the flour to the onions, and cook the roux over medium heat, stirring often, until it's lightly browned, not burned. Add the hot water all at once, stirring constantly until the mixture bubbles and thickens. Blend in the vinegar, tomato paste, and seasonings.

Add the seared meat, potatoes, carrots, and whole garlic cloves, and stir to coat everything with the gravy. Bring the sauce to a boil on the range top, cover tightly, and put the pan on the middle shelf of the oven. Bake for 1 hour, or until the meat and vegetables are tender. *The stew can be made ahead, refrigerated for a day, and reheated on the range top; stir often and gently.*

Remove the bay leaf before serving.

Garlic Snacking Bread

Makes 8 servings whether cut into squares or wedges.

Here's a zesty bread you can whip up in just a few minutes. It's great with soups and stews, and if there happens to be any left over, a hunk of this bread can really liven up a cottage cheese lunch.

Quick breads (which are leavened with baking powder or baking soda instead of yeast) have their own requirements. If you want to get things ready ahead of time, for this or any quick bread/muffin recipe, keep the dry ingredients separate from the liquids until the last moment. Then stir them together until just blended and quickly spoon the batter into a prepared pan.

¼ cup olive oil
1 tablespoon finely minced (not pressed) garlic

1 cup whole-wheat flour
1 cup unbleached all-purpose flour
1 tablespoon baking powder
½ teaspoon salt
1 teaspoon mixed dried herb leaves (not ground herbs), your own combination—rosemary and marjoram, thyme and dill, or tarragon and basil are possibilities—or store-bought Italian seasoning
1 cup milk (can be low-fat)
1 egg or ¼ cup prepared egg substitute

Preheat the oven to 400° F. Choose a heavy 11-by-7-inch pan or 10-inch cast-iron skillet. Pour in the oil. Sprinkle with garlic. Put the pan on the range top on warm until the garlic sizzles and softens. (This will also grease the pan.) Let the mixture cool to lukewarm while taking the next steps.

Sift together both flours with the baking powder and salt. Stir in the herbs.

In a separate bowl, combine the milk and egg. Scrape in all of the garlic and oil from the prepared pan, and whisk this together with the milk and egg mixture.

When ready to bake, pour the liquid ingredients into the dry, stir just enough to blend completely, and spoon the batter into the oiled pan. Quickly use a spatula to level the batter, and bake the bread on the top shelf for 20 minutes, or until it's lightly browned and tests dry when pierced with a cake tester.

Note: There are numerous other recipes throughout this book that also use garlic.

GRAPES

GOOD FOR YOU IN ANY FORM—FRESH, DRIED, OR FERMENTED. Nature's original snack food, perfect for juicy, sweet nibbling, has never lacked devotees, especially since the first enterprising vintner discovered grapes' potential as a fermented beverage.

The sweetness of grapes comes from glucose, a form of sugar that causes tryptophan to rush to the brain, producing the relaxing chemical serotonin. So rather than snacking on grapes before that big meeting where you want to be sharp and alert, enjoy them instead as an after-work treat when you're ready to unwind.

Although most of the nutritional experiments with grapes to date have been performed in test tubes and lab cages, some rather promising results have been obtained.

Red grapes are rich in at least two substances that protect animals from cancer. Grape juice, wines, and extracts from grapes (along with apple juice and tea) have the power to polish off intestinal viruses cultivated in test tubes. Dietary studies on human populations show a lower incidence of gum disease among those who regularly snack on grapes and their dried counterparts, raisins. Animal studies credit grape juice with preventing tooth decay caused by bacteria.

Along the line of folk medicine, many arthritis sufferers have claimed for years that a combination of grape juice and powdered pectin (sold in supermarkets for making jelly from fruits that don't have enough pectin of their own) has eased their condition—though this hasn't been scientifically substantiated.

The fermented juice of grapes has laid claim to health benefits, also. Red wine, especially, is a natural antibiotic—but, on the negative side, it can trigger migraines in those people who are sensitive to its tannins.

Alcoholic drinks in general can be good for your heart. A recent study of 51,000 health professionals showed that those who consumed from one-half to two drinks a day (wine, beer, or hard liquor) reduced their risk of heart disease by 26 percent compared with those who abstained. Wine is the staple drink of people of the Mediterranean Basin, whose low rate of heart disease has impressed researchers.

This information, of course, must be balanced against damage to the liver that can result from immoderate drinking. Alcohol consumption is also related to hypertension and may increase the risk of colon cancer.

In the Market

There are several popular varieties of grapes from which to choose. Green seedless Thompsons, a leading table fruit. Calmeria, a long greenish white grape with a firm pulp and a thick skin. Small juicy Perlette grapes, sweet and thin-skinned. Red-purple Emperor grapes, firm-textured, wonderful in cooking if you don't mind seeding them. Bright red Tokay grapes, very thick-skinned and seeded, with a neutral flavor. Tart purple Concord grapes, a favorite for juice and jelly. Ribier grapes, darkest of all, seeded, superbly flavored.

The peak months for grapes are July through November, although you'll probably find some not-so-great grapes for sale all year long. Grapes don't ripen after they're picked, so look for well-formed bunches with crisp fruit and bright color. Dark varieties should show no tinge of green; bunches of green grapes should not harbor any yellow fruit. But color isn't everything, and you'll never know if the grapes you're buying are truly sweet unless you taste one.

In the Kitchen

To prevent a big bunch of grapes from looking ravaged, snip it into small clusters (three to six grapes, depending on how they grew) before the snackers attack it.

If you put grapes in a bowl with other fruits, they will soon spoil. It's best to refrigerate grapes until just ready to serve; they will keep for three to four days.

Grapes seem to be the very symbol of fall (as strawberries usher in the spring). In the good grape months, I like to brighten an appetizer tray of cheeses by surrounding it with bunches of different varieties.

Grapes just seem to be a natural garnish to decorate any dish, from the first course to the last. For a dessert garnish, you can "frost" grapes by dipping clusters into slightly beaten egg white, then rolling them in sugar. Allow the clusters to dry before serving. Or, for a quick, cool treat, combine seedless grapes with honey and yogurt in a stemmed glass. Anything made with grapes just seems to be delightfully simple! ▬

Braised Chicken with Dark Grapes and Walnuts

Makes 4 servings.

Here's a company dish you can put together while carrying on a conversation (and allowing someone else to seed the grapes).

2 whole skinless, boneless chicken breasts, cut into halves

2 tablespoons olive oil

1 onion, finely chopped

½ cup Marsala wine (optional)

½ cup chicken broth (1 cup if not using wine)

½ teaspoon fresh thyme or ¼ teaspoon dried thyme leaves

salt and pepper to taste

½ cup cold water

2 tablespoons lemon juice

1 tablespoon cornstarch

½ cup walnut halves

1 cup dark, sweet grapes, such as Ribier, halved and seeded

In a large skillet, brown the chicken on both sides in the oil over medium-high heat. When the second side is brown, reduce the heat, add the onion to the skillet, and sauté until it's translucent.

Add the Marsala, broth, thyme, salt, and pepper. If you're not using Marsala, increase the broth to 1 cup. Simmer very slowly, with cover ajar, for 15 to 20 minutes, turning the chicken once, until just cooked through.

Remove the chicken and measure the pan juices; there should be ½ cup. If there's less, add chicken broth to make ½ cup and return the juices to the skillet; bring to a boil. In a cup, mix the water, lemon juice, and cornstarch until there are no lumps. Pour all at once into the skillet and stir constantly until the sauce is thickened.

Add the walnuts; return the chicken to pan. Cook 3 minutes longer. Stir in the grapes.

Veal Véronique

Makes 4 servings.

The term *Véronique* is applied to any dish containing green grapes. And grapes go well in many dishes—besides the fruit bowl!

1½ pounds veal stewing meat
cut into cubes
¼ cup flour
2 tablespoons olive oil
3 shallots, finely minced
salt and white pepper to taste
pinch of dried thyme leaves
1 cup chicken broth
¼ cup dry vermouth
1½ cups seedless green grapes

Put the veal in a plastic bag with the flour and shake to coat. Shake off excess flour. In a large skillet, brown the veal in the oil slowly and thoroughly in several small batches. Don't rush this step. Just before the veal is browned, add the shallots; continue to fry until the shallots have softened.

Add salt, pepper, thyme, ½ cup of the broth, and the vermouth. Cook, uncovered, stirring often, until the veal is quite tender, about 45 minutes, adding more broth as needed. Add the grapes and just bring to a simmer; remove from the heat and serve.

Poached Swordfish with Grapes

Makes 4 servings.

The crisp, slightly acid flavor of green grapes complements an "oily" fish (like swordfish, mackerel, or smelt) very nicely.

1 tablespoon olive oil
4 scallions, chopped
1 cup dry white wine
2 tablespoons lemon juice
¼ teaspoon salt
white pepper to taste
1½ to 2 pounds swordfish cut into
4 serving pieces
1 tablespoon cornstarch
½ cup cold water
½ teaspoon dried tarragon leaves
1 cup seedless green grapes

Heat the oil in a large skillet, and sauté the scallions until they are softened. Add the wine and lemon juice; stir in the salt and pepper.

Put the swordfish steaks in the skillet, and poach them, covered, in barely simmering wine for 5 to 10 minutes, until they are just cooked through.

Gently remove the fish with a spatula to a heated platter and keep the steaks warm.

Stir the cornstarch into the cold water until there are no lumps. Bring the pan juices to a boil, add the cornstarch mixture all at once, and cook, stirring constantly, until the sauce bubbles and thickens. Crush the tarragon leaves between your fingers and stir them in. Reduce the heat and simmer for 3 minutes. Add the grapes and cook another minute. Pour the sauce over the fish before serving.

Grape and Arugula Salad with Mustard Vinaigrette

Makes 4 servings.

The zesty flavor of this salad goes well with a shellfish entrée.

4 large leaves red leafy lettuce
2 cups coarsely chopped arugula
4 scallions, chopped
2 cups red grapes, seedless or seeded

For the vinaigrette:

2 tablespoons Dijon mustard
3 tablespoons red wine vinegar
⅓ cup olive oil
freshly ground black pepper to taste

Tear the red leafy lettuce into bite-size pieces and make a bed of it on 4 salad plates. Divide the arugula and scallions among the salads. Put the grapes on top.

Thoroughly whisk the mustard into the vinegar, then slowly whisk in the oil and add the pepper.

Dress the salads with the vinaigrette.

Fresh Grape Tart

Makes 6 to 8 servings.

A perfect dessert for autumn, when many varieties of grapes are available and you can experiment with taste and color combinations.

1¼ cups pastry cream (see Basics)
2 tablespoons Marsala wine
1 baked tart shell (see Basics)
about 2 cups grapes of 3 different kinds, such as seedless green, seedless red, and Ribier grapes
¼ cup apple jelly

Make the pastry cream and flavor it with the Marsala. When the filling has cooled to lukewarm, spread it in the tart shell.

Lightly press whole seedless grapes and halved, seeded Ribier grapes in a pattern of alternating circles over the pastry cream.

Melt the apple jelly in a microwaveable cup, about 1 minute on high in the microwave, or in a small saucepan over low heat. Brush the jelly over the grapes.

Let the tart chill until the filling is set, about 2 hours.

Green Grape Sangria

Makes nearly 2 quarts.

This is a light refresher, halfway between a drink and a compote. You can serve the fruit with the liquid in a stemmed goblet—or serve the two separately in wine glass and dessert bowl. Either way, spoons are in order.

1 quart or liter of dry white wine

¼ cup fruit-flavored liqueur, such as Midori (melon-flavored) or curaçao (orange-flavored)

1 cup seedless green grapes

1 cup honeydew melon balls

1 large ripe pear, peeled, cored, and diced

1 apple, peeled, cored, and diced

1 lime, very thinly sliced and seeded

10 to 15 ice cubes

Combine all the ingredients except ice cubes in a large pitcher, stir, and chill for at least 30 minutes to combine flavors. Even longer—as much as 6 to 8 hours—is better.

Add ice a few minutes before serving.

If you serve this outdoors, as one would be tempted to do, keep the pitcher well-covered—fruit flies will come from a hundred miles away for this drink!

Red Grape Sangria

Substitute dry red wine for white, red grapes (seeded if necessary) for green, cantaloupe for honeydew, 2 peaches for pear and apple, and an orange for the lime. Use curaçao rather than Midori for the liqueur.

For another grape recipe, see the following: Concord Grape Yogurt

GREENS

VERSATILE VEGETABLES OF MANY VIRTUES. "Eat your greens!" was a phrase I heard often as a youngster, as I sat hunched over a dish of boiled greens dressed with olive oil, having finished all of the foods on my plate that I considered more appetizing. My mother was "into" health food long before it became a widespread concern. As I look back, I realize that she had an amazing instinct for choosing foods that were later to become the superstars of nutrition. I feel grateful now for all those bowls of greens I so reluctantly consumed. But I also know that the wise family cook will vary the way greens are served in the interest of making them a welcome part of the menu. Fortunately, greens are capable of infinite variety!

We're not talking of anemic iceberg lettuce here, but of the dark, leafy greens that are chock-full of compounds to build up our resistance to disease: curly kale, versatile spinach, tender broccoli rabe, mild collards, peppery dandelions, slightly bitter mustard greens, red-stemmed beet greens, and big-leafed Swiss chard.

They're all rich in vitamins and minerals. Among those minerals, greens can provide a good source of calcium for people who want to cut down on dairy foods. (A cup of cooked kale contains almost as much calcium as a cup of whole milk.) Among those vitamins, greens offer significant amounts of beta carotene. The dark green color of chlorophyll—a substance that may fight cancer—masks the characteristic orange of beta carotene, but it's there!

In a study done in the 1970s, over 1,200 Massachusetts residents older than 60 were evaluated in a "food-frequency" questionnaire that tabulated their intake of foods high in beta carotene. After following this elderly group over a five-year period for incidence of cancer mortality, the researchers concluded that there was indeed a trend toward decreased cancer risk with increased intake of beta carotene.

Other studies have indicated a decreased risk in lung, stomach, bladder, colon, cervix, and prostate cancers among people who consume greater amounts of dark green and orange vegetables.

How does beta carotene work? It's been postulated that beta carotene may deactivate some molecular troublemakers. When these substances are rendered unable to damage cells, a chain of events that could lead to cancer is broken. Or, beta carotene may act during later stages of carcinogenesis. Or both. Scientists are not sure just how beta carotene works, but they have considerable evidence that it does, even among older people.

Kale and mustard greens are especially potent; they both carry a double-edged sword against cancer. Besides containing hefty amounts of beta carotene and chlorophyll, they're also members of the cruciferous family (along with cabbage and Brussels sprouts). The recently discovered chemical sulforaphane, found abundantly in cruciferous vegetables, has been identified as a substance that stimulates protective enzymes known to guard against tumors.

All of which is more than enough reason to "eat your greens!"

In the Market

Different greens are available all through the year, from tender young spinach in spring to winter kale, which is sweeter if harvested after the first frost, so you can always find a dark, leafy vegetable that's in season. At the market, choose greens that are crisp, not wilted, with no signs of yellowing or rusting. Some greens, such as spinach, are sold in cellophane bags "for your convenience," but you will get better greens with fewer thick, tough stalks if you buy an unbagged bunch instead. In larger markets, greens are often "misted" periodically, giving them a fresher appearance temporarily. But soggy greens rot faster, so misted greens need to be inspected for leaves that have turned dark and wet with decay.

In the Kitchen

Wet greens may decay faster, but dry greens wilt. I've found the best way to prevent both rot and wilt is to wrap the greens (this includes parsley and all kinds of lettuce) in a clean kitchen towel before placing them in an unfastened plastic bag. The cloth keeps the greens from drying out entirely but absorbs any excess moisture. Put the greens in your crisper or on the bottom shelf of the refrigerator. They will keep quite fresh and crisp from two days to a week, depending on kind.

Also in the interest of delaying decay, don't wash greens until you're ready to cook them. Some locally grown leafy greens can be very sandy, and nothing spoils a carefully prepared and otherwise delicious dish more than the feel of grit between one's teeth. Put the greens in a sinkful (a salad spinner isn't big enough) of *lukewarm*, not warm, water and swish them about. Drain, and repeat, but this time and for subsequent washings use cold water, until no more sand remains at the bottom of the sink. If the leaves are curly, finish by washing each one under running water. (Cookbooks of the old school called for seven to 12 washings for greens. Although the produce we get today is usually cleaner, four to five washings are not excessive.)

Frozen greens may be nice and clean already, but only whole-leaf or cut-leaf (rather than chopped) frozen spinach offers something like the quality of cooked fresh spinach. (Even if you need chopped spinach, buy the whole leaf and chop it yourself for better flavor.) Other frozen greens are inferior in taste and texture.

Many greens can be exchanged for one another in recipes, as long as you are aware that some have a stronger flavor than others.

I like tender young spinach best in salads, either alone or mixed with other greens. I've found, too, that even a greens-hating child may enjoy the dreaded vegetable in salads.

Dandelions make a salad that's especially enjoyed by Italians; the peppery leaves are teamed up with a really vinegary vinaigrette and lots of raw onion. Italian salads are served *after* the entrée; wine is not served with that course, since the vinegar would throw off its flavor. A sharp salad of slightly bitter greens is a kind of macho palate refresher, instead of, say, a miniscoop of sorbet.

An easy way to cook greens is to steam them in the water that clings to their leaves after washing, a technique that's called for in some of the following recipes.

Broccoli Rabe and Potato Soup with Meatballs

Makes about 3 quarts.

Here's a robust fall soup that cooks in just 30 minutes. Try it as an entrée accompanied by a salad of late local tomatoes *(pages 270-273)* and a hearty rye bread from a good bakery.

Broccoli rabe is an Italian green with a slight bite; it's sometimes called rapini.

2 cloves garlic, pressed

¼ cup olive oil

4 cups chicken broth (or two 13-ounce cans)

2 pounds potatoes, peeled and cut into 1-inch chunks

1 bunch of broccoli rabe (about 1 pound) well-washed, tough stems removed, roughly chopped

¼ teaspoon or more freshly ground black pepper

For the meatballs:

1 pound ground turkey

2 slices whole-wheat bread, crumbed

1 small onion, finely chopped

2 tablespoons grated Parmesan cheese

1 tablespoon minced fresh flat-leafed parsley

1 egg, beaten, or 3 tablespoons prepared egg substitute

½ teaspoon dried marjoram

salt to taste (the cheese provides salt, too)

Combine and blend the meatball ingredients. Roll the mixture into walnut-size meatballs. Refrigerate until needed.

In a large pot, sauté the garlic in oil for 1 minute. Add the broth, potatoes, and greens. Bring to a boil. Add the meatballs one at a time, keeping the soup bubbling. Reduce the heat to a simmer. Cook for 20 minutes. Remove about half the potatoes, mash them well, and return them to the soup to thicken it. Stir gently with a wooden spoon. Simmer an additional 10 minutes.

Just before serving, stir in the pepper.

Note: I often make a double batch of small meatballs, freeze them in one layer on a foil-lined tray, then store them in a plastic bag. They can be added to a soup without thawing.

Vegetable Chowder with Shredded Spinach

Makes about 1½ quarts.

Spinach is one of the few greens that's available all year round, making this off-the-shelf soup a good choice for a quick winter lunch.

1 tablespoon butter

1 medium onion, chopped

2 medium potatoes, diced

1 cup water

¼ teaspoon salt

one 16½-ounce can creamed corn

one 14-ounce can imported Italian tomatoes, coarsely chopped (including juice)

1 teaspoon dried marjoram
½ teaspoon dried dill
¼ teaspoon white pepper
⅛ teaspoon black pepper
a few dashes of cayenne pepper
½ cup milk (whole or skim)
*2 cups shredded raw spinach,
 stems removed*

Melt the butter in a 3-quart saucepan, and sauté the onion until it's wilted but not brown. Add the potatoes, water, and salt; cook until the potatoes are tender.

Stir in the corn, tomatoes, and seasonings, and simmer the soup, uncovered, for about 8 minutes, stirring often. Blend in the milk while stirring constantly. (It won't curdle because of the thickening in the creamed corn.)

Stir in the spinach and immediately remove the soup from the heat. Serve at once.

Florentine Meat Roll

Makes 8 servings.

This meat roll goes together easily and makes an attractive buffet dish with the "jelly roll" swirl of spinach in every slice. The recipe can be doubled and cooked in a glass roasting pan that works as a server (the cooking time will be exactly the same).

2 tablespoons olive oil
1 clove garlic, pressed or finely minced
*1 pound fresh spinach, well-washed,
 tough stems removed*
2 slices whole-wheat bread
1½ pounds ground turkey
1 medium onion, chopped
2 eggs or ⅓ cup prepared egg substitute
*⅓ cup coarsely grated
 Monterey Jack cheese*
2 tablespoons grated Parmesan cheese
*1 teaspoon each dried cilantro
 and tarragon*
*½ teaspoon salt (may be reduced
 or omitted)*
*¼ teaspoon each ground sage and
 black pepper*

Heat the oil and garlic in a skillet. Braise the spinach in this mixture, stirring until it is wilted. Drain the spinach and squeeze all the moisture out of it. Chop the spinach.

Preheat the oven to 350° F. In a food processor or with a grater, reduce the bread to coarse crumbs.

Mix the bread with the ground turkey and all the remaining ingredients; blend well. (This can all be done in the processor, with on/off turns of the motor.)

Spoon the meat mixture onto a large sheet of foil. Pat it out into an oblong roughly 10 by 8 inches. Layer the spinach on top. Gently lift one side of the foil (and keep lifting) to roll the 10-inch side of the meat over the filling. Pat the ends to make them an even thickness with the center. Use two spatulas (or the foil itself) to lift the meat roll into a roasting pan, seam side down.

Bake the roll in the center of the oven for 45 minutes, or until just cooked through.

Let it stand 10 minutes before slicing.

The meat roll can be kept warm, covered, for 30 minutes.

Braised Chicken with Collards

Makes 4 servings.

A skillet dinner that's ready in 30 minutes. A ripe-tomato and onion salad *(page 270)* makes a good accompaniment.

> *1 pound collard greens, well-washed, tough stems removed*
>
> *½ cup chicken broth*
>
> *½ cup unbleached all-purpose flour*
>
> *2 teaspoons Italian seasoning (available in supermarkets or see Basics)*
>
> *¼ teaspoon dried rosemary*
>
> *2 whole chicken breasts, skinned and halved*
>
> *2 tablespoons olive oil*
>
> *salt and pepper to taste*

Put the collards and broth in a large pot and cook until the greens are wilted and tender, watching carefully that the broth does not boil away, about 10 minutes. Drain the greens.

Combine the flour, Italian seasoning, and rosemary in a plastic bag. Add the chicken, hold the bag tightly closed, and shake it to coat the pieces. Remove the chicken with tongs, shaking off any excess coating.

Heat the oil in a large skillet. Brown the chicken pieces on one side. Salt and pepper them. When they're brown, turn the pieces, cover the skillet, and cook 15 to 20 minutes, or until the chicken is cooked through. Add the drained collards to the pan, turning the leaves in the pan juices. Cover and heat through.

Kale with Tomato Risotto

Makes 4 servings.

The microwave makes a beautifully creamy risotto with no stirring, but if you don't have a microwave, follow the alternative directions.

> *½ pound kale*
>
> *1 teaspoon salt*
>
> *one 13-ounce can chicken broth*
>
> *½ cup "kitchen-ready" chopped canned tomatoes*
>
> *2 tablespoons olive oil*
>
> *1 medium onion, chopped*
>
> *1 clove garlic, minced*
>
> *1 cup plus 2 tablespoons Arborio rice*
>
> *2 tablespoons grated Parmesan cheese*

Wash the kale and cut off the stems below the leaves. Fill a large pot halfway with water and add 1 teaspoon of salt. Bring the water to a boil and blanch the kale for 5 to 8 minutes, until tender. Drain well and chop the kale.

Combine the broth and the tomatoes in a saucepan, and bring the mixture to a boil. Have it ready at a low simmer.

Microwave method: In a 3-quart casserole, microwave the onion and garlic in the oil on high for 3 minutes, or until the onion is soft. Add the rice and stir well to coat it with the flavored oil. Add the hot broth, cover, and microwave on high for 6 to 7 minutes, until boiling. Change the setting to medium and continue to cook for about 10 minutes, until the rice is just tender and the liquid has been absorbed. Blend in the cheese, then stir in the kale. Cover and let stand about 5 minutes before serving.

Alternative method: Sauté the onion and garlic in a medium-size saucepan, and stir in the rice. Add about 1 cup of the hot broth and cook at a low boil (but not as low as a simmer), uncovered, stirring frequently, until the liquid is almost all absorbed. Add half the remaining broth and repeat the procedure. Pour in the last of the broth and cook until the rice is tender. Total cooking time should be 12 to 14 minutes. Add the cheese and the kale.

The risotto can be kept warm, covered, for 30 minutes.

Spinach Lasagna

Makes 8 servings.
An extra layer of nutrition for this old favorite!

12 pieces curly lasagna (but cook a couple of extras to allow for breakage, about ¾ pound)

one 1-pound bag cut-leaf frozen spinach

1 clove garlic, crushed

1 tablespoon olive oil

freshly ground black pepper

2 pounds ricotta cheese

2 eggs, beaten, or ½ cup prepared egg substitute

¼ teaspoon white pepper

2½ cups tomato sauce (from a jar or see Basics)

2 tablespoons grated Parmesan cheese

½ pound mozzarella, coarsely shredded

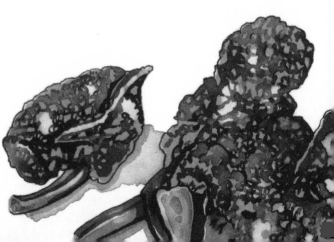

Cook the lasagna according to package directions. After draining, lay the pieces out in a single layer on foil or plastic wrap.

Cook the spinach according to the package directions, adding the crushed garlic to the cooking water. Drain well; discard the garlic. Season with olive oil and freshly ground black pepper.

Mix the ricotta cheese with the eggs and white pepper.

Use a stainless steel or glass baking pan, about 12 by 8 by 3 inches. The size may vary a bit, but the pan should have a 3- to 3½-quart capacity. Spoon ½ cup of tomato sauce over the bottom of the pan. Lay 3 pieces of lasagna over it and spread them with half the ricotta. Add 3 more pieces of lasagna. Spoon the well-drained spinach over that and sprinkle it with Parmesan cheese. Layer 1 cup of tomato sauce over the spinach, followed by 3 more pieces of lasagna and the rest of the ricotta. Top with the remaining 3 pieces of lasagna and another cup of tomato sauce, and sprinkle the mozzarella over the top.

Bake the casserole for 45 minutes to 1 hour (if it's been refrigerated) in a preheated 350° F. oven—or until the ricotta is set. If it's still runny, the lasagna must be cooked longer.

Let it stand for 10 minutes before cutting it into squares. *The lasagna can be kept warm, covered, for up to 1 hour.*

Crustless Swiss Chard Quiche

Makes 4 servings.

Swiss chard has a hearty, beetlike flavor that combines well with other foods.

1 pound Swiss chard, well-washed
½ cup water
1 onion, chopped
1½ cups loosely packed sliced mushrooms
2 tablespoons olive oil
4 eggs or 1 cup prepared egg substitute
¼ cup water
¼ teaspoon hot red pepper sauce
salt and pepper to taste
2 tablespoons seasoned breadcrumbs (store-bought or see Basics)
¼ cup coarsely grated Gruyère cheese

In a large covered pot, cook the chard in water until tender, about 15 minutes. Drain. Then sauté the onion and mushrooms in oil until lightly browned.

Preheat the oven to 350° F. Put the chard in an oiled 8-inch quiche pan. With a knife and fork, chop the vegetable to bite-size pieces. Top with onion and mushrooms.

Mix the eggs, water, hot red pepper sauce, and seasonings. Beat until frothy. Carefully pour the egg mixture over the vegetables. Sprinkle with crumbs and cheese.

Bake for 25 minutes, or until set at the center. Let the quiche stand for 5 minutes, then cut it into wedges to serve.

Colcannon

Makes 6 servings.

This Irish dish is traditionally served on Halloween. Colcannon can be made with cabbage as well as kale, but the kale gives a pleasing color contrast.

1 bunch kale (about 1 pound)
2 tablespoons olive oil
¼ cup minced shallots (about 2 large)
6 potatoes (about 2 pounds)
1 teaspoon white or cider vinegar
½ teaspoon salt
about ½ cup hot milk (can be low-fat)
salt and pepper to taste

Wash the kale very thoroughly and chop it, discarding any tough stems.

Heat the oil in a 12-inch skillet, and sauté the shallots until they are softened but not brown. Add the kale, which should still have some water clinging to it.

Cover and braise the kale 5 to 8 minutes, stirring several times. Add more water if needed. Remove from the heat as soon as the kale is tender to the bite. Keep the kale warm until the potatoes are ready.

Peel and cut the potatoes into uniform pieces. Cover with water to which you've added the vinegar and ½ teaspoon of salt. Boil the potatoes until they are tender. Drain, mash, and whip the potatoes, adding milk as needed to make them fluffy. Add salt and pepper.

Vigorously stir in the kale to keep the texture light. Serve piping hot.

Kale with Sweet Red Pepper and Balsamic Vinegar

Makes 4 servings.

Whether you grow it or buy it, fresh kale tastes best when harvested after the first frost. Its sharp flavor makes a pleasant contrast to sweet orange winter vegetables like squash and carrots.

2 tablespoons olive oil
1 large sweet red pepper, seeded and cut into triangles
2 cloves garlic, minced
1 bunch kale (about 1 pound)
freshly ground black pepper
¼ cup balsamic vinegar

Wash the kale very thoroughly and chop it, discarding any tough stems.

Heat the oil in a 12-inch skillet and sauté the red pepper until the oil begins to turn pink. Add the garlic and kale, which should still have some water clinging to it.

Cover and braise the vegetables for 5 to 8 minutes, stirring several times. Add more water if needed. Remove the pan from the heat as soon as the kale is tender to the bite. Season to taste with freshly ground black pepper.

Just before serving, drizzle on the vinegar.

Beet Greens with Blueberries

Makes 4 servings.

Unsweetened blueberries make a pleasantly tart complement to beet greens. An easy August dinner might combine this piquant vegetable dish with Grilled Fish Steaks *(pages 124-125)*, Carrot Slaw *(page 82)*, and crusty rye bread—a nutrition-packed menu to perk up one's energy in late summer!

1 bunch of beet greens (about 1 pound), well-washed

1 onion, chopped

2 tablespoons olive oil

1 cup water

1 cup fresh or frozen blueberries

Cut off the tough stem ends of the beet greens and cut the bunch into fourths crosswise.

In a large pan, sauté the onion in the oil until it is softened, about 3 minutes. Add the beet greens and water. Cover and simmer for 8 to 10 minutes. Add the blueberries and continue to cook for 5 minutes, until the fruit is cooked but not mushy.

Serve in bowls with some of the pan juice.

Spinach with Olives, Raisins, and Pine Nuts

Makes 4 servings.

Of all the greens, the one most capable of in-finite variety is definitely spinach. This recipe, for instance, may be served as a vegetable dish or tossed with a half-pound of cooked vermicelli as a pasta course.

1 pound fresh spinach, well-washed, tough stems removed

1 clove garlic, mashed

salt and pepper to taste

2 tablespoons olive oil

2 tablespoons pitted, sliced Kalamata olives

2 tablespoons golden raisins

2 tablespoons pine nuts

Steam the spinach in just the water that clings to the leaves after washing, adding the mashed garlic to the pan. Stir often; add more water if needed.

Drain the spinach and remove the garlic. Season with salt and pepper to your taste. (You can omit salt entirely.)

Heat the oil in a large skillet; cook the olives, raisins, and pine nuts until the nuts are golden; don't let them brown. Add the cooked spinach and sauté 1 minute before serving.

For other greens recipes, see: Curried Chicken Salad with Mangoes and Toasted Cashews; Down-Home Oyster Pie à la Rockefeller; Grape and Arugula Salad with Mustard Vinaigrette; Linguine with Broccoli Rabe and Garlic; Mushroom and Barley Soup with Escarole; Ziti with Cannellini Sauce

LEGUMES

NOT HAUTE CUISINE, BUT REALLY HEALTHFUL. Legumes, otherwise known as plain old beans, along with pasta and grains, are the "fillers" so important among hard-working farm folk of many cultures. Fortunately for everyone's good health, beans have gradually made inroads on citified menus, as various provincial cuisines are "discovered" from time to time.

The mushrooming interest in vegetarian cooking has helped a lot to bring about this resurgence of beans. When legumes are combined with grains, they form the whole protein that otherwise could be obtained only from meat and dairy products. Legumes are a satisfying meat substitute, too—any bean dish redolent of garlic, peppers, and herbs, as prepared in many cuisines, from *Frijoles de Olla* to *Pasta e Fagioli*, looks like a main dish and fills up the hungriest diners.

Each culture and region has its own bean specialties. There are certainly plenty of legumes from which to choose! Black beans go over big in Brazil, while adzuki beans are simmering in China. Fava beans are an Italian favorite, but it's usually pintos being refried in Mexico. The American South enjoys black-eyed peas; Bostonians favor navy beans (pea beans), but if you're down East, that would be yellow-eyes in the big brown pot. But wait, there are more: cranberry beans, *flageolets*, Great Northern beans, red and white kidney beans, lima beans, mung beans, red beans, soybeans, lentils, and pigeon peas.

Green peas and split peas are legumes, too—so special that they're covered in a chapter of their own. A soup made from split peas is practically the national dish in Holland.

One of the cheapest foods in the world, and so good for you! Researchers have declared that a cup of beans a day lowers both LDL cholesterol and blood pressure; soluble pectin is thought to be the agent of these desirable effects. But beans also contain lots of insoluble fiber, which speeds food through the digestive tract. This prevents constipation and may help to avert colon cancer. Legumes are also packed with protease inhibitors, enzymes that fight cancer formation at the cellular level. Because they raise blood sugar so slowly, beans regulate insulin, too, and so are an excellent food for diabetics.

In the Market

If you were going to make beans from scratch every time, you probably wouldn't eat them as often as health concerns dictate—except lentils, which take less than an hour to cook. Many canned beans are excellent products and great timesavers. I particularly like the Italian brands for chickpeas, kidney beans, shell beans, and cannellini. There are also some good canned pinto beans and kidney beans among American brands. But so-called New England baked beans (pea beans or yellow-eyes) are much tastier when made from scratch. The alternative is to doctor up canned baked pea beans with lots of chopped onion, green pepper, dry mustard, and molasses, then bake them for a half-hour.

In the Kitchen

One big advantage to making bean dishes from scratch, however, is that you can cut down on the problem of intestinal gas that plagues many people who don't digest bean sugars readily. Simply soaking the beans overnight in water and then discarding the liquid to cook the beans in fresh water removes some of the gas-producing sugars that cause the problem. Soaking is an important step that ought never to be overlooked; the beans cook in less time, too. It's also true that if beans are introduced gradually but *persistently* into the diet, most people will find that the digestion learns to adapt to those complex sugars, and there's no more discomfort.

All dried beans must be cooked before they are eaten, because uncooked beans contain toxins called lectins, which can make you ill. They also need to be picked over for any foreign matter such as small stones that may have got mixed in when they were processed. The easiest way to do this is to spill them into one layer on a large tray. After sorting, rinse them in a strainer; if you rinsed them first, they would stick together, making your quality control operation more difficult.

Dried beans probably keep better than any other food you may store. You only need to shelve them in a cool, dry place, and they'll keep for months. The only problem with *very* long storage is that the beans will dry even more and take longer to cook. Dried beans will actually be good for a year, but since the store may have had them for a while, using them within six months is a good rule.

It's also a good idea to write the date of purchase on canned beans and any other canned goods that you may not use immediately. Use an indelible marker to note the date on the top of the can. That way, no matter how cans get switched around in your pantry, you'll always be able to use the oldest first. No more standing there, in a cook's paranoia, sniffing an open can and wondering, *Now when exactly did I buy this and is it still good?* (Your nose can't answer this.)

The countless ways of using dried or canned legumes, multiplied by the abundant varieties, could easily fill a whole book. What follows are a few of my special favorites. ■■■

Lentil Soup with Shiitake Mushrooms and Raw Scallions

Makes 4 to 5 cups.

Woodsy shiitake mushrooms give this soup an unexpectedly rich taste, and the scallions give it bite.

4 large dried shiitake mushrooms (stocked in the produce section of most large supermarkets)

½ cup finely diced celery

2 tablespoons chopped shallots

2 tablespoons vegetable oil

1 cup lentils, picked over and washed

6 cups water

½ cup dry white wine

1 beef bouillon cube

1 large carrot, scraped and cut into thin coins

½ cup finely chopped scallions, including some green tops

Reconstitute the mushrooms by soaking them in lukewarm water for an hour or so. Save the soaking water and measure it as part of the 6 cups of water needed for the soup. Discard the mushroom stems and dice the mushrooms.

In a medium-size pot, sauté the celery and shallots in oil for 2 to 3 minutes. Add the mushrooms, lentils, water, wine, and bouillon cube.

Cook the soup, with cover ajar, stirring occasionally, for 1 hour.

The soup can be prepared in advance to this point and refrigerated. Reheat, stirring often.

Add the carrot slices and cook until they are tender but still crunchy, remove the soup from the heat, and taste to correct the seasoning. The single bouillon cube adds a little salt; you may want more. Stir in the scallions just before serving.

Braised Veal Breast with White Beans

Makes 4 servings.

This one-pot meal may take time to braise, but while it's cooking you can read a novel or write one, because you hardly need to pay attention to what's going on in the oven.

Plain rice (*Arborio is an excellent choice —see Basics*) and a mixed green salad are all you need for accompaniments.

3½- to 4-pound meaty veal breast, bone in

2 tablespoons olive oil

1 large onion, chopped

2 carrots, chopped

2 stalks celery, chopped

1 clove garlic, minced

peel of 1 lemon (zest only, no pith), cut into strips

one 14- to 16-ounce can whole Italian-style tomatoes with juice

salt and pepper to taste

sprigs of fresh basil, thyme, and marjoram, or 1 teaspoon dried Italian seasoning (see Basics)

one 20-ounce can Italian cannellini (white
beans), drained and rinsed

In a large skillet, brown the veal on all sides in
hot oil. Put the veal in a roasting pan about 3
inches larger all around than the meat.

Meanwhile, heat the oven to 350° F.

In the same skillet, slowly sauté the onion,
carrot, celery, and garlic until softened.
Scoop the vegetables into the roasting pan.
Pour in the tomatoes, add the lemon zest, and
sprinkle with salt and pepper. Lay sprigs of
fresh herbs on top of meat.

Cover the pan tightly with foil, place it in
the middle of the oven, and braise for 2½
hours. (The juices will not boil away if the foil
is well-sealed.)

Then remove the foil, stir the beans into
the pan juices, re-cover, and cook for 30 to 40
minutes more. The veal should be superbly
tender. *This dish can be kept warm, covered,
for 30 minutes.*

To serve, carve the veal on a platter;
spoon the bean mixture into a separate dish.

Chicken, Garbanzo, and Pepper Stew

Makes 4 servings.

Let's face it—hardly anyone has time to make
soup stock anymore. Canned broth is a perfectly good substitute, except that it tends to
be too salty. Choose a low-salt brand.

8 skinned chicken thighs
2 tablespoons olive oil
2 green peppers, seeded and chunked
1 large onion, chopped
2 cloves garlic, minced
one 13-ounce can chicken broth
½ cup chopped canned tomatoes
*one 19- to 20-ounce can garbanzo beans
(chickpeas), drained and rinsed*
½ teaspoon dried marjoram
¼ teaspoon dried thyme leaves
¼ teaspoon crushed red pepper
*1½ cups uncooked whole-wheat
elbow macaroni*
*2 tablespoons minced fresh
flat-leafed parsley*

In a heavy pot or Dutch oven, brown the
chicken pieces in oil a few at a time. Add the
green pepper, onion, and garlic; sauté 3 minutes. Add all the remaining ingredients except
the macaroni and parsley. Simmer, covered,
for 30 minutes, or until the chicken is cooked
through. *The stew can be prepared ahead to
this point and reheated.*

Meanwhile, cook the elbows according to
package directions. Add the elbows and parsley to the stew, stir well, and serve.

Ziti with Cannellini Sauce

Makes 6 servings.

This hearty dish is winter fare. Even the plum tomatoes are the kind that can still be found in the market in December. One of the few dishes in which the unyielding firmness of winter tomatoes is not a liability.

¼ cup olive oil

1 large onion, chopped

3 cloves garlic, minced

6 fresh ripe plum tomatoes, peeled and chopped

one 1-pound bag cut-leaf frozen spinach or 4 cups fresh spinach, loosely packed

one 20-ounce can Italian cannellini (white beans), drained and rinsed

2 tablespoons tomato paste

½ cup water

¼ teaspoon crushed red pepper flakes

¼ teaspoon freshly ground black pepper

salt to taste

one 1-pound package ziti, cooked according to package directions

grated Parmesan cheese

Heat the olive oil in a large skillet, and sauté the onion and garlic until they are sizzling. Add the chopped tomatoes and cook, uncovered, until the tomatoes soften, 5 minutes.

Add the spinach, beans, tomato paste, and water; simmer uncovered until the spinach is cooked, 5 minutes. Add the pepper flakes. Taste to correct the seasoning. You may want to add salt and more pepper.

Toss the ziti with half the sauce, put it in a serving dish, and spoon the remaining sauce on top. Pass grated cheese at the table.

Nancy Hindle's Shell Bean Succotash

Makes 4 to 6 servings.

Made from sweet, fresh vegetables, this is a much more pleasing dish than the usual lima bean-canned corn combo. Shell beans, which have creamy-white pods marked with purplish red patches, come into the market just about the same time as fresh corn.

The Hindles usually make this dish with salt pork but have allowed me to substitute onion and savory instead.

¼ cup (½ stick) butter or low-cholesterol margarine

1 large onion, chopped

1½ pounds fresh shell beans, shelled (about 2 cups)

½ teaspoon salt

½ teaspoon dried summer savory

3 cups water

5 ears corn (about 2 cups kernels)

¼ teaspoon white pepper

Melt the butter in a large, heavy pot, and sauté the onion until it's yellowed but not brown. Add the shell beans, salt, summer savory, and water; bring to a boil and simmer, covered, for 20 minutes.

Cut the corn kernels from the ears, not too close to the cobs. Add the corn to the pot, cover, and cook an additional 10 minutes. Stir in white pepper. Serve hot in bowls.

Succotash with Tomatoes

Prepare as above, substituting 1 cup of chopped peeled fresh tomatoes for ½ cup of the water. A tablespoon of minced fresh basil makes a nice addition.

New England Baked Beans, Vegetarian Style

Makes 4 to 5 cups.

Dark, rich, sweet, and fragrant—baked beans are easy to make and give the cook a sense of homespun accomplishment. By all means, invest in a real bean pot; it looks handsome on the shelf when not in action and can be pressed into service as a kitchen utensil holder.

You have to think ahead when you're going to make beans, because they must be soaked in water overnight. Although you can mix up the ingredients in 10 minutes, beans need long, slow cooking. I often make two kinds at once to make best use of the oven heat. Beans will keep a week in the refrigerator, or they can be frozen in serving-size containers for six months.

Homemade brown bread *(pages 283-284),* codfish cakes (made with fresh not salt cod), and coleslaw complete a nostalgic New England Saturday night supper and provide a half-dozen superfoods in one great meal.

In this version, the traditional hunk of fatty salt pork is replaced by vegetable oil. You can choose between yellow-eye beans, favored by down-easters, or navy beans, preferred by Bostonians.

1 pound of dried yellow-eye beans or
navy beans (also called pea beans)
1 large onion, halved
¼ cup brown sugar
1 teaspoon each dry mustard and salt
¼ teaspoon pepper
⅓ cup molasses
⅓ cup pure maple syrup
¼ cup vegetable oil

Pick over, rinse, and drain the beans. Put them in a pan with 2 quarts of cold water and let them stand overnight.

The next morning, drain the beans and discard the water. Put a kettle of fresh water on to boil and set the oven at 300° F.

Start with half the onion on the bottom of a bean pot or Dutch oven, and then add the beans. In a cup, mix together the brown sugar, mustard, salt, and pepper. Add this to the beans, followed by the molasses, maple syrup, and oil. Push the second onion half into the top of the beans. Add enough boiling water to cover the beans.

Put the lid on the pot and bake the beans for five hours, checking occasionally (once an hour, beginning with the second hour, is sufficient) to add more water as the beans absorb it.

Remove the lid and bake another hour, or until the beans are perfectly tender but not mushy. Add more water as needed, checking each half-hour.

The beans can be prepared ahead for later use. Reheat in a conventional oven (350° F. for about 30 minutes) or in a microwave oven (time will vary according to the amount reheated) or in a skillet on the range top over low heat. If the beans seem dry, add a little water.

Baked Beans from the North End of Boston

Makes about 5 cups.

In the Italian section of Boston, a pot of baked beans is translated into an entirely different dish, served with fresh white bread and a salad of mixed greens and vegetables. *Delizioso!*

1 pound navy (pea) beans
1 large onion, chopped
1 large sweet pepper (any color), seeded and chopped
1 or 2 cloves garlic, minced
1 dried whole hot red pepper (cayenne, available in specialty stores and some supermarkets)
¼ cup olive oil
1 teaspoon salt
½ teaspoon each oregano and summer savory
¼ teaspoon black pepper
one 28-ounce can whole Italian-style tomatoes with juice, heated in a saucepan

Pick over, rinse, and drain the beans. Put them in a pan with 2 quarts of cold water and let them stand overnight.

The next morning, drain the beans and discard the water. Put a kettle of fresh water on to boil, and set the oven at 300° F.

Combine all the ingredients in a bean pot or Dutch oven. Add boiling water to cover the beans. Cover the pot and bake the beans for 5 hours, checking once an hour to add water as the beans absorb it. These beans should be juicier than those in the previous recipe.

Remove the lid and bake another hour, or until the beans are tender but not mushy. Add water as needed, checking each half-hour.

Remove the hot pepper before serving.

The beans can be prepared ahead for later use. Reheat in a conventional oven (350° F. for about 30 minutes) or in a microwave oven (time will vary according to the amount reheated) or in a skillet on the range top over low heat. If the beans seem dry, add a little water.

Kidney Beans with Sweet and Hot Red Peppers

Makes 4 servings.

The body manufactures protein from a range of amino acids, which must be in a particular ratio to one another and must be consumed in those proportions at one meal. Meat, fish, and eggs provide complete sets of amino acids, but no single vegetable does. When beans and grains are combined, however, each makes up for what the other lacks. The kidney beans and brown rice in this dish complement each other to provide a complete plant protein.

1 tablespoon olive oil

1 sweet red pepper and 1 green pepper, seeded and diced

1 large onion, chopped

one 19-ounce can kidney beans, drained and rinsed

2 tablespoons brown sugar

2 tablespoons crushed hot red pepper relish (wet pack, similar to pickle relish— found in the Italian foods section of the supermarket)

hot cooked brown rice as an accompaniment (see Basics)

Heat the oil in a medium-size skillet, and sauté the sweet red and green peppers with the onion until they have softened. Add all the remaining ingredients and simmer for 10 minutes. Serve with rice.

Cannellini in Caper Vinaigrette

Makes 4 servings.

Adding legumes to one's daily diet has been shown to lower cholesterol, but that doesn't mean having to endure a boring sameness. Putting them in salads is one way to give beans a new twist. A handful of drained chickpeas is a good addition to any tossed green salad—or try an all-bean salad, like the following.

one 20-ounce can Italian cannellini (white beans)

2 roasted red peppers (see Basics or buy oil-packed peppers in a jar), diced

½ sweet onion (such as Vidalia), chopped

For the caper vinaigrette:

⅓ cup olive oil

3 tablespoons red wine vinegar

1 tablespoon drained capers

¼ teaspoon dry hot mustard

salt and pepper to taste

Drain and rinse the beans. Combine them with the peppers and onion in a serving dish.

Combine the dressing ingredients in a jar. Shake well and pour over the salad. Toss, cover, and marinate for at least an hour, stirring occasionally.

For other bean recipes, see the following: Take-It-Easy Minestrone; Tomato, White Bean, and Tuna Salad

MANGOES AND PAPAYAS

TEMPTING TROPICAL HEALTH FOODS. The mango, a member of the cashew family, is widely cultivated in the tropical world and deeply interwoven with the folklore and religion of India. Buddha himself reposed in a mango grove. This oval fruit may weigh as much as a pound; it contains one large flat stone to which the flesh adheres quite stubbornly. The mango's flavor is something like that of a tangy peach.

Mangoes are a rich source of vitamins A, C, and D. That deep orange color, of course, demonstrates the presence of beta carotene, one of our foremost food fighters against cancer. Mangoes are also antiviral: When mango juice is poured into a test tube containing viruses, they're put out of action in short order.

The papaya, also called the pawpaw, is another treat from the tropical zones. It's pear-shaped, with a mild, sweet flavor, something like that of muskmelon, and has many wrinkled black seeds at the heart of the fruit.

Unripe papayas, which can be baked like squash, contain a milky substance from which we get papain, a protein-digesting enzyme with many uses. It's the predominant ingredient in meat tenderizers, and it's also included in many aids to digestion, being very much like the human digestive enzyme pepsin. A paste made of papain-based meat tenderizer is good first aid for a bee sting. Papain is even used in enzyme-cleaning agents for soft contact lenses.

The papaya (along with the cantaloupe) stands out among fruits for being especially "nutrition dense"—when vitamin content is compared with caloric value, papayas give you the most nutrition for the least calories. Orange-fleshed papayas also contain lots of cancer-fighting beta carotene, and a single serving—half a papaya, 58 calories—also gives you nearly twice the recommended dietary allowance of vitamin C to help build and maintain body tissue.

Because of their high enzyme content, papayas and fresh papaya juice are natural digestive aids. In addition to the pepsinlike enzyme that breaks down meat proteins, papayas also contain an enzyme like human rennin, which breaks down milk protein. In animal studies, papaya has shown some promise as an anti-ulcer food.

If you cook a sliced papaya, preferably one that's a bit unripe, with a pot roast, it will use that same papain to tenderize the meat—not to mention adding its own exotic flavor to the dish. Don't use raw papaya in a gelatin dish, however, because it won't gel unless the papaya is cooked first.

In the Market

The peak season for papayas is April through July. Those of highest quality are free from blemishes and half yellow, with no acrid odor.

The mango season is from May through August. Mangoes should have a smooth outer skin, be at least five inches in diameter, and free from cracks and bruises. Since mangoes don't ripen very well after picking, choose one that has tinges of yellow and red on its deep green skin. Its aroma should be sweet.

If you're going to use papayas or mangoes for a specific occasion, you'll probably have to buy them two days or more ahead of time, since most of the fruits you'll encounter in the market will still be too firm to use.

In the Kitchen

Ripen papayas to full yellow at room temperature. Mangoes, too, will benefit from time spent on the kitchen counter getting softer and juicer. When ready to eat, these fruits should yield slightly to the pressure of your thumb. At this point, you can refrigerate papayas or mangoes, if desired, for a day or two longer.

Besides being enjoyable in themselves, mangoes and papayas add a touch of glamour to many dishes, from simple salads and desserts to elegant (but easy!) entrées. ■

Oven-Fried Chicken with Mangoes and Leeks

Makes 4 servings.

Mango's zesty flavor and juicy texture are right at home in savory entrées.

*1 cup seasoned breadcrumbs
(store-bought or see Basics)*
2 tablespoons wheat germ
1 teaspoon sweet or hot paprika
8 skinned chicken thighs
2 tablespoons vegetable oil
2 leeks
1 mango

Preheat the oven to 375° F. Mix the breadcrumbs, wheat germ, and paprika. Put half the mixture in a plastic bag with half the chicken and shake to coat. Repeat with the remaining crumbs and chicken.

Coat a baking pan with oil. Add the chicken in one layer. Wash and trim the leeks; slice them thin using only the white part. Scatter the leeks over the chicken.

Bake for 25 minutes. Meanwhile, thinly peel the mango. Cut slices lengthwise off the stone in the center. Turn the chicken, arrange the fruit among the chicken pieces, and cook an additional 20 minutes, or until the chicken is cooked through. *The dish can be kept warm, covered, for 30 minutes.*

Pot Roast with Papaya

Makes 8 servings.

Among its other attributes, papaya tenderizes meat because it breaks down protein. Store-bought meat tenderizers are made of papain, an enzyme from the juice of unripe papayas.

3- to 4-pound pot roast, trimmed of all fat
2 tablespoons oil
1 large onion, chopped
1 cup beef broth or prepared bouillon
3 tablespoons cider vinegar
2 tablespoons brown sugar
salt to taste (optional)
1 bay leaf
*2 papayas, peeled, seeded, and cut
lengthwise into slices*
*1 tablespoon cornstarch stirred into
¼ cup cold water until dissolved*

Preheat the oven to 350° F. In a Dutch oven (or any ovenproof, heavy covered pan), brown the meat on all sides in hot oil. Add the onion and fry until golden. Add the broth or bouillon, vinegar, sugar, and salt, if using. Put the bay leaf in the broth. Lay the papaya on top of the meat.

Bring the broth to a boil, cover the pan, and place it in the heated oven. Bake about 2½ hours, or until the meat is quite tender. Remove the papaya to a dish. *The pot roast can be prepared ahead and reheated in the oven at 350° F. until hot, about 30 minutes. Add the papaya during the last 10 minutes.*

Remove the pot roast to a platter and discard the strings, if any. Let the roast stand 10 minutes before slicing; keep it warm. Surround the meat with papaya slices.

Remove and discard the bay leaf; bring the pan juices to a boil on the range top, add the blended cornstarch mixture, and cook, stirring constantly, until thickened. Lower the heat and simmer at least 3 minutes. Serve the gravy with the pot roast.

Curried Chicken Salad with Mangoes and Toasted Cashews

Makes 4 servings.

Two pounds of skinned chicken thighs and/or bone-in breasts will yield about the right amount of chicken, and you'll have the broth, too *(see Basics).*

3 tablespoons mayonnaise
3 tablespoons cold chicken broth
2 tablespoons yogurt
½ teaspoon curry powder
2 cups cooked, cubed chicken
(well-packed measure)
1 mango
fresh, young spinach leaves, stems removed
½ cup cashews

Whisk together the mayonnaise, chicken broth, yogurt, and curry until well-blended. Stir into the chicken until all pieces are coated.

Peel and slice the mango from its stone. Cube the mango to about the size of the chicken pieces. Gently stir into the chicken. Arrange the salad on a bed of raw spinach leaves. Refrigerate until ready to serve.

Toast the cashews under the broiler (watch carefully!) or in a toaster oven set for medium toast. Sprinkle them over the salad.

Papaya Salad with Raspberry Vinaigrette

Makes 4 servings.

A beautiful combination of tastes and colors for a luncheon salad.

3 tablespoons raspberry vinegar
⅓ cup salad oil
salt and pepper to taste
1 small head Boston lettuce
1 large ripe papaya, peeled and seeded
2 carrots, scraped
fresh raspberries for garnish (optional)

Combine the raspberry vinegar, oil, salt, and pepper in a small jar.

Layer washed lettuce leaves on 4 salad plates. Slice the papaya and divide among the plates. Coarsely grate the carrots and heap some on each plate.

Shake the salad dressing in its closed jar. Spoon 2 tablespoons of dressing over each plate, stirring each time to recombine the vinegar and oil evenly. Garnish with fresh raspberries, if desired.

Frozen Mango-Banana Mousse

Makes 6 servings.

Both mango and banana have a pleasingly creamy texture suitable for frozen desserts, that substitute for real ice cream.

1 envelope unflavored gelatin
⅔ cup cold water
⅓ cup sugar
one 6-ounce can frozen orange juice concentrate, undiluted
1 mango, peeled and chunked
1 banana, peeled and chunked
1 cup low-fat yogurt
2 tablespoons orange liqueur
6 ice cubes
6 thin slices of lime

In a small saucepan, sprinkle the gelatin over the water and let it stand for 5 minutes. Place the saucepan over low heat, stirring until the gelatin is completely dissolved.

Pour the mixture into a blender or food processor. With the motor running, add the sugar and blend well. Add the remaining ingredients except the ice cubes and lime, and blend until the mousse is puréed, light, and frothy. Add the ice cubes one at a time, continuing to blend until dissolved.

Divide the mixture among six 8-ounce plastic cups and freeze the mousse. To serve, thaw slightly and unmold into dessert bowls.

Garnish each portion with a slice of lime.

Note: A blender works better and faster for puréeing mixtures with a liquid base to which you're adding solid chunks of food. When you begin with a solid food and add liquid, a food processor is the first choice.

Papaya Meringue Pie

Makes 4 to 6 servings.

Pies should be made on the day they're to be served, and that's especially true of meringue pies. An *unfilled* pie crust, however, can be made the day ahead and stored in a breadbox or on the kitchen counter. Lightly cover the pie crust with wax paper, but don't swathe it in plastic wrap!

Egg whites whip up more easily when at room temperature. Fat retards volume, so be certain that not a speck of egg yolk remains in the white and there's not a trace of grease on the beaters.

2 cups pastry cream (1½ times recipe, see Basics)
2 tablespoons lemon juice
1 teaspoon grated lemon zest
one 9-inch baked pastry shell (see Basics)
1 ripe papaya
pinch of cream of tartar
¼ cup sugar
2 egg whites

Omit other flavorings from the pastry cream recipe, substituting lemon juice and ¾ teaspoon grated zest. Cool the mixture slightly, then spoon half of it into the baked pie shell.

Peel, seed, and dice the papaya. Layer it over the pastry cream, pressing down slightly. Spoon in the remaining pastry cream, smoothing to cover all the papaya. Chill until set.

Preheat the oven to 400° F. Mix the sugar with the remaining ¼ teaspoon of grated zest. Beat the egg whites until foamy; add the cream of tartar. Continue beating until the egg whites are stiff, then gradually add the sugar and grated zest. When ready, the meringue should be glossy and stand in peaks that curve over slightly. Pile it lightly over the pie so that the meringue touches the rim of the crust all around (to prevent shrinking) and has those attractive hills and valleys over the surface.

Bake on the middle shelf of the oven for 6 minutes, until delicately brown all over. Watch carefully! Ten seconds one way or the other makes a difference.

Cool completely on a wire rack before serving. Cut with a wet knife.

Refrigerate any leftovers.

Baked Papaya with Ricotta and Citron

Makes 4 servings.

This delectable dessert is quite filling without being fattening.

> *2 small ripe papayas*
> *1 cup low-fat ricotta cheese*
> *1 egg, beaten, or ¼ cup prepared egg substitute*
> *3 tablespoons brown sugar, sifted to remove lumps*
> *2 tablespoons chopped candied citron (sold with chopped candied fruits in the baking ingredients or produce section of the supermarket)*

Preheat the oven to 350° F. Peel the papayas, cut them in half, and scoop out the seeds. Place them in a baking dish that will hold them snugly upright.

Blend together the remaining ingredients and spoon the cheese mixture into the papayas' cavities.

Bake for 40 minutes, or until the papayas are tender and the cheese lightly golden on top. Allow the dessert to cool until it is just warm before serving.

For other mango and papaya recipes, see: Mango-Orange Yogurt; Papaya Yogurt

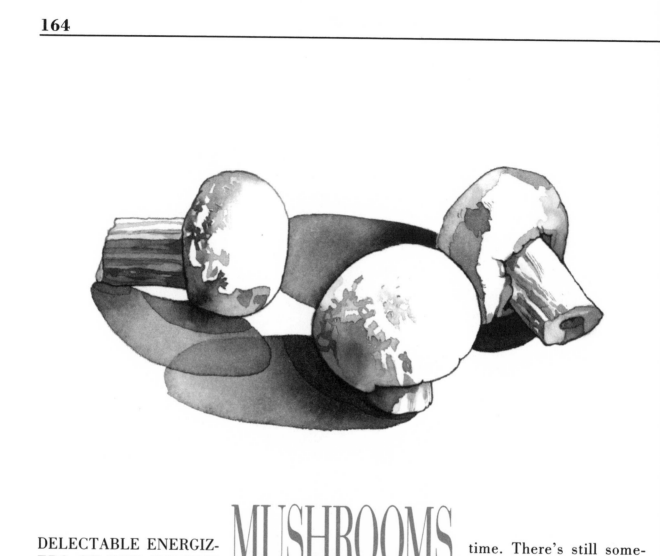

MUSHROOMS

DELECTABLE ENERGIZERS OF THE IMMUNE SYSTEM. Because mushrooms spring to life "magically" overnight, the ancient Egyptians believed that these umbrella-shaped fungi would confer godlike powers upon them. Mushrooms were therefore a prized dish the nobles reserved for themselves. But since mushrooms pop up at random in the fields, the common Egyptians may very well have managed to enjoy their rich flavor in the evening stew from time to time. There's still something special about the way mushrooms lift any dish from the commonplace into haute cuisine.

With their "meaty" texture, mushrooms make a satisfying meat substitute. Just think of how well they can replace pepperoni on a pizza and be so much better for you. A richly flavored mushroom pâté can fill in nicely for liver. Three big stuffed mushrooms will take the place of a lunchtime burger.

Mushrooms are often dismissed as having

an insignificant nutritive value, yet they do offer a respectable amount of fiber and B vitamins as well as quite a lot of heart-protecting potassium. One cup of mushrooms (at only 20 calories) is equal to a half banana in potassium content and compares favorably in B vitamins with a slice of whole-wheat bread. They're also a good source of germanium (as is garlic), a trace mineral with antitumor and antiviral properties. Germanium also enhances cells' ability to generate energy. If you haven't heard much about germanium, it's probably because the mineral wasn't synthesized organically until 1967 and most of the research on it has been done in Japan.

Among the different varieties of mushrooms, the Asian ones have shown the most health benefits, but they've also been the most thoroughly studied. The shiitake, also known as the golden oak, revs up the immune system to produce more interferon, which defends the body against viral and bacterial infections as well as tumors.

Recent Japanese studies on mice have found several mushrooms, including the shiitake, the oyster, and even the plain old button variety, to help protect the body against carcinogens that may lead to cancer.

In the Market

The first rule in selecting mushrooms is to buy them in a market, unless you're a mushroom expert. Among those that grow wild in the fields after a rain are some nice-looking white mushrooms that contain deadly alkaloids. It takes a lot of experience to separate the good mushrooms from the fatal ones.

But right there in the supermarket is a nice choice of cultivated mushrooms for every culinary purpose. Gone are the days when all you'd find were the ubiquitous white buttons and an occasional basket of big white "stuffers." Fresh shiitake, oyster, and portobello mushrooms also enliven the mushroom selection these days, and colors include golden and brown as well as white.

Whatever the variety, choose mushrooms that are free from blemishes, with short stems and unopened veils at the base of the caps. Mushrooms with spots, darkened flesh, or exposed gills will not keep well or taste fresh when cooked.

When fresh shiitake mushrooms are not available, dried ones can be obtained in many supermarkets and in Asian grocery stores. Freshening them is a simple matter of soaking them for a half-hour in warm water. The tough stems are usually discarded.

Frozen mushrooms, breaded and unbreaded, are available. I wouldn't advise paying good money for all that breading, but the plain frozen mushrooms are a good product, if somewhat spongy.

Canned button mushrooms, either whole, sliced, or "stems and pieces," are also sold, but they are all quite tasteless. Owing to cultivation, fresh mushrooms are abundantly available all year, so there's little need for the canned product anyway. But if you want to have mushrooms "at the ready," it would be far better to poach fresh mushrooms in a half-cup of water and a tablespoon of oil for the freezer than to stock canned mushrooms. Lightly cooked mushrooms and the accumulated pan juices can be packed in small plastic containers for the freezer.

In the Kitchen

Very fresh mushrooms will keep two to three days in the refrigerator. But don't wash mushrooms until you're ready to cook them because excess moisture hastens their decay.

Mushrooms are porous and soak up water when washed. Use a salad spinner to spin out that moisture so that it won't delay the browning of sautéed mushrooms.

If you've bought too many mushrooms and they're in danger of decaying before you can use them, a nice way to keep them a day or two longer (or for months frozen) is to turn them into a duxelles, a finely chopped mixture of mushrooms and shallots fried to a nice brown in butter or oil and flavored with thyme. Duxelles imparts a lovely flavor to soups, sauces, and stuffings. Try them as the stuffing in fillet of sole roll-ups.

Shiitake Stuffed Mushrooms

Makes 4 to 6 servings.

The flavor of white mushrooms is enriched with a shiitake stuffing—and lots of wheat germ. The meaty taste of this dish makes it a good choice to enhance a meatless meal.

4 large dried shiitake mushrooms

twelve 2-inch white stuffing mushrooms

2 tablespoons olive oil

2 tablespoons minced shallot

⅔ cup dry herb stuffing mix (not the stovetop variety) reduced to finer crumbs in a food processor or blender (about ½ cup)

¼ cup toasted wheat germ

¼ teaspoon dried thyme leaves

salt and pepper to taste (the stuffing mix is well-seasoned)

Reconstitute the shiitake mushrooms by soaking them in lukewarm water for 30 minutes. Drain them and reserve the soaking water. Discard the stems and finely dice the caps.

Wash and pat dry the stuffing mushrooms. Remove and reserve the stems. Put the caps in an oiled pan that will hold them in one layer.

Cut off the woody bottom part of the reserved stems. Finely dice the rest of the stems and put them into a medium-size skillet with the olive oil. Fry them until they begin to brown, add the shallots, and continue cooking for about 3 minutes. Remove from the heat and stir in the crumbs, wheat germ, shiitake mushrooms, and thyme. Add enough of the shiitake soaking water so that the stuffing will just hold together but is not soggy. Stuff the mushrooms with the mixture, mounding it up.

The mushrooms can be prepared several hours ahead and refrigerated. When ready to cook, preheat the oven to 350° F. and bake the mushrooms for 25 minutes.

Greek-Style Marinated Mushrooms

Makes about 1 pint.

The spicy flavor of oregano is integral to Greek cooking. A member of the mint family, oregano is a wild herb that, when cultivated, becomes mild-mannered marjoram. Herbalists use oregano to treat colds and chest congestion and as a digestive aid. You'd never guess from oregano's peppy flavor that it's actually a calming rather than a stimulating herb.

*2 packages small white mushrooms
(most packages are 12 to 13 ounces)*

olive oil

1 onion, chopped

1 teaspoon oregano

*salt and freshly ground lemon pepper to
taste (found in the spice section of the
supermarket or in gourmet food shops)*

juice of 1 lemon

3 cloves garlic, peeled and crushed

Wash and dry the mushrooms very well. Slice
off the woody ends of the stems.

Cover the bottom of a large skillet with a
thin coating of oil. Add the mushrooms, and
cook over medium-high heat, stirring often,
until the mushrooms give off their juice and it
evaporates. At that point the mushrooms will
begin to fry and brown.

Add the onion. When the onion is golden,
add the oregano, salt, and lemon pepper. Remove the mixture from the heat.

Spoon the mushrooms into a jar or deep
bowl. Add the lemon juice, garlic, and enough
oil so that the juice nearly covers the mushrooms. *Refrigerate for a day before using, stirring once or twice.*

Spiced Turkey with Shiitake Mushrooms

Makes 4 servings.

Just the dish to whip up during the flu season!
The shiitake mushroom contains a substance
that puts up a natural defense against viruses.

*2 turkey cutlets (about 1 pound)
partially frozen*

½ cup chili sauce

¼ to ½ teaspoon hot red pepper sauce

¼ cup soy sauce

¼ cup sweet-and-sour sauce

6 large dried shiitake mushrooms

2 large peppers (different colors are nice)

1 large onion

2 tablespoons vegetable oil

1 tablespoon cornstarch

½ cup cold water

Cut the partially frozen turkey into thin strips.
Mix the chili, hot red pepper, soy, and sweet-
and-sour sauces. Stir the mixture into the turkey to coat all of the pieces; marinate the turkey in the refrigerator 1 hour or more, turning
occasionally.

At least 30 minutes before cooking, soak
the shiitake mushrooms in warm water to cover. Drain the mushrooms. Discard the stems.
Slice and reserve the caps.

Seed and slice the peppers, then cut the
strips into roughly triangular shapes. (Don't
fuss!) Slice the onion thin.

Heat 1 tablespoon of oil in a wok or skillet. Stir-fry the peppers and onions until tender-crisp. Remove them and keep them warm.

Use another tablespoon of oil to stir-fry the mushrooms and turkey until the meat is cooked through. Mix the cornstarch in water until there are no lumps. Pour the mixture into the hot turkey over medium heat and stir constantly until the pan juices become a thick glaze. Add the reserved vegetables.

Serve with hot cooked brown rice, more sweet-and-sour sauce, and Hot Mustard Sauce *(see Basics).*

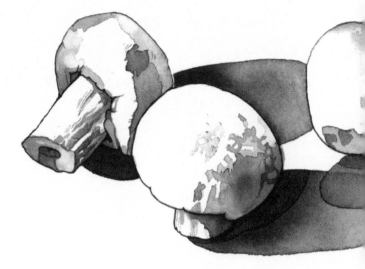

Baked Pasta with Shiitake Mushroom Sauce

Makes 4 servings.

A happy marriage of two cuisines.

> *4 ounces fresh shiitake mushrooms*
> *2 tablespoons olive oil*
> *1 clove garlic, minced*
> *½ pound penne or ziti without lines, cooked according to package directions*
> *1 tablespoon cornstarch*
> *one 12-ounce can evaporated skim milk*
> *1 cup tomato sauce (from a jar or see Basics)*
> *1 roasted sweet red pepper (from a jar or see Basics), diced*
> *¼ teaspoon hot red pepper flakes*

Preheat the oven to 350° F. Wash the mushrooms, discarding stems, and slice them. Shake or spin them dry. Heat the oil in a medium skillet and fry the mushrooms until they are brown, adding the garlic during the last minute of cooking.

Meanwhile, cook the penne according to the package directions.

Stir the cornstarch into the milk until there are no lumps. Add the mixture to the mushrooms, and cook over medium heat, stirring constantly, until the sauce boils and thickens slightly. Then stir in the tomato sauce, roasted pepper, and pepper flakes.

Combine the sauce and the pasta in a 3½-quart casserole and bake, covered, for 30 minutes, or until bubbly throughout.

The casserole can be kept warm, covered, for 20 minutes.

Cantonese Egg Foo Yung

Makes 2 large servings.

For lunch or a quick supper, try this with Carrot and Ginger Soup *(page 80)* as a starter.

*3 ounces oyster mushrooms, bottoms
of the stems trimmed*

1 cup finely diced bok choy stalks or celery

1 sweet red pepper, diced fine

½ onion, chopped

about 3 teaspoons vegetable oil

*4 large eggs or 1 cup prepared
egg substitute*

1 tablespoon dry sherry or dry vermouth

For the sauce:

1 cup chicken broth

*1 tablespoon each soy sauce and
chili sauce*

hot red pepper sauce to taste

1 tablespoon cornstarch

To make the sauce, combine ½ cup of the chicken broth with the soy, chili, and hot red pepper sauces, and bring the mixture to a boil. Mix the cornstarch with the remaining ½ cup of cold broth until there are no lumps. Pour it all at once into the boiling sauce, stirring constantly until it bubbles and thickens. Reduce the heat and simmer 2 to 3 more minutes, whisking. Correct the seasoning. Put the sauce in a gravy boat and keep it warm.

Prepare the vegetables. Heat 1 teaspoon of oil in a seasoned 9-inch cast-iron or non-stick skillet (if you use another kind of pan, you'll need more oil), and stir-fry the mushrooms, bok choy, pepper, and onion together until they are tender-crisp. Remove them from the pan and let them cool slightly.

Put the eggs in a bowl with the sherry or vermouth. If you're using whole eggs, stir as little as possible to blend the whites and yolks. Do not beat the eggs or egg substitute. Add the cooled vegetables. *The recipe can be prepared ahead to this point and refrigerated until ready to cook.*

Heat 1 teaspoon of oil in the frying pan and tilt the pan to coat the bottom. When the oil is hot, ladle in half the egg mixture, smoothing it with a spatula over the pan, and cook on medium heat until the bottom is brown, loosening it from time to time with the spatula. Turn the omelet (you may have to do this in 2 pieces) and cook until the eggs are set and the second side is brown. Keep it warm.

Scrape any crust from the pan, add the remaining 1 teaspoon of oil, and proceed as above to cook the second omelet. Pass the sauce with the egg foo yung.

Mushroom Salad with Herb Vinaigrette

Makes 4 servings.

Lots of mushrooms give this salad a nice potassium punch. Potassium-rich, low-sodium foods like mushrooms help to keep blood pressure under control.

4 cups (about ½ head) red leaf lettuce torn into bite-size pieces (or part lettuce and part tender young spinach)

croutons

2 cups sliced mushrooms

1 tablespoon vegetable oil

2 tablespoons white wine

½ cup chopped sweet onion

½ cup chopped sweet red pepper

For the vinaigrette:

⅓ cup olive oil

2 tablespoons red wine vinegar

1 teaspoon Dijon mustard

¼ teaspoon black pepper

¼ teaspoon sugar

2 tablespoons chopped fresh herbs: choose at least 2 from marjoram, oregano, thyme, tarragon, basil, and parsley

In a large skillet, sweat the mushrooms in the oil and wine until they are tender.

Combine the mushrooms, onion, and red pepper in a salad bowl. Combine the vinaigrette ingredients in a small jar. Shake the dressing well and pour it over the vegetables. Toss them with the dressing. Put the lettuce and croutons on top, but don't toss the salad again until just ready to serve. The unmixed lettuce and croutons will stay crisp. *Refrigerate the salad until needed.*

For other mushroom recipes, see: Bean Sprout and Carrot Stir-Fry; Broccoli with Mushrooms and Lemon-Pepper; Brown Rice Risotto with Asparagus and Porcini Mushrooms; Brussels Sprouts Dijon; Cabbage Stir-Fry with Shiitake Mushrooms; Cream of Broccoli Soup with Smoked Turkey and Shiitake Mushrooms; Cutlets with Fresh Pineapple Sauce; Japanese-Style Noodle Soup; Lentil Soup with Shiitake Mushrooms and Raw Scallions; Mushroom and Barley Soup with Escarole; Sweet and Sour Pork

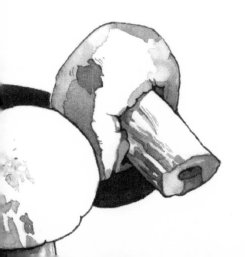

NUTS

HIGH-ENERGY SNACKS WITH MINERAL MAGIC. Nature has put something special into each of its seed foods—a package of nutrients whose compactness rivals any ration NASA can come up with to sustain its orbiting astronauts. And why not? Nuts and seeds, after all, have evolved to provide all that is needed to generate life and perpetuate each food species.

Some people avoid nuts because they're high in fat, but most of that fat is unsaturated. Almonds, filberts, and pistachios are sources of monounsaturated fats: They lower the destructive LDL cholesterol and raise the helpful HDL cholesterol. Chestnuts are the leanest nuts, with 5 percent fat. Brazil nuts have the most fat, but coconuts have the highest proportion of *saturated* fat and hardly any unsaturated fat; avoid them if you're watching your cholesterol.

Nuts are a source of manganese, a mineral that helps prevent osteoporosis, which afflicts some postmenopausal women.

A great meat substitute, nuts are rich in protein, with peanuts topping the list. (Botanically speaking, peanuts aren't nuts, but try telling that to a squirrel. They're so much like nuts in popular opinion and they share so many of the same nutrients, they're generally lumped together.) A cup of peanuts will give you about as much protein as half of a chicken breast.

Plant sources of the important trace mineral selenium are generally dependent on the selenium content of the soil in which the foods have been grown, but there's one plant that is a dependable source. The Brazil nut is always high in selenium. (The best sources are swordfish, lobster, salmon, and tuna.)

Dutch studies found that selenium has a negative effect on the development of atherosclerosis. Studies in the United States found a relationship between a selenium-enriched diet and a reduced incidence of schizophrenia.

Nuts are also a good source of vitamin E. In recent Russian studies, the dynamic duo of selenium and vitamin E has shown promise in protecting the heart. These two antioxidants also have been found to work together in an enzyme system that is both antiaging and anticancer.

In fact, all nuts and seeds protect against tumors because they have protease inhibitors—proteases are enzymes that carry on normal functions in the body, but which a cancerous cell can use for unchecked growth. If protease *inhibitors* are present at the site, the cancer cell doesn't have this advantage.

Lab tests with animals and population dietary studies both have shown that nuts and seed foods in general protect against cancers of the breast, digestive tract, liver, reproductive system, and respiratory organs.

Peanuts are rich in choline, a chemical that crosses the blood-brain barrier to enhance memory. Along with walnuts, peanuts are an important source of vitamin B_6. Associated with the production of gamma amino butyric acid, a brain chemical that has calming and stabilizing effects, vitamin B_6 is thought to be a sleep vitamin. Peanuts also are an excellent food for diabetics because they help to regulate blood sugar and insulin.

Walnuts are rich in heart-protecting omega-3 fatty acids. Cashews and almonds are high in zinc, a trace mineral that promotes cell growth and is involved in sperm production. Nuts are also good sources of heart-protecting fiber and potassium.

So there you have it in a nutshell: A handful of nuts a day helps keep illness away.

In the Market

Buying shelled nuts when they're available makes the cook's job easier, but not all nuts are packaged without those pesky shells.

Shelled hazelnuts can be found in health-food stores but are not usually available in supermarkets, which is a shame; they add class to ordinary baked goods. After shelling hazelnuts, warm and then rub them briskly in a terry towel to slip off the dark inner skins. This works best if the nuts are fresh, not dry.

I've gone into the shelling of chestnuts elsewhere *(see Basics).* Canned shelled chestnuts are available in a few specialty stores.

Brazil nuts can be purchased by the bagful, but not shelled. Freezing them overnight makes for easier shelling.

Shelled cashews, walnuts, pecans, and almonds are widely available. Almonds are sold whole, blanched whole, and slivered.

Unless you must have them for a party, avoid buying nuts that have been roasted or salted. You don't need the extra fat and sodium, and those processes throw off the taste of nuts you might want to use in cooking.

Unsalted, unroasted shelled peanuts can often be found near the peanut butter machines in the supermarket. Since we started making our own peanut butter in a food processor—plain peanuts and nothing else—none of the national brands taste as good.

In the Kitchen

Nuts will keep a few weeks on the shelf, if they haven't already been kept for a while in the store. Refrigerated nuts will keep for one to two months. If you bake a lot and have the freezer space, buy a variety of nuts for cooking and keep them in the freezer, where they'll stay fresh for six months or more—for all the times when you're inspired to make some crunchy nut treat.

Basque Chicken with Almonds and Olives

Makes 8 servings.

One of my favorite buffet dishes, this recipe can be doubled, using four skillets for the preliminary steps and two roasting pans to bake.

3 pounds boned, skinned chicken breasts

one 35-ounce can Italian plum tomatoes (whole, not crushed), with juice

zest of 1 lemon

¼ cup olive oil, plus more for frying

1 large onion, chopped

1 to 2 cloves garlic, minced

½ cup stuffed green olives

one 4-ounce can pitted black olives, drained

1 tablespoon drained capers

1½ teaspoons salt (can use less, if desired)

½ teaspoon pepper

1 cup slivered almonds

about 1 cup flour

½ teaspoon dried thyme leaves

Wash the chicken in cold salted water. Rinse and drain well. Cut the whole breasts into quarters lengthwise (or sixths if they're large). Cut the tomatoes into chunks. Use a vegetable peeler to cut the zest from the lemon, with no white pith; cut the zest into thin strips.

Heat ¼ cup of olive oil in a large skillet. Add the onion and garlic, and sauté on medium heat until the vegetables are yellow. Add the tomatoes and juice, green and black olives, capers, lemon zest, 1 teaspoon (or less) of salt, pepper, and ½ cup of the almonds. Cook uncovered over medium heat for about 30 minutes, stirring occasionally. The mixture should have a sauce-like consistency.

Meanwhile, mix the flour, thyme, and remaining ½ teaspoon salt, if using. Put about a third of the mixture in a plastic bag and add about a third of the chicken pieces. Close the bag tightly and shake it to coat the chicken. Prepare the remaining chicken the same way, in 2 more batches. The coating should be thin; shake off any excess.

In a second large skillet, heat a small amount of olive oil and brown the chicken *lightly* on both sides, in batches. Don't crowd the pan; don't cook the chicken through. Add oil as needed (the thinner the flour coating, the less oil needed).

Spoon half the sauce into a large roasting pan (glass or ceramic) from which you can serve. Lay the chicken on top. Spoon the remaining sauce over it. Sprinkle with the remaining ½ cup almonds. *The recipe can be prepared ahead to this point and refrigerated until needed.*

Preheat the oven to 350° F. Bake for 30 minutes, or until the chicken is cooked through but not dry. *If the casserole is cold, this may take 40 minutes.*

Pork Cutlets with Chestnuts and Sweet Potatoes

Makes 4 servings.

A skillet dinner that needs only a mixed green salad to complete the meal. The chestnuts turn dark and sweet when cooked with sweet potatoes and cider.

8 boneless pork chops (about 1½ pounds)

1 egg beaten with 2 tablespoons water or ⅓ cup prepared egg substitute

about ½ cup fine dry breadcrumbs

2 tablespoons olive oil

2 large shallots, minced

½ teaspoon Chinese five-spice powder

3 medium sweet potatoes (about 1½ pounds) peeled and sliced ¼ inch thick

1 cup cooked, shelled chestnuts (use canned unsweetened ones or see Basics for freshly cooked chestnuts)

1 cup or more of cider or apple juice

Trim all visible fat off the cutlets. Dip them into the egg, and then the breadcrumbs, coating all surfaces.

Heat the oil in an ovenproof skillet (no wooden handle) and sear the cutlets over medium-high heat, just enough to brown them on both sides. When you turn the pork, add the shallots to the pan and sprinkle a pinch of five-spice powder over each cutlet.

Remove the meat from the skillet. Pour off any excess fat. Preheat the oven to 375° F.

Lay the sweet potatoes over the bottom of the skillet and add the chestnuts. Pour in enough cider or apple juice to reach almost to the top of the potatoes. Lay the cutlets on top. Bring the liquid to a boil on the range top.

Cover the pan tightly with foil and bake for 30 minutes. Uncover and bake an additional 20 minutes, or until the cutlets are very tender.

Alternative method: If you don't have an ovenproof skillet, you can transfer everything to a 2-inch-deep baking dish, *not glass*, so that you can still bring the casserole to a boil on the range top.

Peanut-Crusted Chicken

Makes 4 servings.

A crusty, savory chicken without fatty skin. Gratin of White Turnips, Carrots, and Rice *(page 278)* cooks at the same temperature and would go alongside very compatibly.

*4 skinned chicken leg quarters,
not separated*

about ½ cup flour

*2 eggs, beaten, or ½ cup prepared
egg substitute*

2 tablespoons water

¼ teaspoon cayenne pepper

1 cup very finely chopped peanuts

Preheat the oven to 375° F. Coat a baking dish with olive oil.

Lay out two pieces of wax paper with a flat soup bowl between them. Put the flour on one sheet of wax paper. Mix the egg with water and cayenne pepper in the bowl. Put the peanuts on the second sheet of paper.

Dip the chicken in the flour, then in the egg mixture, and finally in the peanuts. (There's no way around it—this is a messy job that's best done with the hands, not two forks.) Lay the leg quarters round side up on the prepared pan. *The recipe can be prepared ahead to this point and refrigerated until needed.*

Bake for 45 minutes without turning, or until there is no pink at the joint.

Pasta al Sugo d'Estate (Pasta with Summer Sauce)

Makes 4 large servings as an entrée.

This "summer pasta" dish should be made only with vine-ripened, locally grown tomatoes.

3 pounds ripe tomatoes

½ cup olive oil

¼ cup minced fresh basil

*one 4-ounce can pitted black olives,
drained*

2 cloves garlic, pressed

½ teaspoon salt

*¼ teaspoon each freshly ground black
pepper and cracked red pepper flakes*

1 pound medium shell macaroni

*½ pound mozzarella, cubed (can be
skim-milk mozzarella)*

1 cup walnuts, toasted

*grated Romano cheese as
an accompaniment*

Pour very hot water over the tomatoes and let them stand until the skins loosen. Drain, peel, and chop the tomatoes. Mix them with the olive oil, basil, olives, garlic, and seasonings. Let the sauce marinate at room temperature for about an hour.

Cook the shells according to the package directions. Stir in about ½ cup of the juices accumulated in the sauce. Stir in the mozzarella and toss the hot macaroni until the cheese begins to melt. Stir in the remaining sauce and the toasted walnuts. Serve immediately. Pass grated Romano cheese at the table.

Serve any leftovers at room temperature; the dish should not be reheated.

Orange and Brazil Nut Salad with Basil

Makes 4 servings.

Brazil nuts are very rich in selenium, a mineral that's shown itself to be toxic to tumors.

4 large dark leaves of romaine lettuce
4 navel oranges
4 tablespoons olive oil
4 fresh basil leaves, plus 4 sprigs for garnishing (if fresh basil is unavailable, sprinkle a pinch of dried basil over each salad)
8 Brazil nuts, shelled and sliced thin (they will slice if they're fresh)
freshly ground black pepper to taste

Tear the lettuce into bite-size pieces and divide them among 4 salad plates. (Whole leaves look nice but are hard to cut with a salad fork, so they languish on the plates.)

Use a knife to peel the oranges right down to the flesh, removing not only the peel but also the pith. Slice them into rounds and overlap the rounds on top of the lettuce.

Drizzle a tablespoon of oil over each salad. Top with thinly shredded fresh basil and a goodly sprinkling of ground pepper.

Sprinkle the sliced nuts over all and garnish each portion with a sprig of basil.

Tonno and Brazil Nut Salad with Sweet Red Pepper Dressing

Makes 4 servings.

This could almost be called a selenium salad—both tuna and Brazil nuts are especially high in this cancer-fighting mineral.

one 6½-ounce can tonno (Italian tuna)
red wine vinegar for "rinsing" the tuna,
plus 2 tablespoons more for the dressing
¼ cup olive oil
1 sweet red pepper, seeded and diced
1 tablespoon drained capers
1 small head of curly-leafed lettuce
4 Brazil nuts, sliced or
coarsely chopped

Drain and discard the oil from the tuna. Put the tuna into a strainer, and "rinse" the fish with red wine vinegar.

In a small skillet, heat the oil and stir-fry the red pepper for 3 minutes, or until *barely* cooked and still crisp. Remove the skillet from the heat; add the capers and 2 tablespoons of red wine vinegar. Allow the peppers to cool to room temperature.

Wash and shake or spin-dry the lettuce. Arrange a bed of bite-size pieces of lettuce on 4 salad plates.

Divide the tuna among the plates. Spoon on the red pepper dressing. Top with the nuts.

Biscotti Anise with Hazelnuts

Makes about 2 dozen cookies.

Hazelnuts are a favorite with Italian bakers and chocolatiers. These nut-and-cherry studded *biscotti* go beautifully with espresso.

2½ cups unbleached all-purpose flour
3 teaspoons baking powder
½ teaspoon salt
½ cup (1 stick) butter or low-cholesterol margarine
¾ cup sugar
3 eggs or ¾ cup prepared egg substitute
1½ teaspoons anise extract
1 cup shelled hazelnuts
½ cup candied cherries, halved

Sift together the flour, baking powder, and salt.

Cream the butter, gradually adding the sugar, then the eggs and anise extract.

Blend the flour into the creamed mixture. Incorporate the nuts and cherries into the dough with a light touch. Chill the dough until it can be shaped.

Grease and flour a jelly roll pan. Preheat the oven to 375° F.

Shape the dough into 3 small loaves and place the loaves on the prepared baking sheet. Bake them for 20 to 25 minutes, until they are pale gold, like shortbread.

Cool the loaves completely on wire racks. Slice into cookies about 1 inch wide.

If desired, the slices can be toasted by

placing them upright but separated on a baking sheet in a 350° F. oven for 10 minutes. Store in an airtight container.

Brazil Nut Tartlets

Makes 12 tartlets.

Nut mixes usually have a few—but only a few—Brazil nuts among the many peanuts. Around the winter holidays, however, bags of Brazil nuts sometimes can be found—a good time to make these delicious morsels!

pastry for a 1-crust pie (margarine pastry preferred, see Basics)

For the filling:

1 tablespoon cornstarch
½ cup cold water
½ cup dark brown sugar, firmly packed
2 tablespoons butter or low-cholesterol margarine
½ teaspoon vanilla
½ cup coarsely chopped Brazil nuts

Preheat the oven to 400° F. You'll need 12 tartlet pans, 2-tablespoon capacity each. Roll out the pastry so that the sheet is the size of a page of typewriting paper and cut it into 12 squares. If necessary, roll each square a bit larger to fit the pans. Line and trim the tartlet pans; prick the pastry with a fork to keep it from bubbling while it bakes. Put the tartlet shells on a baking sheet, and bake them on the middle shelf for 10 minutes, or until golden brown. Cool them completely in the pans.

In a small saucepan, stir the cornstarch into the water until there are no lumps. Add the brown sugar and bring the mixture to a boil, stirring constantly. Lower the heat and simmer for 3 minutes, stirring. Remove from the heat; stir in the butter and vanilla until blended, then the chopped nuts.

Cool the mixture slightly before filling the tartlets and chill until set. Gently remove the tartlets from the pans before serving.

For other nut recipes, see: Apple-Almond Tart with Apricot Glaze; Banana Cake with Peanuts; Barley with Green Beans Parmesan; Braised Curried Savoy Cabbage with Toasted Peanuts; Cauliflower with Hot Peanut Sauce; Chicken Sauté with Figs and Almonds; Coffee-Can Fig and Nut Bread; Crunchy Eggplant-Walnut Pâté with Whole-Wheat Pita Bread; Curried Chicken Salad with Mangoes and Toasted Cashews; Jamaican Chicken with Sweet Potatoes; Maple-Nut Rice Muffins; Maple Walnut Carrots; *Pastiera*; Spaghetti with Walnut-Parsley Sauce; Twice-Baked Butternut Squash with Pecans

A RISING STAR OF THE HEALTHY HEART DIET. Those of us who were raised on hot oatmeal breakfasts were not surprised when recently oats were "discovered" as an important health food. We remember being bright and alert for that first morning class, not half-asleep like youngsters who "couldn't eat a thing in the morning." The same would be true of our first working hour today if we still started the day with that energizing meal. A combination of whole-grain oats and low-fat milk's good protein, perhaps rounded out with a sliced banana and a glass of orange juice, is a real power breakfast—unlike, say, eggs Benedict. Low fat is important, because fat makes your mind feel slowed down just when your body is revving up for action. Oats are low in both fat and sodium.

Speaking of brainpower, oats are a good source of choline, chemical precursor of the neurotransmitter acetylcholine, which plays an important role in memory function.

But there's a good deal more to oats than merely being a super breakfast food. Oatmeal is a whole grain, meaning it contains its original bran, germ, and endosperm—everything that nature put into this little package of goodness. Oats contain seven B vitamins, vitamin E, and nine minerals.

Oats benefit the heart as well as the brain: A good-sized bowl of oatmeal at breakfast lowers the artery-clogging LDL cholesterol shortly after eating and, later on, raises the artery-cleaning HDL cholesterol. For an even better effect, introduce oatmeal in some form into a second meal or snack during the day.

Oatmeal is also a good food for diabetics because it stabilizes blood sugar and insulin.

Besides what it does for you on the *inside,* oatmeal is also a topical skin healer with anti-inflammatory action. An oat-starch bath, in which the bathwater is run through a cheese-cloth bag filled with a cup of oat flour, is mighty soothing for a sunburn, a rash, or the winter itches.

In the Market

Since oat bran's recent rise to fame, its share of the supermarket cereal aisle has expanded considerably. These days, you're presented with a plethora of oatmeal and oat-bran products. When choosing between all those new cold cereals featuring oat bran in big print, always read the ingredients panel to see if oat bran tops the list and whether sugar or salt has been added.

Plain oat bran, served as a hot cereal, re-duces cholesterol better than any other form of oats. It can be used in cooking as well as for breakfast. I especially like its slight crunch in a pizza crust. A tablespoon or two of oat bran can also be added to a cup of any breading or crumb mixture or stuffing.

Oatmeal comes in three basic forms: *old-fashioned* (whole oat flakes that cook in five minutes), *quick* (cut oat flakes that cook in one minute), and *instant* (to which you just add boiling water). Old-fashioned oats have the nuttiest flavor, especially for a toasted oat topping or in a granola mix. Quick oats are useful for adding to meat loaf or when you want to whip up some oat flour—which is oatmeal ground to a powder in a food processor. Both are equally nutritious. Instant oatmeal comes in various flavors, with sugar and salt added, to mask the fact that it doesn't taste as great as the other two.

In the Kitchen

You can store oats in the original container for a month or more on the pantry shelf, or in the refrigerator in a tightly closed jar for up to a year. But you shouldn't have to keep oatmeal that long if you use it in new and interesting ways—as well as for that heartwarming bowl of hot cereal on a winter's morning. ■

Meat-Loaf "Pie" with Ricotta Filling

Makes 6 servings.

Think of naturally nutritious oats for stuffings and meat "extenders" of every purpose.

1½ pounds ground turkey or very lean beef

¾ cup uncooked quick-cooking oats

1 cup finely chopped canned tomatoes

¼ cup minced shallots

2 eggs or ½ cup prepared egg substitute

*2 tablespoons freshly grated
Romano cheese*

*1½ teaspoons Italian seasoning
(store-bought or see Basics)*

*½ teaspoon salt (optional—the cheese
is salty)*

¼ teaspoon black pepper

1 cup low-fat ricotta

⅛ teaspoon white pepper

dash of nutmeg

Preheat the oven to 350° F. Mix together the ground meat, oats, ½ cup of the tomatoes, shallots, 1 egg or ¼ cup egg substitute, cheese, 1 teaspoon of the Italian seasoning, salt, and black pepper until well-blended. Pat half the mixture into a straight-sided, 1-inch-deep, 9-inch-diameter round glass baking pan or 10-inch glass pie plate.

Blend the remaining egg or ¼ cup egg substitute with the ricotta, white pepper, and nutmeg. Spoon the mixture over the meat.

On a sheet of wax paper, pat the remaining meat into a round layer about the same size as the pan. Use the paper to flip the meat layer on top of the ricotta.

Spread the remaining tomatoes on top. Sprinkle with the remaining Italian seasoning.

Bake for 40 minutes, or until the ricotta layer is set. If you use the egg substitute, this may take 5 minutes longer.

Let the pie stand 10 minutes before cutting into wedges to serve.

Chiliburgers

Makes 6 servings.

Whether broiled or grilled, beef or turkey, burgers are juicy and flavorful with the addition of oatmeal.

1½ pounds ground turkey or very lean beef

¾ cup uncooked quick-cooking oats

½ cup chopped onion

¼ cup ketchup or tomato sauce

2 tablespoons chopped canned chilies, mild or hot

1 egg or ¼ cup prepared egg substitute

½ teaspoon each dried cilantro, ground cumin, and salt

black pepper to taste

6 hamburger buns, toasted

Mix together all the burger ingredients and form the meat into 6 patties. *The recipe can be prepared ahead and refrigerated or frozen until needed. If frozen, thaw in the refrigerator or, better yet, in a few minutes in a microwave oven on the defrost setting.*

Broil or grill the patties 5 minutes per side for well-done turkey or medium-rare beef. Cutting a patty is the only sure test that they are done to perfection. Serve on toasted buns.

Sunshine Oat Bran Pizza

Makes 10 slices.

If you've been thinking of pizza as a junk food, think again! Homemade pizza, made with low-fat mozzarella and no sausage or pepperoni, is a health food in disguise. Even the anchovies, if you use them, are near the top of the list of fish containing the healthful omega-3 oils.

I make pizza almost every Sunday evening, particularly if there's a good adventure film to watch on TV. Making a yeast dough used to be a project, even with electric dough hooks—but you can whip it up in 10 minutes with the aid of a food processor!

For the dough:

1 envelope dry yeast

1 teaspoon sugar

1 cup very warm water

½ cup oat bran hot cereal, uncooked (plus a tablespoon more to sprinkle on the pan)

3 cups unbleached all-purpose flour
¾ teaspoon salt
2 tablespoons olive oil

For the topping:

1½ cups meatless tomato sauce (see Basics)
crushed red pepper to taste (optional)
1 teaspoon dried oregano
1 large yellow pepper, seeded,
cut into strips
1 can flat anchovies, drained,
rinsed in vinegar (optional)
½ pound low-fat mozzarella,
coarsely grated

Stir the yeast and sugar into the warm water. Let it stand 5 to 10 minutes; the yeast should bubble up to show that it's active.

Combine the oat bran, flour, and salt in the work bowl of a food processor fitted with the steel blade. Process just long enough to blend. Coat a medium-size bowl with a little of the olive oil; pour the rest into the flour mixture. Process to blend. With the motor running, pour the yeast mixture down the feed tube. Process 10 to 15 seconds, until the mixture forms a ball that cleans the sides of the work bowl. (If the flour does not adhere in a ball, add a little water, 1 teaspoon at a time.) Continue to process, counting 30 seconds, or until the dough is elastic and springy.

Knead just enough to smooth the surface. Place the dough in an oiled bowl, turning it around to grease all sides, and cover with plastic wrap. Let it rise in a warm place until double in bulk, about 1 hour and 15 minutes.

Preheat the oven to 425° F. (400° F. if your pan is black steel bakeware). Punch down the dough and roll it into a circle to fit a 15-inch-diameter round pizza pan (or oblong to fit a jelly roll pan) that has been coated with olive oil and sprinkled with oat bran. Let it stand 10 minutes to relax the gluten; pull the dough out to fit the pan, a little thicker at the edges.

Layer the tomato sauce on the dough. Sprinkle with red pepper, if using, and oregano. Alternate strips of yellow pepper and anchovy. Top with a layer of cheese.

For a crisp crust, bake immediately. For a breadlike crust, let the pizza rise an additional 30 minutes. Bake on the lowest shelf for 25 minutes (20 minutes if your pan is black steel bakeware), or until the top is bubbly and the bottom is browned. (Lift the crust with a spatula to check the bottom.)

Oatmeal Cinnamon Rolls

Makes 14 rolls.

Sneaking real nutrition into a sweet favorite!
The directions are long, but if you've ever made
yeast bread, you'll find these fairly easy.

1 cup uncooked oatmeal
("old-fashioned" preferred)

1 cup water

9 tablespoons brown sugar

3 tablespoons butter or
low-cholesterol margarine

1 package dry yeast

½ cup very warm water

3 cups unbleached all-purpose flour

2 tablespoons wheat germ

1 teaspoon salt

½ cup raisins

½ teaspoon cinnamon

In a saucepan, combine ½ cup of the oatmeal
and 1 cup of water; cook on the range top—or
use a bowl and cook the cereal in the microwave—according to the package directions.
Stir in 2 tablespoons of the brown sugar and 2
tablespoons of the butter. Cool to lukewarm.

Stir the yeast and another tablespoon of
brown sugar into the ½ cup of very warm water and allow it to stand until it bubbles up.

In a food processor fitted with the steel
blade, blend the flour, wheat germ, and salt in
the work bowl. Process to blend in the cooked
oatmeal mixture. With the motor running,
pour the yeast mixture down the feed tube.
Process 10 to 15 seconds, until the mixture
forms a ball that cleans the sides of the work
bowl. (If the dough doesn't adhere in a ball,
add a little water, 1 teaspoon at a time.) Continue to process, counting 30 seconds, or until
the dough is elastic. (If it's too sticky to handle, add flour, ¼ cup at a time.) Blend in the
raisins with 2 or 3 on/off turns of the motor.
They may chop up a bit, but that's okay.
Knead just enough to smooth the surface.

Alternative method: Add ingredients in
the same order and blend well. Knead 5 minutes with dough hooks or 10 minutes by hand.

Place the dough in a buttered bowl, turning it to grease all sides, and cover with plastic
wrap. Let it rise in a warm place until doubled
in bulk, about 1 hour and 15 minutes.

Meanwhile, toast the remaining ½ cup of
uncooked oats in a 350° F. oven 10 to 12 minutes, or until they are golden but not brown.

Punch the dough down and knead just
enough to smooth it out. With a rolling pin,
roll the dough out on a floured board into a

12-by-12-inch square. (If it's too sticky to roll, knead in a little flour.) Sprinkle the square with the remaining 6 tablespoons (⅓ cup) of brown sugar, the cinnamon, and the toasted oats. Roll it up like a jelly roll. Stretch the roll out a bit so that it's at least 14 inches long.

Use the remaining tablespoon of butter to generously grease two 9-inch cake pans.

Cut the dough roll into fourteen 1-inch slices. Fit 7 slices into each pan, 1 in the middle and 6 around the sides. Cover them and let them rise until the rolls fill the pan, about 1 hour and 15 minutes.

Preheat the oven to 375° F. Bake the rolls in the top third of the oven for 25 minutes, or until risen high and browned. Turn the rolls out of the pans onto wire racks to cool or serve them warm—irresistible!

Irish Brown Oatmeal Bread

Makes 2 loaves.

This firm-textured soda bread slices well and is delicious for breakfast. Try it with an all-fruit spread instead of butter.

2 cups whole-wheat flour
2 cups unbleached all-purpose white flour
¼ cup sugar
1 tablespoon baking soda
1 teaspoon each baking powder and salt
1 cup each oatmeal and dried currants
½ teaspoon caraway seeds
¼ cup vegetable oil
about 1½ cups buttermilk (or sour milk made by stirring 2 tablespoons of white vinegar into plain whole milk)

Preheat the oven to 350° F. Grease a baking sheet or jelly roll pan.

Sift together the first 6 ingredients into a large bowl. Stir in the oatmeal, currants, and caraway seeds.

Stir in the oil. Add just enough buttermilk to make a soft dough. Knead briefly and form 2 round loaves; place them on a prepared pan. Cut an inch-deep cross in each loaf.

Bake 30 to 35 minutes, until lightly browned and dry inside when tested with a cake tester. Cool on wire racks before cutting.

Lucy's Apricot Oatmeal Bars

Makes 24 bars.

Homemade desserts taste best and can offer some real nutritional value. Two superfoods in one cookie make this a guiltless treat.

2 cups uncooked oatmeal
1 cup sifted unbleached all-purpose flour
1 cup firmly packed dark brown sugar
1 teaspoon baking soda
½ cup (1 stick) unsalted margarine, melted
½ jar of apricot preserves

Preheat the oven to 375° F. Butter an oblong baking pan—11 by 7 inches or 12 by 8 inches.

Mix together the oatmeal, flour, sugar, and soda until well-blended. Pour the melted margarine over the dry ingredients and mix until moistened throughout. (Mixing with the hands works best.)

Layer half the oat mixture over the bottom of the pan. Top with a thin layer of apricot preserves. Pat into place the remaining oat mixture to form a top layer.

Bake on the middle shelf for 20 minutes. Cool on a wire rack before cutting; don't remove the bars from the pan until they're cool enough to hold together. Store the bars in a covered tin with wax paper between layers.

Oatmeal Crunchies

Makes about 6 dozen cookies.

Of all my cookie recipes, this seems to be everyone's favorite—and also the easiest to make and bake. These cookies travel well, pack in as many high-energy, nutritious ingredients as a granola bar, and disappear like magic.

This recipe is my answer to chocolate chip cookies, but you may wish to omit the chocolate if you're watching cholesterol. Chocolate, by the way, induces a euphoric feeling similar to being in love. No wonder folks crave it!

1½ cups sifted unbleached
all-purpose flour
1 cup sugar
1 teaspoon cinnamon
½ teaspoon each baking soda and salt
1¾ cups uncooked oatmeal
½ cup each raisins and unsalted peanuts
(if chocolate chips are omitted, increase
this amount to ¾ cup)
½ cup chocolate chips (optional)
½ cup vegetable oil
½ cup (1 stick) unsalted margarine, melted
1 egg or ¼ cup prepared egg substitute
¼ cup milk

Preheat the oven to 350° F. Sift the flour, sugar, cinnamon, soda, and salt into a large bowl.

In another bowl, mix the oatmeal, raisins, peanuts, and chocolate chips.

In a third bowl, whisk together the oil, margarine, egg, and milk.

Pour the liquid ingredients into the flour mixture and blend well. Stir in the oatmeal mixture until no part appears dry.

Spoon the batter by tablespoons onto a greased or nonstick baking sheet, leaving space between. Flatten the cookies slightly. Bake 10 to 12 minutes, until the bottoms are golden and the tops are lightly browned. Repeat with each batch. Cool on wire racks.

Store the cookies in a cookie jar (it doesn't have to be airtight) or canister. They also freeze well and thaw in minutes.

Apple Oatmeal Crisp

Makes 6 servings.

As tasty as an apple pie, but much easier to make and lighter in calories. For a really crisp topping, buy "old-fashioned" oatmeal, which has bigger flakes.

4 cooking apples, such as Granny Smith
¼ cup granulated sugar
¼ teaspoon cinnamon

For the topping:

⅓ cup unbleached all-purpose flour
⅓ cup firmly packed brown sugar
⅛ teaspoon salt
¼ teaspoon cinnamon
3 tablespoons unsalted butter or
no-cholesterol margarine
½ cup uncooked "old-fashioned" oatmeal
¼ cup finely chopped walnuts

Preheat the oven to 375° F. Peel and thinly slice the apples. Mix them with the granulated sugar and ¼ teaspoon cinnamon. Spoon them into a 9-inch pie plate and press them flat.

Mix the flour, brown sugar, salt, and ¼ teaspoon cinnamon. Cut in the margarine with a pastry cutter or 2 knives until the consistency is fine. Stir in the oatmeal and walnuts.

Sprinkle the topping over the apples; press into a flat layer.

Bake for 35 minutes, or until the topping is brown and the apples are tender. Serve warm or at room temperature.

1 cup sifted unbleached all-purpose flour
1 teaspoon each ginger and cinnamon
¾ teaspoon baking powder
½ teaspoon salt
½ cup oat flour
¾ cup molasses
½ cup vegetable oil
2 eggs or ½ cup prepared egg substitute
⅓ cup brown sugar with no lumps in it
½ teaspoon baking soda
½ cup boiling water
applesauce as a topping (optional)

Old-Time Oat-Flour Gingerbread

Makes 9 servings.

Oat flour can be substituted for up to a third of the flour in quick breads and unfussy cakes that don't depend on an extremely light texture, as sponge cake does. Baked goods made with oat flour will be more tender and crumbly than others, but delicious. Try oat flour in carrot cake, banana cake, spice cake, and this gingerbread. Stir the oat flour into the dry ingredients *after sifting*, so that you won't sift out the germ and bran.

Oat flour can also be substituted for all the flour in thickened gravies, soups, and stews, as well as puddings.

To make ground-oat flour, put 1 to 2 cups of quick-cooking (not instant) oats in a food processor or blender. Process or blend for about 1 minute, until the oats are ground to a flour consistency.

Preheat the oven to 350° F. Butter and flour a 9-by-9-inch or 8-by-8-inch baking pan.

Sift together the all-purpose flour, ginger, cinnamon, baking powder, and salt. Stir in the oat flour.

Beat together the molasses, oil, eggs, and brown sugar.

Pour the molasses mixture into the dry ingredients and blend well.

Put the baking soda in a cup; add the boiling water and stir. Pour all at once into the batter, whisking to blend; the batter will be thin.

Pour the batter into the prepared pan, and bake in the middle of the oven for 25 minutes, or until the gingerbread shrinks slightly away from the sides of the pan and a cake tester inserted in the middle comes out dry. Serve with applesauce.

For other oat recipes, see the following:
Peach and Raspberry Cranachan; Whole-Wheat, Oatmeal, and Apple Muffins

OLIVE OIL

GOLDEN "HEAL-ALL" OF THE VEGETABLE KINGDOM. Of all the superfoods that promote good health, none is more super than the golden oil of the olive. With a history interleaved with mystical legend, it's also one of the most venerable; the first olive trees were cultivated in Syria and southern Iran around 6000 BC.

The ancient Israelites used olive oil in their consecrated lamps. The Egyptians, to whom the olive came from Cretan traders around 1700 BC, nevertheless called it a gift from their goddess Isis; Tutankhamen wore a garland of olive branches. By 1000 BC, the Greeks were crediting their goddess Athena for the golden oil that to them symbolized holiness and courage. And an olive branch still to this day is identified with peace and hope.

With such a record of reverence, wouldn't you expect olive oil to be good for you? It is!

To explain why, first we have to look at the composition of fats. Solid fats are classified as "saturated"; meat fat and butter are mostly saturated fats. Fats called "unsaturated" remain liquid at room temperature. This classification is divided further, according to a difference in molecular structure, as "polyunsaturated" or "monounsaturated." Corn, soybean, and safflower oil, and some margarines, are mostly polyunsaturated fat. Olive oil is largely monounsaturated, and it contains the beneficial oleic acid.

In their first experiments with the effects of fats on cholesterol, scientists were pleased to note that unsaturated fats lowered the cholesterol count. Subsequently, they learned that polyunsaturates did not discriminate; they lowered *all* cholesterol—the "good" HDL as well as the "bad" LDL—which was not such a great health benefit after all. And then they found that monounsaturates were (as Goldilocks would say) "just right." While lowering LDL cholesterol, they raised HDL, making the monounsaturates the fat of choice for people concerned about their cholesterol.

But improving the cholesterol count isn't olive oil's only virtue—Homer didn't call it "liquid gold" for nothing! In recent studies, it's been confirmed that regular olive oil consumption produces a significant lowering of arterial blood pressure. Olive oil also blocks the tendency of the blood to clot and therefore protects against strokes.

Gastric tolerance is higher for olive oil than for any other fat, and this superfood may even be beneficial for ulcer patients. In a study involving 102 ulcer patients, the replacement of animal fats by olive oil produced a reduction of lesions in one-third of the cases.

Olive oil may play a protective role against gall bladder disease (especially cholesterol gallstones) because it activates bile flow and raises HDL cholesterol.

Olive oil contains antioxidant substances that fight against the cellular damage and genetic "errors" that cause cancers and the effects of aging. The life expectancy of mice fed on olive oil has been shown to be longer than that of mice fed sunflower and corn oil.

Does all this mean that one should increase the proportion of fat in one's diet? (In the form of monounsaturates, of course.) *No!* Although fats are necessary to maintain life, most Americans are in no danger—they are eating too much fat already. The idea is to *replace* other, less healthful fats with "heal-all" olive oil while at the same time trimming back on the proportion of total fat in one's diet. And olive oil has such a rich taste, it's easy to use a small amount! As an example, suppose you're used to putting a few pats of butter or gobs of sour cream (some people use both!) on a baked potato. Try it instead with extra-virgin olive oil and some chopped fresh chives, and you'll find that a teaspoon of oil is enough. The bottom line is less total fat—and fat that's better for you, too!

In the Market

Extra-virgin olive oil is the finest (and most expensive) grade, with not more than 1 percent acid and a fruity flavor that can vary from subtle to strong. Once you find the brand that has the right intensity of flavor for your taste, it's wise to stick to it; new brands may be too mild or too strong for your taste. Extra-virgin oil is great as an accent, on an antipasto or a cold vegetable dish, wherever its distinctive taste can be made to count.

Virgin olive oil is much the same as extra-virgin but is allowed a 2 percent acidity. It's a waste to use extra-virgin or virgin olive oil in cooked dishes where it will have a supporting, not a starring, role.

"Olive oil" or "pure olive oil" is a blend of refined olive oil and extra-virgin or virgin olive oil. It's an excellent product for most of your cooking needs, and certainly for all frying. I usually buy pure olive oil by the gallon and extra-virgin (preferably "cold-pressed") by the half pint. At home, I pour some olive oil from the gallon into a green glass container for easy access and store the rest.

Olive pomace oil is extracted from the olive pulp with the use of solvents and then blended with virgin olive oil to improve its flavor. It's the lowest grade of olive oil, and while it has the same nutritional benefits, I recommend using pure olive oil instead.

One company markets a "Mild & Light" olive oil for those who really don't like the taste of olive oil but would like to share in its health benefits. The word *light*, in this case, refers to flavor; it has as many calories as any other olive oil. "Mild & Light" can also be used for dishes in which the distinctive taste of olive oil would not be an asset, such as in pastry *(see Basics)* or in cakes that call for vegetable oil.

In the Kitchen

Olive oil should be stored in a cool, dark place. It's the longest lasting of oils, the least likely to go rancid, and will keep for a year under the correct conditions. But if you're worried about storage, you can refrigerate olive oil. It will turn cloudy and thick, but returning it to room temperature will restore its normal consistency. If you flavor some of your salad oil with a clove of garlic, you must refrigerate the oil and use it within a week or so.

A wise health move is to experiment with gradually replacing the fats you use with olive oil. It can replace butter to flavor popcorn, to baste turkey, to dress cooked vegetables, and even to drizzle over corn on the cob. Olive oil dressings are wonderful, too, on macaroni or potato salads. The combination of olive oil, which keeps well, and vinegar, which retards spoilage, will keep those picnic favorites fresh longer than other salad dressings.

Speaking of salad dressings, in countries around the Mediterranean Basin, that term simply means olive oil, vinegar, salt and pepper—sprinkled directly on the salad, not premixed. This improvisation requires some experience and control on the part of the salad maker. Salads made this way often vary with one's mood and are never quite the same twice. In making a salad dressing in the Mediterranean manner, the proverbial recipe still rings true: "A spendthrift for the oil, a miser for the vinegar, a wise man for the salt, and a madman to toss it together."

Tuna Tapenade

Makes about 1¼ cups.

Serve this savory spread/dip with toasted French bread or with raw vegetables, especially cherry tomatoes.

1 clove garlic, sliced

one 6½-ounce can tonno (Italian tuna packed in oil), drained

½ cup pitted black olives

2 tablespoons red wine vinegar

1 tablespoon drained capers

3 to 4 sprigs fresh flat-leafed parsley, no stems

about ¼ cup extra-virgin olive oil

In a food processor with the motor running, toss the garlic slices down the feed tube to mince them. Add the tuna, olives, vinegar, capers, and parsley, and process to chop as fine as possible.

With the motor running, slowly pour the olive oil down the feed tube until a spread consistency is reached. Stop the motor to scrape down the sides of the work bowl once or twice.

Fresh Spinach Fettuccine with Bread Sauce

Makes 2 to 4 servings, depending on what else you are having.

This simple dish has a quick sauce and is meant to be served at room temperature, making it perfect for a lazy summer evening.

2 cups fresh breadcrumbs from about 3 slices Italian bread

6 tablespoons extra-virgin olive oil

2 cloves garlic, finely minced or pressed

6 juicy ripe tomatoes, peeled and chopped

¼ cup chopped fresh flat-leafed parsley

2 tablespoons minced fresh basil

½ teaspoon salt

freshly ground black pepper to taste

8 ounces fresh spinach fettuccine

In a large skillet, heat 4 tablespoons of the oil and sauté the garlic until it just begins to sizzle. Add the breadcrumbs and stir-fry them until they are golden; be sure the garlic is well-distributed and not clumped somewhere among the crumbs. Allow the finished crumbs to cool.

To make the uncooked tomato sauce, combine the tomatoes, parsley, basil, salt, pepper, and the remaining 2 tablespoons of oil. *The recipe can be prepared ahead to this point and kept at room temperature for 2 hours.*

Cook the fettuccine according to the package directions until it's al dente. Do not overcook. Stir in the tomato mixture. Toss with half of the crumbs and sprinkle the rest on top. Serve at room temperature.

Parsley *Pistou*

Makes about ½ cup.

This is a piquant purée to make in winter when parsley is the only fresh herb in sight. Serve a dollop of fragrant *pistou* in bowls of bean or vegetable soup—such as Tomato Rice Soup *(page 250)*.

1 to 2 cloves garlic, sliced
1 well-packed cup of fresh flat-leafed parsley leaves, no stems
1 teaspoon dried basil
¼ cup or more extra-virgin olive oil

Two different methods are given because the blender purées better when a liquid base is included, whereas the processor needs to chop the solids before liquid is added.

Blender method: Purée the garlic, parsley, and basil with ¼ cup of oil. Add more oil through the feed hole as necessary to make a sauce texture. Stop the motor to scrape down the sides of the blender once.

Processor method: Chop the garlic, parsley, and basil fine. Slowly pour ¼ cup of oil down the feed tube, adding more as needed to make a sauce texture. Stop the motor to scrape down the sides of the bowl 2 or 3 times.

Spaghetti with Walnut-Parsley Sauce

*Makes 2 servings as an entrée,
4 as a first course.*

Although oil-based pasta sauces are among
the quickest and easiest to make, they're
quite flavorful—and usually spiced up with
lots of pepper.

*⅓ cup extra-virgin or regular olive oil
2 cloves garlic, finely minced
½ cup walnut halves
½ cup loosely packed, chopped fresh
flat-leafed parsley
¼ teaspoon each freshly ground
black pepper and hot red pepper flakes
½ pound thin spaghetti, cooked according
to package directions*

In a small skillet, sauté the garlic in the oil
over very low heat until the garlic is barely
golden but not brown, about 5 minutes.

Stir in the walnuts, parsley, and both kinds
of pepper. *The sauce can be prepared ahead
and kept at room temperature for 2 hours.*

While the pasta is cooking, dip out ¼ cup
of the cooking water and add it to the sauce.

Toss the cooked spaghetti with the sauce,
saving a few walnuts for the top.

Vermicelli all'Olio

Makes 2 to 4 servings.

If you'd like to try this but don't care for anchovies, you can omit them, substitute garlic
for shallots, and throw in a handful of toasted
pine nuts as you finish the sauce.

*¼ cup extra-virgin or regular olive oil
6 anchovy fillets, rinsed in wine vinegar
2 large shallots, minced
½ cup sweet red pepper, finely diced
½ cup sliced pitted black olives
2 tablespoons raisins
2 tablespoons minced fresh
flat-leafed parsley
hot red pepper flakes to taste
(¼ teaspoon or more)
½ pound vermicelli, cooked according to
package directions*

In a large skillet, heat the oil, and sauté the anchovies, shallots, sweet red pepper, olives, and raisins over very low heat until the anchovies have dissolved into the oil and the vegetables are soft. Turn off the heat; stir in the parsley and the hot red pepper flakes. *The sauce can be prepared ahead and kept at room temperature for 1 hour.*

Have the water boiling but wait to cook the vermicelli until you can watch it, because it takes only a few minutes. Save ½ cup of the cooking water when you drain the vermicelli and add it to the sauce. (This keeps an oil-based sauce from making the pasta gummy.)

Scoop the vermicelli into the skillet and blend it well with the sauce.

Caesar Salad with Radicchio and Toasted Parmesan Crumbs

Makes 4 to 6 servings.

The strong flavor of radicchio stands up very nicely to this spicy dressing (minus the raw egg), which can be prepared in advance without the fuss of bringing all these ingredients to the table. If you miss the mystique, you could grind the black pepper on the salad at the last moment.

1 crusty roll of Italian or Portuguese bread
1 cup olive oil
1 clove garlic, pressed
1 to 2 tablespoons grated Parmesan cheese
1 clove garlic, sliced
4 to 6 anchovies, rinsed in vinegar
(optional but traditional)
juice of ½ lemon
½ teaspoon Worcestershire sauce
¼ teaspoon dry mustard
freshly ground black pepper to taste
1 head romaine lettuce, torn into
bite-size pieces
1 cup shredded radicchio

Olive Oil Mayonnaise with Garlic

Makes about 1 cup.

All you need is a blender and a steady hand to have homemade mayonnaise in minutes!

1 whole egg plus 1 egg yolk or
⅓ cup prepared egg substitute
2 tablespoons red wine vinegar
½ teaspoon each dry mustard and salt
¼ teaspoon white pepper
1 clove garlic, sliced
¾ to 1 cup olive oil

Coarsely grate the roll without being too fussy about evenness of size. In a large skillet, heat ¼ cup of the oil and sauté the pressed garlic until it just begins to sizzle. Add the crumbs and stir-fry them until they are golden. Sprinkle with cheese, and allow them to cool.

In a blender, purée the sliced garlic and the anchovies in the lemon juice, blending in the Worcestershire sauce and dry mustard, until the mixture is really smooth. Through the feed hole at the top, with the motor running, very slowly add the remaining ¾ cup of oil to emulsify the dressing. Pour it into a small pitcher and stir in the pepper.

Put the lettuce and radicchio in a salad bowl, and chill until needed.

When ready to serve, pour the dressing over the salad and toss well. Sprinkle the crumbs on top.

Put the eggs in the blender. With the motor running, add the vinegar, spices, and garlic, one at a time, through the feed tube in the lid, and blend until the garlic is puréed.

Pour the oil into a small pitcher. With the motor running, add the oil in a slow, steady stream through the feed tube until the mayonnaise is thick and will incorporate no more oil.

To store, pour boiling water into a clean jar and lid, and invert them. When they are dry, spoon in the mayonnaise, which will keep about 2 weeks in the refrigerator.

Note: There are numerous other recipes throughout this book that use olive oil.

ONIONS, LEEKS, AND SHALLOTS

INDISPENSABLE AIDS TO FLAVOR AND HEALTH. These three "country cousins" of the lily family may not boast of elegant perfume, but they're prized for the earthy fragrance they've imparted to cooking since ancient times. No Egyptian pharaoh considered his tomb complete unless it contained wooden replicas of onions and garlic to season his meals royally in the afterworld. According to the Old Testament, even the children of Israel, led to freedom by Moses, recalled with nostalgia: "We remember the fish, which we did eat in Egypt . . . the cucumbers, and the melons, and the leeks, and the onions, and the garlic."

Onions and leeks probably traveled out of Egypt and shallots out of Asia (bypassing the ancient Greeks, who considered all of these pungent bulbs vulgar) to Europe, where there's scarcely a soup or stew today in which they are not included. The leek, as a matter of fact, eventually became the national emblem of Wales.

Good health traveled with them. Ancient doctors began prescribing onions and garlic for practically anything that ailed their patients. Medicine was empirical in those days: If patients got well, the prescription worked; if they died, the doctor gave up the remedy.

Onions and their relatives seemed to promote health, and modern studies have confirmed this. For one thing, they reduce the incidence of blood clots that lead to strokes. When three groups of vegetarians were studied in India in the 1970s, those who ate no onions and garlic had the shortest blood coagulation time. But clotting was inhibited in those who ate onions liberally.

An extract of onions has been shown to raise HDL cholesterol levels. Onions contain a prostaglandin that lowers blood pressure.

If you put onion juice in a test tube with some nasty bacteria such as salmonella, the bacteria will lose its punch. In experiments with humans, onion juice has lessened the effect of allergens and inhibited bronchial asthma. There is evidence, too, that onion oils inhibit the formation of tumors.

The very substance in onions that makes you cry as you peel them also breaks up mucus congestion. This means that an old-time cough medicine that consisted of onion juice and honey was nothing to sneeze at after all.

Leeks and shallots, containing so many of the same compounds as onions, are good heart medicine and may also help to prevent cancer.

Although they're de rigueur in European kitchens and American cooking magazines, leeks aren't often found in the average American kitchen—and that's a shame, because the leek has a delicacy (unlike the rest of its robust relatives) that enhances without overwhelming companion foods.

In the Market

Buy leeks that are one and a half inches in diameter or less; bigger ones will be tough. Look for healthy green stalks, but discard the green part. A two-pound bunch of leeks yields one pound trimmed and cleaned.

Scallions, which resemble leeks, are sweetest when the bulbs are thinnest. Look for green tops with no sign of yellow or decay.

Shallots are the gourmet bulb, tender and mild. Buy them loose so you'll be able to weed out any with soft spots or sprouts.

Vidalia onions, available in the spring and early summer, are so sweet and flavorful that one wishes their season were longer. Local summer onions are second best; the flat rather than round ones are sweetest. Bermuda onions and red onions are "salad onions" that look great with leafy greens but are not as sweet as Vidalias. Yellow onions arrive in the fall; they are good for every cooking purpose, and wonderful keepers, but too strong to be eaten raw unless they've been "sweetened" by marinating in vinegar, wine, or ice water.

Don't buy onions that have begun to sprout or smell acrid. Check Bermuda and red onions for soft spots, indicating there is rot within that may not show outside.

In the Kitchen

All onions should be stored in a cool, dry, dark place, not the refrigerator. Vidalia onions will keep well for two weeks or more, yellow onions for a month.

To store scallions, trim off the tough outer membrane, the base, and about halfway down the green top; wrap scallions in a towel within a plastic bag and keep them in the refrigerator for up to a week. Scallions are welcome in winter salads when onions are just too strong; use the green tops, too.

Shallots cook quickly and are ideal in a white sauce that will be cooked for only a few minutes. They will keep three weeks.

When you wash leeks, look out for grit between the fleshy white layers. As with scallions, wrap leeks in a towel within a plastic bag and refrigerate them for up to a week.

Of all the dishes that onions flavor so well, salads especially need the crisp bouquet of sweet onions or scallions to be truly great. As Sydney Smith wrote in *Recipe for a Salad:* "Let onion atoms lurk within the bowl / And, scarce-suspected, animate the whole." ▬

Scrod Baked with Onions, Lemon, and Rosemary

Makes 4 servings.

A fast, flavorsome entrée with a Mediterranean influence.

2 tablespoons olive oil
2 fillets of scrod (about 1½ pounds)
1 large sweet onion, very finely sliced
½ teaspoon dried rosemary
salt and pepper to taste
1 lemon cut into paper-thin slices

Preheat the oven to 400° F. Put 1 tablespoon of the oil in a baking pan that will hold the scrod in a single layer. Turn the scrod in the oil to coat all sides.

Arrange the onion over the fish in overlapping slices. Drizzle the remaining 1 tablespoon of oil over the onion. Sprinkle with rosemary, salt, and pepper. Remove any seeds from the lemon slices and lay them over all.

Bake for 15 to 20 minutes, or until the fish flakes apart easily at the center.

Red Snapper with Rosemary-Scented Shallot Confit

Makes 4 servings.

Like most fish dishes, this one is convertible—make it with flounder or sole or whatever fillets look fresh and beautiful at the market.

12 shallots, peeled
1 cup chicken broth
2 tablespoons olive oil
½ teaspoon rosemary
1½ pounds potatoes
salt and freshly ground lemon pepper
1½ to 2 pounds red snapper fillets
½ cup seasoned breadcrumbs
(store-bought or see Basics)
paprika

Put the shallots in a small covered casserole with the broth, oil, and rosemary. Bake in a 300° F. oven for 30 minutes or in the microwave for 10 minutes on high—until the shallots are quite tender but still retain their shape. If you use the microwave, reduce the amount of broth to ½ cup.

Meanwhile, peel and slice the potatoes ¼ inch thick. Parboil the potatoes in salted water for 5 minutes. Drain and layer them in the bottom of a 2-inch-deep, 10- to 12-inch-long rectangular baking dish from which you can serve. Season the potatoes with salt and freshly ground lemon pepper to your taste.

Preheat the oven to 400° F. Rinse the snapper fillets and lay them on top of the potatoes. Pour the juice from the casserole over all, and place the shallots among the fillets. Sprinkle with the crumbs and paprika.

Bake for 20 minutes, or until the fish and potatoes are cooked through.

Sicilian Pearl Onions with Golden Raisins

Makes 4 servings.

Instead of the traditional creamed onions, try serving this piquant dish with turkey.

1 bag frozen pearl onions
2 tablespoons olive oil
1 tablespoon tomato paste
2 tablespoons red wine vinegar
1 tablespoon sugar
¼ cup golden raisins

In a medium-size skillet, sauté the unthawed onions in oil for 3 to 5 minutes, until the liquid evaporates. Add the tomato paste and cook, stirring, for 2 minutes. Add the vinegar, sugar, and raisins. Continue to cook, stirring occasionally, until the onions are tender-crisp. Serve warm or at room temperature.

Note: This is one of those pesky recipes that use a single tablespoon of tomato paste. If you've had to open a can of it, what to do with the rest? Spoon leftover paste by tablespoons onto wax paper on a tray and freeze it. Then, store the frozen lumps of paste in a plastic container. Very handy for future recipes!

An even easier way to solve the problem is to buy tomato paste in a tube.

Fresh Pickled Onions

Makes about ½ pint.

Once the season for sweet spring onions has passed, you may find yellow onions a bit too strong to eat raw. If so, here's a way to make them milder for salads and sandwiches.

1 large yellow onion
1 tablespoon sugar
½ cup wine vinegar

Peel and thinly slice the onion into rings. Cover with cold water and soak for 30 minutes. Drain.

In a small bowl (ceramic, not plastic, which would hold the smell forever), stir the sugar into the vinegar until dissolved. Add the drained onion. Cover tightly with foil and refrigerate for a few hours, stirring once or twice and pushing the onion rings under the vinegar. Use for salads or any dish requiring raw onion.

Sage and Onion Tart

Makes 8 servings.

A savory appetizer or accompaniment to soup. Fresh sage is less fussy than many other herbs and can be grown in a pot on a sunny window sill. In folk medicine, sage has been used as a remedy for headache, gastrointestinal and respiratory ailments, insomnia, and mental illness. Modern herbalists recommend a sage gargle to treat a sore throat, sage tea for depression, and sage as an aid to digestion. Perhaps the last prescription tells us why the annual Thanksgiving feast traditionally includes a sage-scented turkey dressing.

¾ cup milk

3 large eggs or ¾ cup prepared egg substitute

1 teaspoon dry mustard

3 large yellow onions (about 1 pound), peeled and ringed

2 tablespoons butter or low-cholesterol margarine

2 tablespoons dry sherry or dry vermouth

½ tablespoon very finely minced fresh sage leaves or ½ teaspoon ground sage (the fresh sage is much better)

one 9-inch pie shell, baked until golden (not browned) and cooled (see Basics)

2 tablespoons grated Parmesan cheese

paprika

Beat together the milk, eggs, and dry mustard. Let the mixture stand until the bubbles subside, about 15 minutes.

In a large skillet, stir-fry the onions in the butter over low heat until the rings are separate. Add the sherry or vermouth, and continue to sweat the onions over very low heat, stirring occasionally, until they are quite tender but not brown, about 20 minutes. If necessary, add more sherry. Distribute the sage evenly among the onion rings.

Preheat the oven to 375° F. Put the onions into the partly cooked pastry shell and carefully pour the egg mixture over the rings. Sprinkle with the grated cheese and paprika. Bake the tart on the middle shelf of the oven for 25 minutes, or until the filling is set. If you use an egg substitute, it may take 5 minutes longer to set. Serve at room temperature.

Scallion Cornmeal Pancakes

Makes 10 large cakes.

Plain or with yogurt, these savory cakes make a tasty accompaniment to fish or chicken.

1 bunch scallions
1 tablespoon vinegar
1 cup milk
1 cup boiling water
¾ cup coarse yellow cornmeal
1½ cups sifted unbleached all-purpose flour
1 tablespoon baking powder
1 teaspoon salt
¼ teaspoon baking soda
2 eggs, beaten, or ½ cup prepared egg substitute
3 tablespoons vegetable oil

Wash the scallions and trim off the root ends. Thinly slice the scallion bulbs with about 3 inches of green tops.

Stir the vinegar into the milk to sour it; let it stand 5 minutes or more.

In a medium-size bowl, pour the boiling water over the cornmeal, whisking to blend.

Sift the remaining dry ingredients together.

Whisk the sour milk, beaten eggs, and oil into the cornmeal. Stir in the dry ingredients and the scallions.

Heat a nonstick griddle to 400° F. (or use an oiled nonstick skillet). Drop the batter from a spoon onto the griddle and cook until bubbles form on top. Turn and cook until brown.

Hot Onion Bread

Makes 8 servings.

A wonderful accompaniment to a hearty soup, this bread is best when made in a cast-iron skillet, which is my favorite for a number of quick, hot breads. Not only that, every time you cook in cast iron, you're adding a trace of iron to your diet—yes, the same stuff that's in vitamin pills.

If you don't have a cast-iron skillet, use a 9-inch-square baking dish.

2 large onions sliced (about 2 cups)
2 tablespoons olive oil
½ teaspoon rosemary
⅔ cup unflavored yogurt (low-fat can be used)
1 egg or ¼ cup prepared egg substitute
white pepper and cayenne pepper to taste
1 cup whole-wheat flour
1 cup unbleached all-purpose white flour
1 tablespoon baking powder
½ teaspoon salt
¼ cup vegetable oil
½ cup milk plus about 4 tablespoons more milk

In a 10-inch cast-iron frying pan, slowly fry the onions in olive oil until they are limp and golden but not brown. Sprinkle the cooked onion with rosemary. Remove and reserve the onion. Don't wash the frying pan, which is now oiled and ready for the bread dough.

Preheat the oven to 450° F. Mix together

the yogurt and beaten egg. Add white pepper and cayenne pepper to your taste (at least ⅛ teaspoon each).

Sift together the flours, baking powder, and salt. Combine the oil and ½ cup of milk. Stir the liquid mixture into the dry ingredients. Add additional milk by tablespoons to make a soft dough that can be handled. Knead the batter briefly, flatten it into a 10-inch round, and place it in the skillet. Layer onions over the top. Pour the yogurt mixture on top, smoothing it with a spatula.

Bake for 25 minutes in the top third of the oven. The bread should be risen, light brown, and dry inside when tested with a toothpick.

Basil-Scented Summertime Green Bean and Onion Salad

Makes 4 to 6 servings.

This crunchy salad absolutely requires fresh Vidalia onions, crisp green beans, and fresh basil. It's perfect for a summer buffet table, right beside the potato salad. Better make plenty, because people will eat more of this salad than you ever would expect, as I found out to my dismay the first time I set out a dish of it on a buffet. I'd made only 4 pounds, and the last few people to the table got none.

2 pounds fresh green beans
1 large Vidalia onion, peeled and thinly sliced
10 to 12 leaves of fresh basil, shredded
½ cup olive oil or more to taste
salt and freshly ground black pepper to taste
¼ cup red wine vinegar or more to taste

Wash the beans and snip off the ends. Steam them over an inch of boiling water from 4 to 7 minutes, depending on thickness, until tender-crisp. Taste is the best test. It's vital not to overcook the beans. Immediately rinse the beans in cold water to stop the cooking action and drain well.

Slip the onion slices into rings and combine them with the beans in a salad bowl. Toss with the basil, oil, salt, and freshly ground pepper.

Here's where you have a choice to make. If you add the vinegar an hour or so before serving, you'll get a nice pickled flavor but the beans will lose their color. Otherwise, add the vinegar at the last moment to preserve that bright green.

You must taste this salad to correct its seasoning, adding more oil, vinegar, salt, or pepper to your taste.

Serve the salad at room temperature. If it must be held for several hours, refrigerate it but bring it out 30 minutes before serving.

Note: There are numerous other recipes throughout this book that use onions, leeks, and shallots.

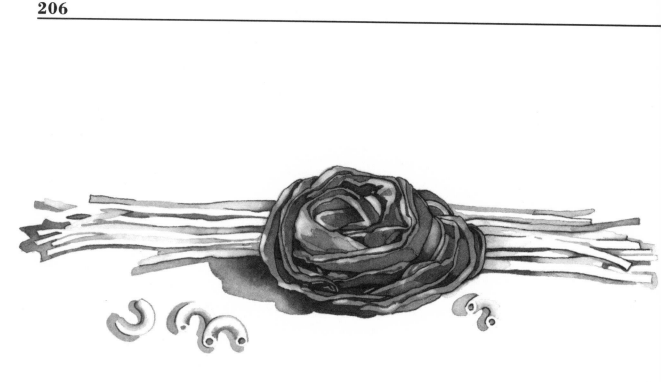

PASTA

THE GOOD-MOOD FOOD. The umbrella term *pasta* has come into the limelight rather recently as an upscale name for spaghetti and macaroni, those imaginative shapes created to be dressed in so many different sauces. The general rule is: The thicker the sauce, the bigger the macaroni can be; the finer the sauce, the thinner the spaghetti. Then there are the nice distinctions. A medium shrimp curls perfectly into a medium pasta shell; peas look like tiny pearls nestled within small shells. The long, flat shape of fettuccine complements asparagus spears, whereas buds of broccoli florets combine nicely with fusilli.

Each shape suggests an ideal sauce.

Pasta itself is made of nothing but hardy semolina flour and water (egg noodles excepted). So how can it be considered a superfood? Because it's an all-time favorite complex carbohydrate food that, when used correctly, can help relieve what may be our number-one health problem: stress. *Stress* is a term that covers a host of negative feelings—worry, frustration, anxiety, and anger—that arise, as Hamlet put it, from "the slings and arrows of outrageous fortune." And, without doubt, unchecked stress has an effect on our physical health.

Pure carbohydrate, when not combined

with protein, is a drugless tranquilizer that relieves tension almost as fast as a couple of aspirins relieve a headache. Under stressful conditions, the brain uses up chemicals that stabilize states of mind. When carbohydrates are eaten without protein, the brain begins manufacturing more serotonin, which promotes a calm, cheerful mood that puts one's problems into perspective.

Studies done by Dr. Judith J. Wurtman at the Massachusetts Institute of Technology set the tranquilizing carbohydrate "dose" at one and a half ounces of *pure* carbohydrate—two and a half ounces if one is overweight. As soon as this carbohydrate is absorbed into the bloodstream, the chemical reaction begins. If a protein food is consumed at the same time, its amino acids slow down this process.

Feeling at your wit's end? Curl up with a comforting bowl of vegetable soup thickened with lots of macaroni (I suggest tubettini or pastina)—and relax. Want to prevent a child from getting too keyed up before a party? Serve elbow macaroni and a low-fat tomato sauce (*not* cheese sauce) for lunch.

Notice how people crave starchy foods in winter? The fact that an increase in serotonin helps relieve depression may explain why people desire more carbohydrates in winter, when the decreased light of shorter days brings on a condition known as seasonal affective disorder. SAD, as it's called, shows itself in symptoms of irritability, moodiness, and depression.

Pasta is a good food choice, too, for those who are trying to quit smoking and who will probably experience similar discomforts.

A glass of warm milk is not the ideal beverage for insomniacs. Actually, digesting the protein in milk is liable to keep you awake. Carbohydrate foods like pasta, on the other hand, encourage relaxation.

Worried about the extra calories? A cup of cooked macaroni has only 140 calories, compared with 370 for a small club steak. It's what you put *on t*he macaroni that racks up the calories. Pasta dressed with one of the vegetable sauces (including tomato), made with a reduced amount of oil, is a satisfying, sensible entrée that fits into most diets better than the leanest beef.

Athletes on high-carbohydrate diets have been shown to experience greater vigor and less anxiety—a winning combination—than those on high-protein diets.

A plateful of pasta provides a significant amount of some important minerals: manganese, iron, phosphorus, copper, magnesium, and zinc. Enriched pasta is fortified with some B vitamins as well—thiamine, riboflavin, and niacin. You'll get even more of the B complex if you buy whole-grain pastas. Supermarkets usually have one or two varieties, but "whole food" markets have a much better selection of whole-wheat shapes.

B complex is the "stress vitamin"; a vitamin B deficiency can cause nervousness, irritability, and fatigue. B vitamin supplements have been used to treat nervous and mental disorders such as migraine headaches and senile dementia. Thiamine (vitamin B_1) has been used to relieve symptoms of psychiatric disorders. Since sugar and alcohol destroy B vitamins, Americans need a good supply of B complex in their daily diets that enriched pasta can help provide.

In the Market

In buying pasta, brand loyalty rather than shopping the sales makes the most sense. That's because not all pastas are created equal. Some of them get mushy and break apart by the time they're cooked through. Nor are imported brands *necessarily* superior to American. You really have to experiment with different brands, American and imported, to find the ones that offer good quality, and then stick to them.

Fresh pasta is much more expensive than dried, so keep in mind that although it's delicious for a simple dish like fettuccine Alfredo, the fresh variety is by no means desirable in all (or even most) pasta dishes.

Some brands of frozen pasta—ravioli, manicotti, tortellini, and gnocci—are excellent, and so comforting to have in the freezer!

In the Kitchen

Dried pasta can be kept on a cool, dry pantry shelf for a year, but use it within six months, since you don't know how long the store has stocked that batch. Dried whole-wheat pasta should be kept for less time; whole-grain products retain oils that can cause an "off" taste as they age. Fresh pastas must be refrigerated and used within a week.

There are two cardinal rules of pasta cooking: Always use plenty of water (seven quarts for a pound) and always have the water at a rapid boil. A tablespoon of olive oil in the cooking water prevents sticking and boiling over. The addition of a teaspoon to a tablespoon of salt provides flavor. No amount of salt applied later will add as much, so if you're cutting down on sodium, it's better for the taste of the finished dish to leave it out of the sauce rather than the cooking water.

About the mystique of al dente: Don't feel it's necessary to serve half-cooked pasta in order to reach some culinary ideal. Pasta should be cooked just long enough to suit your own taste, whether you prefer it chewy or tender—but never soft and sticky, of course! If the package directions give a cooking time (many do not), consider the number of minutes suggested as a guide only. The only way to test for doneness is to taste a small piece. For a perfect test, turn that bit of pasta around in a spoonful of sauce before tasting it.

Pasta must be sauced immediately to prevent its sticking together. If that's not possible, add just enough olive oil to coat the pasta.

Hot sauced pasta that stands in the pot for even a few minutes will continue to cook, so you must either serve it at once or, if it must be held for 10 minutes or so, undercook it a bit. The same may be said for pasta that will be recooked in a casserole.

One of the things I like best about pasta is the way it combines with vegetables to make some terrific dishes that even those who shy away from health foods find enjoyable. ■■■

Japanese-Style Noodle Soup

Makes 4 servings.

Japanese soup uses a broth made from *konbu* (seaweed) and bonito flakes (dried fish), for which I've substituted the more readily obtainable clam juice. Japanese noodles and shiitake mushrooms, however, can be found in many supermarkets.

3 to 4 fresh or dried shiitake mushrooms
one 8-ounce bottle clam juice
4 cups water
4 cups loosely packed chopped bok choy
2 tablespoons sake or dry white wine
1 tablespoon soy sauce
½ teaspoon salt or more, to taste
½ pound Japanese noodles
1 cup cooked, slivered chicken
2 scallions, thinly sliced

If you're using the dried mushrooms, reconstitute them by soaking them in warm water for 30 minutes. Sliver the mushrooms, discarding the tough stems.

Combine the mushrooms, clam juice, 3 cups of the water, the bok choy, wine, soy sauce, and salt in a large saucepan. Bring the broth to a boil, reduce the heat, and simmer for 5 minutes.

Bring the broth back to a rolling boil, add the noodles, and immediately add the remaining 1 cup of cool water to reduce the broth to a simmer. Cook the noodles at a simmer for 3 to 5 minutes, watching that the broth does not boil over. (Lift it off the heat for a moment if it bubbles up too high.)

Taste for seasoning: You may want more soy sauce or salt. Stir in the chicken and scallions. As soon as the chicken is heated through (30 seconds or so), remove the soup from the heat and serve at once.

Take-It-Easy Minestrone

Makes about 1½ quarts.

This is an emergency soup for when you're too tired to cook but really need a nourishing, comforting, meal-in-a-bowl soup. Better keep the makings in your pantry right through the winter. The root vegetables, too, ought to be on hand at all times.

2 tablespoons olive oil

1 clove garlic, minced

1 large onion, chopped

two 13-ounce cans chicken broth

one 16-ounce can tomatoes with juice, chopped

2 medium carrots, sliced

½ teaspoon dried basil

¼ teaspoon black pepper

salt to taste

1 cup canned kidney beans or chickpeas, drained and rinsed

1 cup small elbow macaroni, cooked according to package directions

1 cup or more of leftover green vegetables, such as peas, green beans, and zucchini

grated Parmesan cheese

In a large saucepan, sauté the garlic and onion in the oil until they're translucent. Add the broth, tomatoes, carrots, basil, and pepper. Simmer with the cover ajar for 20 minutes. Correct the seasoning, adding more pepper, basil, and salt to your taste.

Stir in the kidney beans, separately cooked macaroni, and 1 cup or more of almost any green vegetable you happen to have left over in the refrigerator—or frozen vegetables.

Simmer the soup a few minutes longer to blend the flavors, or if you've used frozen vegetables, until they're tender. Serve with grated cheese and a good crusty bread.

Greek-Style Shrimp with Shells

*Makes 2 servings as an entrée,
4 as a first course.*

This dish is *so* elegant—and so easy!

Until recently, shellfish were thought to elevate blood cholesterol, but this is not true. They have a high concentration of the omega-3 fatty acids that help prevent blood clots, and their pure protein stimulates brain activity.

If you don't care for shrimp, you can substitute cooked, cubed swordfish.

1/4 cup olive oil

1 large clove garlic, minced

4 large fresh ripe tomatoes, peeled
and chopped (not seeded), or
one 1-pound can imported Italian
tomatoes, chunked, with juice

12 Greek olives, pitted

1 teaspoon dried oregano

1/4 teaspoon (or more) red pepper flakes

salt and black pepper to taste

1/2 cup dry white wine

2 tablespoons minced fresh
flat-leafed parsley

3/4 pound cooked, shelled large shrimp
(see note below)

1/2 pound medium shell macaroni, cooked
according to package directions

1/2 cup loosely packed crumbled
feta cheese

Heat the oil in a large skillet. Sauté the garlic but don't brown it. Add the tomatoes, olives, and seasoning. Simmer uncovered for 10 minutes. Add the wine and simmer 10 more minutes. Add the parsley and shrimp, bring back to a simmer, and remove from the heat.

Spoon the hot cooked macaroni into a serving dish. Stir in the feta cheese; ladle the sauce over the top.

Note: This dish will be easiest to make if you buy cooked, shelled shrimp, but it will taste best if you cook the shrimp yourself. Rinse the shrimp and put them in a pot with 1 teaspoon of peppercorns, 1/2 sliced lemon, and a bay leaf; add enough water to make 2 inches in the bottom of the pan. Bring the pot to a boil and cook, covered, 5 minutes, or until all the shrimp are pink. Cool, peel, and devein the shrimp. *Refrigerate until needed.*

Fillets of Sole with Linguine

Makes 4 servings.

A quick and flavorful entrée that goes well with a vinaigrette-dressed broccoli salad.

4 fillets of sole (1 1/2 to 2 pounds)

1/2 cup unbleached all-purpose flour

1/4 cup olive oil

salt to taste

1 clove garlic, minced

1/2 cup bottled clam juice

1/2 cup white wine

1 cup peeled, chopped tomatoes,
fresh or canned

crushed red pepper to taste

freshly ground black pepper to taste

6 fresh basil leaves, minced, or
1/2 teaspoon dried basil

1/2 pound thin linguine, cooked according
to package directions

Dip the fish in the flour to coat. Heat the oil in a large skillet and fry the fish over medium-high heat until golden on both sides. Salt the fillets, then remove them from the skillet and keep them warm.

Add the minced garlic to the skillet and sauté it over low heat. When the garlic is sizzling but not brown, add the clam juice and wine. Cook on high heat, scraping the pan, until the liquid is reduced to about ½ cup. Add the tomatoes. Reduce the heat and simmer while the linguine is cooking.

Add red and black pepper (try ¼ teaspoon of each) and the basil to the sauce. Reserve ¼ cup of the sauce and toss the cooked linguine in the rest. Put the linguine on a serving platter. Slide the fish on top, spooning a tablespoon of sauce onto each fillet.

Shells with Tuna and Peperoncini

Makes 2 servings as an entrée, 4 as a first course.

Peperoncini are Italian pickled peppers that look like jalapeños but are pale green and only mildly hot. They add a deliciously spicy note to this quick tuna entrée. If you make this dish in summer, by all means choose fresh ripe tomatoes rather than canned. A dish of sautéed zucchini or tender-crisp steamed broccoli would go well on the side.

1 tablespoon olive oil

one 6½-ounce can imported Italian tuna,
drained, reserving oil

1 clove garlic, minced

one 28-ounce can Italian-style tomatoes
(not in purée), drained and chopped,
or 2 cups fresh peeled, chopped tomatoes

4 peperoncini (found among imported
Italian foods in the supermarket)

¼ teaspoon each dried oregano and
freshly ground black pepper

½ pound shell pasta

Heat the olive oil in a large skillet, add 2 tablespoons of the tuna oil, and sauté the garlic until it is sizzling but not brown. Add the tomatoes and cook over medium-high heat, stirring often, for 10 minutes.

Reduce the heat to a simmer. Break the tuna into chunks. Add the tuna, peperoncini, oregano, and black pepper, and cook over low heat for 10 more minutes.

Meanwhile, cook the shell pasta according to the package directions. Drain the pasta and put it into a serving dish. Toss it with the finished sauce, arranging some of the tuna and the peperoncini on top.

Fusilli with Broccoli, Sun-Dried Tomatoes, and Black Olives

Makes 4 to 6 servings as a side dish.

This is one of those extremely convenient off-the-shelf (and out of the freezer) dishes to make for unexpected guests. Grilled fish steaks *(see pages 124-125)* or any grilled meat would make a good accompaniment.

2 cloves garlic, minced

⅓ cup olive oil

two 10-ounce packages frozen
broccoli spears

2 ounces (about ½ cup, loosely packed)
snipped sun-dried tomatoes

3½-ounce can black olives, drained

½ teaspoon crushed red pepper

salt to taste

½ pound fusilli, cooked according to
package directions

grated Romano cheese

In a large skillet, sauté the garlic in oil until it's sizzling. Add all the remaining ingredients except the fusilli and the grated cheese. Cover the pan and cook on low, stirring occasionally, until the broccoli spears are separated and barely tender, about 7 minutes. Remove the cover so the dish won't overcook. With a knife and fork, cut the broccoli into bite-size pieces. Then mix the broccoli with the cooked fusilli; pass the Romano cheese at the table.

Fettuccine with Asparagus

Makes 2 servings as an entrée, 4 as a first course or accompaniment.

This taste of spring can be enjoyed at any time of year, thanks to frozen asparagus. The dish can also be made, of course, with ¾ pound of *fresh* asparagus—but it's handy to have a few recipes for frozen vegetables ready to relieve the between-season vegetable blahs.

Because of its high carotene, selenium, and vitamin C content, asparagus is one of the foods that help to protect against cancer. *And* it's low in calories and sodium!

2 tablespoons olive oil

2 cloves garlic, minced

one 14- to 16-ounce can Italian tomatoes with juice

¼ teaspoon salt

freshly ground black pepper to taste

¼ cup chopped fresh flat-leafed parsley

one 10-ounce package frozen asparagus (preferably whole stalks, but chopped asparagus can also be used) or ¾ pound fresh asparagus

½ pound good-quality fettuccine

2 tablespoons grated Parmesan cheese plus more to pass at the table

Heat the oil in a large skillet and sauté the garlic until it is sizzling but not brown. Add the tomatoes, salt, pepper, and parsley. Cook at a low boil, uncovered, stirring occasionally, for 8 minutes. Break up the tomatoes.

Add the asparagus (frozen or fresh), cover, and simmer until the stalks are not quite tender. Remove the mixture from the heat; the hot sauce will finish cooking the asparagus.

Meanwhile, cook the fettuccine, drain it, and put it into a serving bowl. Spoon out some of the sauce (mostly the tomato part), add 2 tablespoons of cheese, and toss well. Spoon the remaining asparagus and sauce on top. Pass more cheese at the table.

Linguine with Broccoli Rabe and Garlic

Makes 4 servings as a first course or accompaniment, 2 as an entrée.

This is a favorite dish in Italian homes, and yet it's rarely found on Italian restaurant menus. Simple to make, really good for you, and somewhat addictive—it should be a little bit oily and plenty hot.

⅓ cup olive oil

2 cloves garlic, minced

*1 bunch of broccoli rabe (also called
rapini), about 1 pound, well-washed,
tough stems removed, roughly chopped*

*¼ teaspoon each (or more) freshly ground
black pepper and hot red pepper flakes*

½ pound thin linguine

grated Parmesan cheese

In a large pot, sauté the garlic in the oil until it
sizzles, then immediately add the broccoli
rabe with just the water remaining on its
leaves after washing. Cover and braise over
very low heat for 12 to 15 minutes, until tender. Watch carefully that all the moisture does
not evaporate! Add the black and hot red peppers. *The recipe can be prepared ahead to this
point and held at room temperature for 1 hour.*

Meanwhile cook the linguine according to
the package directions and drain it. Add the
pasta to the broccoli rabe and toss well to get
all the oil from the pan before spooning into a
serving dish. Pass the cheese and more hot
red pepper flakes at the table.

Fettuccine with Creamy Ricotta

*Makes 2 servings as an entrée,
4 as a first course.*

Creamy taste without the cream and butter.
Try this sauce in place of the one used on fettuccine Alfredo.

½ pound fettuccine

1 cup low-fat ricotta cheese

*½ cup tomato sauce (either of the 2
sauces in Basics, or from a jar)*

2 to 3 tablespoons milk, if required

*1 tablespoon finely minced, fresh
flat-leafed parsley*

grated Parmesan cheese

Cook the fettuccine according to the package
directions. While it's cooking, make the sauce.

In a food processor or blender, process the
ricotta until it's creamy. Blend in the tomato
sauce and, if necessary, a little milk to achieve
a pourable sauce consistency.

Heat the sauce in a microwaveable measuring pitcher in the microwave or in a saucepan over very low heat on the range top. Don't
let it boil, or the sauce will separate. Stir in
the parsley.

Drain the fettuccine and toss it with the
sauce. Serve immediately. Pass the grated
Parmesan cheese at the table.

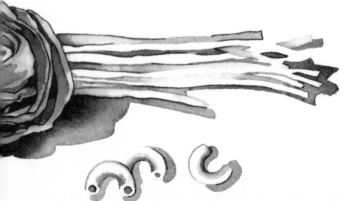

Macaroni with Three Cheeses

Makes 6 servings.

Macaroni and cheese is a real comfort food and a good source of protein for active youngsters. This version is lighter and less salty than the traditional dish, with a little blue cheese providing a lot of flavor. Nevertheless, for those who must be careful about cholesterol, another pasta dish might be preferable.

> 1 tablespoon butter
> 1 tablespoon unbleached all-purpose flour
> ¼ teaspoon dry mustard
> ¼ teaspoon white pepper
> 1 cup hot skim milk
> 1 cup low-fat cottage cheese
> ½ pound low-fat mozzarella, diced
> ¾ cup crumbled blue cheese, loosely packed
> ½ pound elbow macaroni
> paprika for sprinkling

Melt the butter in a saucepan; stir in the flour, dry mustard, and pepper. Cook the roux over low heat, stirring, for 3 minutes; don't let the mixture brown. Blend in the hot milk all at once, and whisk over medium heat until thickened and smooth.

In a food processor, process the cottage cheese until it's smooth and creamy. Pour the sauce down the feed tube and blend.

Cook the macaroni according to the package directions. Spoon it into a buttered 2-quart casserole. Stir in the sauce, then the mozzarella and blue cheeses. Sprinkle the top with paprika.

Preheat the oven to 350° F. Bake the casserole for 30 minutes, or until golden, crusty, and bubbly.

Smoked Salmon Pasta Salad with Peas and Scallions

Makes 8 cups.

Because of the saltiness of the mustard and salmon, no additional salt is needed in this colorful salad, which is a piquant addition to a summer buffet table.

1 cup frozen "petite" peas,
thawed only enough to separate

½ pound penne or ziti
(the smaller size, without lines)

¼ pound Nova Scotia smoked salmon
cut into 1-inch squares

1 sweet red pepper, cut into small dice

inner heart of a bunch of celery, including
leaves, chopped small (about 1 cup)

½ cup chopped scallions, including some
green tops

alfalfa sprouts for garnish

For the vinaigrette:

¼ cup red wine vinegar

1½ tablespoons Dijon mustard

½ teaspoon freshly ground black pepper

1 cup olive oil

In a small bowl, whisk together the vinegar, mustard, and black pepper. Add the oil in a thin stream while continuing to whisk.

Blanch the peas for 30 seconds in a pot of boiling water. Drain and rinse the peas with cold water to stop cooking.

Cook the pasta al dente according to package directions. Rinse the pasta in cold water. Drain well and toss with about ⅔ of the vinaigrette dressing. Reserve the rest of the dressing. Stir in the remaining ingredients except the peas and sprouts. Be sure the salmon is distributed evenly throughout—it tends to stick together. *Refrigerate until needed.*

Let the salad stand at room temperature for 20 to 30 minutes before serving. Stir in the peas and the remaining dressing. Spoon the salad into a large serving dish and edge it with alfalfa sprouts.

For more pasta recipes, see the following: Acorn Squash Soup with Pastina; Baked Pasta with Shiitake Mushroom Sauce; Broccoli and Ziti Casserole; Broccoli Tetrazzini; Carrots with Tomatoes and Elbows; Cauliflower Casserole with Shell Pasta; Chicken, Garbanzo, and Pepper Stew; Lemon Sole with Lemon Pepper Sauce and Egg Bows; *Pasta al Sugo d'Estate;* Peas with Tiny Shells; Rotelle with Four Peppers and Fontina; Spaghetti with Walnut-Parsley Sauce; *Vermicelli all'Olio;* Whole-Wheat Pasta with Gorgonzola; *Ziti alla Siracusa;* Ziti with Cannellini Sauce

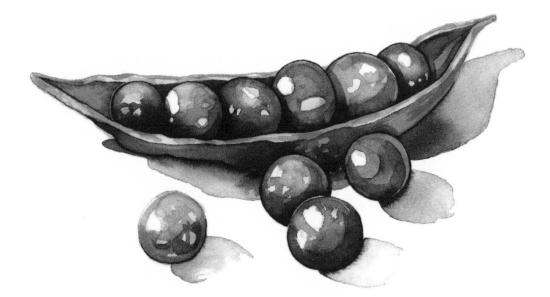

PEAS

IN A CLASS BY THEMSELVES. Truly exquisite fresh peas are those rushed from the garden to the pot in less than two hours, and most of us will only read about them in Thomas Jefferson's notebooks or M. F. K. Fisher's pastoral tributes, such as the one in *An Alphabet for Gourmets*. But if you have a little garden space, peas (along with tomatoes, of course) are a vegetable worth weeding for. By the time peas come to the produce section of your local market, some of their sugar will have converted to starch. Hurry peas into the refrigerator to preserve their remaining sweetness.

A cup of green peas has more protein than a large egg—with none of the cholesterol. Even better, peas also are a great source of soluble fiber and potassium, both of which promote a healthy heart. Soluble fiber lowers cholesterol, and potassium helps to control blood pressure. Peas are also rich in protease inhibitors and carotene, both of which defend the body against carcinogens.

But here's the surprise: Folk medicine has always ascribed contraceptive powers to peas, and modern experiments have demonstrated that there's some truth to this belief. Peas contain antifertility agents that are being studied by Indian scientists hoping to isolate these substances to construct an inexpensive contraceptive.

Peas with edible pods, such as snap peas, are high in vitamin C, especially if you eat them raw, as in salads. Snap peas make a good substitute for pea pods in Asian dishes, where they would be *barely* cooked and so still retain most of their vitamin C.

All peas are a good source of thiamine and niacin, two components of B complex. Thiamine is an antistress nutrient; supplements have been used to help control symptoms of emotional disorders. Niacin has been prescribed to lower blood pressure and increase circulation.

In the Market

Peas arrive in the market for a short stay in early summer—how we wish it were a longer season! Those of the highest quality will have bright green velvety pods. Immature pods are flat; old pods are yellowish.

For the rest of the year, we must content ourselves with frozen peas, which are a pretty good product. The "petite" frozen peas are best. Bland, tasteless canned peas, however, ought to be completely avoided.

On the other hand, dried split peas, which will keep for months on the pantry shelf, make a wonderfully nourishing soup that's equally popular—with subtle variations—in France, Italy, and the Netherlands.

In the Kitchen

Fresh peas keep in the refrigerator for four to five days, but the sooner they're cooked, the tastier they will be. For easy shelling, break off the stem tip and pull the string down the side, pressing open the pod at the same time. One pound yields one cup or a bit more.

Freshly shelled peas should be cooked for the shortest possible amount of time. They can be braised in butter for two to three minutes or blanched three to four minutes. Although they need no dressing up, there are nonetheless many ways to do so, such as adding fresh chopped mint, tiny chunks of carrot, sautéed mushrooms or shallots, or tiny boiled onions, or any combination thereof. ▬▬

Risi e Bisi

Makes 4 servings.

That's Venetian dialect for "rice and peas soup." It should be *almost* thick enough to eat with a fork but thin enough to be served in bowls. You should plan to serve it as soon as it's ready, because the longer the dish stands, the more liquid the rice will absorb.

2 tablespoons olive oil

1 medium onion, chopped

2 pounds fresh peas, shelled, or 2 cups frozen peas, thawed to separate

one 13-ounce can chicken broth

2 cups water

½ teaspoon salt

2 tablespoons chopped fresh flat-leafed parsley

6 very thin pieces of lemon zest, no pith

¾ cup Arborio rice

2 tablespoons grated Parmesan cheese, plus more to pass

freshly ground black pepper to taste

Heat the oil in a deep, heavy pot and sauté the onion until it's pale yellow. Add the peas and stir-fry for about 1 minute.

Add the broth, water, salt, parsley, lemon zest, and rice, and bring the mixture to a boil. Reduce the heat to medium-low and simmer the soup, stirring occasionally, for 12 to 15 minutes, until the rice is al dente.

Stir in the cheese and pepper. Serve immediately and pass more cheese at the table.

Vegetarian Split Pea Soup

Makes 6 servings.

Italian-style split pea soup is often made without ham or sausage. Sautéed vegetables, oil, and seasonings create its robust flavor.

1 cup dried split peas

¼ cup olive oil

2 cloves garlic, minced

1 large onion, chopped

1 stalk celery, with the leaves, chopped

1 carrot, chopped

6 cups water

⅓ cup tomato purée (not paste)

1 teaspoon dried marjoram or ½ teaspoon dried oregano

1 bay leaf

½ teaspoon salt

¼ teaspoon pepper

1 tablespoon minced fresh parsley

croutons for garnishing

Pick over, wash, and drain the split peas.

In a large, heavy pot, heat the oil, and sauté the garlic, onion, celery, and carrot until they are yellow but have not browned. Add all the remaining ingredients except the parsley and the croutons.

Bring the soup to a boil, reduce the heat, and simmer it on low for about 2 hours, with the cover slightly ajar, stirring often, especially toward the end, when it could stick. If the soup gets too thick, add a little water.

Alternatively, you needn't worry about the sticking problem if you microwave this soup. Sauté the vegetables in a small skillet on the range top. (I do sometimes sauté in the microwave, but when intense flavor is needed, the range top is really better.) Put all the ingredients, except the parsley and the croutons, in a 3-quart casserole, and microwave, covered, for 6 to 8 minutes on high (until it boils) and 35 to 45 minutes on medium. Stir 2 or 3 times.

Remove the bay leaf. Stir the parsley into the soup. Top each serving with croutons.

Spezzatino di Vitello con Piselli (Veal Stew with Peas)

Makes 4 servings.

This is real peasant fare; that may be why it's so delicious. It's easy to prepare, too, but you have to hang around the kitchen while it cooks to stir the sauce from time to time. Arborio rice *(see Basics)* is the perfect accompaniment.

The recipe can be easily doubled or tripled (in which case, use two skillets) as a perfect buffet entrée, since it doesn't require guests to struggle with knives while balancing a plate of food.

1½ pounds veal stewing meat, trimmed of sinew and cut into 1-inch cubes

¼ cup unbleached all-purpose flour

2 tablespoons olive oil

1 large onion, chopped

½ cup dry vermouth or dry white wine

one 14- to 16-ounce can Italian tomatoes with juice

2 tablespoons chopped fresh flat-leafed parsley

½ teaspoon salt

freshly ground black pepper to taste

one 10-ounce package frozen "petite" peas, thawed just enough to separate, or 1½ pounds fresh peas, shelled (1½ cups)

Put the veal in a plastic bag with the flour and

Peas with Pesto

Makes 6 to 8 servings.

Pesto fills the senses with the rich taste of basil, an herb that is reported to induce a sense of ease. All herbs are said to produce particular effects, either stimulating or relaxing.

What to do with the leftover pesto? Spoon it into ice-cube trays and freeze it solid. Remove the cubes and store them in a plastic bag in the freezer. What a nice fresh flavor of summer they will add to winter dishes! Add one cube to a tomato sauce or a vegetable dish.

two 10-ounce packages frozen "petite" peas

For the pesto:

2 cups loosely packed fresh basil leaves
2 cloves garlic, peeled
½ cup lightly toasted pine nuts
½ teaspoon salt
¼ teaspoon freshly ground black pepper
about ½ cup extra-virgin olive oil
¼ cup freshly grated Parmesan cheese

shake to coat. Shake off any excess flour. In a large skillet, brown the veal in the oil slowly and thoroughly. Don't rush this step. Just before the veal is browned, add the onion; continue to fry until the onion softens.

Add the wine and cook over medium-high heat, uncovered, stirring often, until the liquid is reduced by half. Add the tomatoes, parsley, salt, and pepper. Reduce the heat and simmer the stew until the veal is tender, about 45 minutes. Stir frequently; add broth or water if the sauce gets too thick.

Add the peas. *The stew can be prepared ahead, refrigerated, and reheated later. If the dish is to be reheated, simply stir the peas into the simmering sauce and turn off the heat. The remaining heat, plus reheating, will cook the peas.* If the stew is to be served immediately, simmer 3 minutes for frozen or fresh young peas. For fresh but large, mature peas, simmer 5 to 7 minutes.

To make the pesto: Rinse and thoroughly dry the basil leaves. In a food processor fitted with the steel blade, with the motor running, put the garlic down the feed tube to mince it.

Stop the motor. Add the basil, pine nuts, salt, and pepper to the work bowl. Process until *very* finely chopped.

With the motor running, slowly pour the olive oil down the feed tube in a thin stream until the mixture reaches a pastelike consistency, neither too thick to drop off a spoon nor runny. You'll have to stop the motor, stir, and check a few times. Transfer the pesto to a bowl. Stir in the cheese.

Cook the peas according to the package directions. Drain. Stir in ¼ cup, or more, pesto, to your taste.

Peas with Tiny Shells

Cook 2 cups of tiny shell pasta according to the package directions. Combine the shells with the peas and pesto. Pass grated Parmesan cheese at the table.

Petits Pois

Makes 6 servings.

These are peas cooked in the French manner, braised on a bed of lettuce, which seems to have a marvelously sweetening effect.

> *2 tablespoons olive oil*
> *¼ cup minced shallots*
> *4 large outer leaves of iceberg lettuce, washed and shredded*
> *3 pounds fresh young peas, shelled (about 3 cups) or two 10-ounce packages frozen "petite" peas, thawed to separate*
> *pinch of basil*
> *salt and pepper to taste*
> *½ cup chicken broth or water*

In a medium saucepan, heat the oil and sauté the shallots until they are yellowed but not browned. Lay the lettuce over the shallots, and top with the peas and seasonings.

Pour the broth over all, cover the pan tightly, and simmer over low heat until the peas are barely tender, 3 to 4 minutes after they reach a simmer.

Transfer the peas to a heated vegetable dish and serve at once.

Some cooks remove the braising lettuce, but I like to stir it right into the peas.

For other recipes using peas, see the following: Paella with Brown Rice; Smoked Salmon Pasta Salad with Peas and Scallions

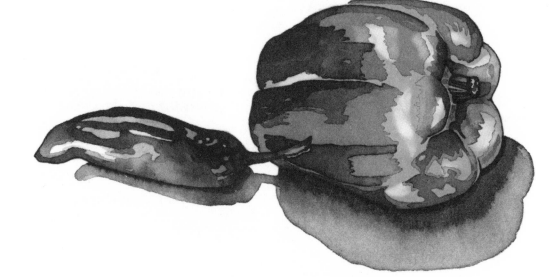

PEPPERS

SWEET OR HOT, THEY'RE FULL OF ZESTY NUTRITION. When Columbus first arrived at the West Indies, he thought he'd discovered that elusive spice route to Asia after all when the local people introduced him to peppers. When he carried these pungent fruits of the Capsicum family back to Spain in triumph, they were promptly renamed Spanish peppers and soon became the rage of European kitchens. Sometime later, when an inspired cook combined tomatoes (also a gift from the New World) and chopped onions in a sauté, the first tomato sauce was created. The rest, as they say, is culinary history.

There are so many varieties of peppers, sweet and hot, that one could write an entire book describing their characteristics and uses. Briefly, most popular in North American cooking are the sweet bell peppers: green peppers, which would turn red if they were allowed to ripen; the pimento red; the bright yellow bell, not to be confused with the long, creamy-colored Cuban banana pepper; and the newer colors, orange and deep purple. For those who have trouble digesting peppers, the yellow seem to cause the least gastric distress.

The Italian frying pepper, with a long, twisted pale green shape, is also a sweet pepper. Its skin is more tender than that of the bell peppers; the latter are often roasted to remove that tough outer membrane.

Sweet peppers are right up there with rose hips and kiwis at the top of the vitamin C list. A cup of chopped sweet red pepper contains over three times the recommended dietary allowance, green pepper over one and a half times the RDA for vitamin C.

Sweet red peppers are a good source of cancer-fighting beta carotene, the plant version of vitamin A.

Chilies are the spicy peppers popular in South American cuisine, although other hot peppers are Italian or Thai favorites. This list includes the mild ancho or poblano, often stuffed to make *chiles rellenos*; the Anaheim, or chile verde, ranging from mild to hot; the pasilla, or chili negro, a long brown, quite hot pepper that's usually dried; the peperoncini, a small, twisted Tuscan pepper marketed as Italian pickled peppers, mild to medium hot; the cherry, also pickled by Italians, pretty hot stuff; the jalapeño, used fresh or dried, very hot; the serrano, dark green or ripened to red, extremely hot; and the cayenne, usually dried whole, crushed, or ground—pure fire. Thai, or Santaka, peppers are tiny, dry peppers that never lose their ferocity no matter how long they're cooked. Scotch Bonnets are the hottest of all.

Scientists have found that capsaicin, the substance that causes the sensation of heat, reduces the activity of neurotransmitters carrying pain messages to the central nervous system. Besides causing a bit of euphoria, hot peppers—despite the fire in your mouth—should help to relieve pain elsewhere in your body. Continual indulgence in fiery peppers can lessen their impact on your tongue.

In folk medicine, hot pepper extract was used as a topical anaesthetic. A drug containing capsaicin has already been approved as a topical treatment for shingles and is being tested for psoriasis.

Capsaicin acts as a nasal decongestant and will help to clear up stuffiness. When you have a cold, add a few dashes of hot red pepper sauce to your chicken soup and you'll have a surefire, double-barreled remedy for congestion. Capsaicin helps to keep the lungs healthy, too; pulmonary diseases are lowest in countries where the cuisine is hottest. It boosts the metabolism, making your body burn calories faster.

Capsaicin also helps to prevent the stickiness of blood that leads to blocked vessels and strokes.

In the Market

Choose peppers that are plump, firm, crisp, and free of blemishes. Both sweet and hot fresh peppers are available all year, with the long peak season being from late spring to early fall. This is probably the only vegetable I'd advise you to buy out of season, because you may get a special benefit from eating fresh peppers during the winter cold and flu season, when the sweet bell peppers will give you extra vitamin C and the hot chilies will keep your respiratory tract clear. With peppers, garlic, and some good chicken soup, you should be able to weather the storms right through to spring.

In the Kitchen

Peppers can be kept in a refrigerator's crisper drawer or in a plastic bag on the bottom shelf of the refrigerator for a week or more.

Removing the seeds and ribs of a hot pepper somewhat diminishes its heat. *Never use your bare hands to handle hot peppers.* Wear rubber gloves, and don't touch your face while seeding and chopping.

Roasted sweet peppers have a deliciously different taste from raw peppers. A neat way to roast peppers is simply to put them whole on the side of a grill, turning them until all sides are browned and blistered, while you're grilling the main course.

Some cooks put peppers on long forks and toast them like marshmallows over a gas burner, but that's much too time-consuming for me. When not using the grill, I prefer roasting peppers in a toaster-broiler oven, where they seem to char to perfection faster even than under a regular oven broiler.

Cool freshly roasted peppers in a sealed bag (brown paper or plastic), and within a few minutes the accumulated steam will make them easy to peel. Then dress the peppers with extra-virgin olive oil, a little salt, and slivers of garlic.

A sandwich of garlic-flavored roasted peppers, aged provolone cheese, and fresh Italian bread is heaven! ▬

Jalapeño-Sweet Potato Bisque

Makes 4 servings.

It may be hard to believe while your mouth is burning, but hot peppers actually are painkillers, suppressing pain messages to the central nervous system. And that's not all; "hot stuff" in the mouth causes the brain to secrete endorphin, a natural morphine, which in turn causes a feeling of euphoria. That's a lot of action from one small jalapeño!

This is one of those "creamy" soups without any cream, a plus for those who are watching their fat intake.

1 pound sweet potatoes (2 medium)

1 or 2 canned jalapeño chilies, seeded and finely minced

two 13-ounce cans chicken broth

½ teaspoon each ground coriander, cumin, cinnamon, and salt

1 tablespoon cornstarch

1 cup milk (can be low-fat)

Bake and cool the sweet potatoes; peel the potatoes and cut them up.

If the jalapeño is not already seeded and minced, use rubber gloves to handle it, and don't touch your face with the gloves.

In a food processor, purée the sweet potatoes with the broth and seasonings. Pour the soup into the top of a large double boiler and heat it to the boiling point over direct heat. Mix the cornstarch with the milk until there are no lumps. Pour it all at once into the boiling soup, stirring constantly, until it bubbles and thickens.

Meanwhile, set 1 inch of water to boiling in the bottom of the double boiler. Place the soup over the boiling water, stir in the chilies, and let the soup heat and develop its flavor for 15 to 20 minutes, stirring occasionally.

Note: 2 tablespoons of milder chopped chilies can be substituted for the jalapeño.

Ossobuco with Crisp Peppers

Makes 4 servings.

Ossobuco, which means literally "bone with a hole" (marrowbone), is a stew made from meaty pieces of veal shank. The ideal way to slow-simmer this veal dish is in a slow cooker, but the peppers must be barely cooked, so that they will retain most of their vitamin C.

4 thick slices (about 3 pounds) veal shank, with marrowbone at the center—choose those with the most meat around the bone and intact skin around the outside

flour for dredging

2 tablespoons olive oil

1 teaspoon butter

1 large onion, chopped

1 large clove garlic, minced

3 large red or yellow peppers (or both), seeded

½ cup chicken broth

1 cup peeled, sliced fresh tomatoes or canned, drained tomatoes

bouquet of fresh rosemary, sage, and oregano leaves, tied together, or a pinch each of the dried herbs

salt and freshly ground black pepper to taste

2 tablespoons lemon juice

Flour the veal generously. Heat the olive oil and butter in a skillet (cast iron is best) and brown the meat well on both sides. Just before it's done, add the onion and garlic to the pan, and cook just until the vegetables are softened a bit. Scoop everything except the oil into the slow cooker.

Cut the peppers into large chunks and stir-fry them for no more than 2 minutes in the same oil. They should be crisp. Remove them from the pan and refrigerate until needed.

Add the chicken broth to the pan and bring it to a fast boil, scraping the browned bits into the broth. Pour this over the veal. Add the tomatoes, herbs, and salt (don't add

the black pepper yet). For the bouquet, use small sprigs (2 to 3 leaves) of rosemary and sage and a large sprig of oregano.

Cook 6 to 8 hours on low. Turn off the heat; stir in the reserved peppers, freshly ground black pepper, and lemon juice.

Alternatively, ossobuco can be cooked on the range top, like any other stew, at a very low simmer for 2 hours or more, until the veal is quite tender.

Arborio rice *(see Basics)* and a mixed-green salad are the perfect accompaniments.

Smothered Chicken with Peppers and Corn

Makes 4 servings.

Corn on the cob is so tasty this way, you won't miss buttering it at all.

2 green peppers

2 tablespoons olive oil

*2 whole skinned chicken breasts cut in half
(4 pieces)*

1 clove garlic, minced

*1 cup ripe tomatoes, skinned and chopped,
or canned, drained tomatoes*

*1 teaspoon each chopped fresh sage and
oregano, or ¼ teaspoon ground sage and
½ teaspoon dried oregano*

salt and pepper to taste

*4 ears fresh corn, husked, each ear broken
into 2 pieces*

*hot cooked plain rice as
an accompaniment*

Seed the peppers and cut them into chunks. Heat the oil in a large Dutch oven (or other flameproof casserole that can be used on the range top) and stir-fry the peppers for no more than 2 minutes. They should still be crisp. Remove and reserve the peppers.

Preheat the oven to 400° F. Fry 2 chicken pieces in the oil until they are lightly brown on both sides. Do the same with the rest of the chicken. Put all the chicken back in the Dutch oven; add the garlic, tomato, sage, oregano, salt, and pepper. Bring the ingredients to a boil. Cover and bake the casserole in the middle of the oven for about 20 minutes, until the chicken is almost cooked through.

Add the corn, bring the stew to a boil on the range top, and return it to the oven, covered, to cook for 8 to 10 minutes. Stir in the reserved peppers and serve with rice.

Aunt Catherine's Pepper, Onion, and Potato Omelet

Makes 4 servings.

What a wonderfully easy Sunday brunch dish! Be sure to pick up a fresh loaf of Italian bread when you get the papers.

This is an omelet that always tastes a little different from the last time, because it depends on leftover bits of this and that in the refrigerator. Only the eggs, pepper, onion, and potato are constants. But lots of foods not listed here could be included, so experiment!

3 tablespoons olive oil

1 medium onion, chopped

2 green peppers, seeded and diced

2 cooked potatoes, diced

*1 cooked Italian sausage, sliced, or
4 slices low-fat ham, diced*

*1½ cups beaten egg (6 large or 8 medium)
or 1½ cups prepared egg substitute*

*salt and freshly ground black pepper
to taste*

*1 cup diced cheese, such as Monterey Jack
or fontina*

1 fresh tomato, diced (needn't be peeled)

Heat the oil in a large skillet, and slowly fry the onion, green peppers, and potato until the potato is browned and the other vegetables are tender. Stir in the sausage or ham when the potato is almost ready.

Beat the eggs with a fork, adding 2 tablespoons of water and salt and pepper to your taste. Stir in the diced cheese.

Pour the eggs all at once over the vegetables and sausage in the hot pan. After the eggs begin to set, stir the omelet (since this is an Italian omelet not a French one), adding the tomato. Stir once more to let the uncooked egg run underneath; when all the egg is set, but not dry, the omelet is ready.

Golden Stuffed Peppers

Makes 6 servings.

If a dish can be light (in fat and calories) and yet hearty (in taste), this one is it! An easy and attractive buffet dish, it can be prepared ahead of time. And you'll find that yellow peppers are the most digestible of the peppers.

2 tablespoons olive oil

2 cloves garlic, peeled and crushed

1½ pounds ground turkey

1 egg

½ onion, minced

1 cup herb stuffing mix (not stovetop variety), slightly moistened with water

2 tablespoons wheat germ

2 tablespoons grated Parmesan cheese

1 teaspoon Italian seasoning (store-bought or see Basics)

½ teaspoon salt-free seasoning (or salt and pepper to taste)

3 large yellow peppers, seeded and quartered lengthwise

one 14½-ounce can stewed tomatoes with juice

additional Italian seasoning

Pour the oil into a large flat casserole or roasting pan; add the garlic.

In a bowl, mix together the next 8 ingredients; blend well. Stuff the peppers with the mixture, mounding it as necessary to use the filling, and place them in the pan. Pour the tomatoes over the peppers. Sprinkle with additional Italian seasoning. *The recipe can be prepared ahead and refrigerated for several hours.*

Preheat the oven to 375° F. Bake for 45 minutes, or until the peppers are tender and the meat is cooked through.

Rotelle Salad with Four Peppers and Fontina Cheese

Makes 4 servings as an entrée.

A hearty salad, bursting with vitamin C, that can be a family supper entrée or the pretty accompaniment to a buffet.

If Greek olives are not too firm, they can often be pitted by squeezing them, which causes the pit to pop out. Try this easy method before cutting out the pits with a knife.

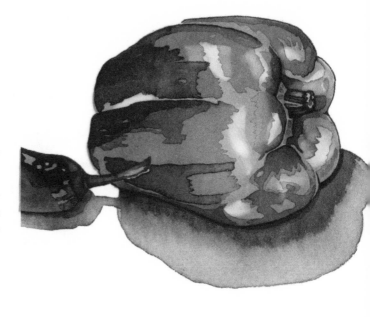

⅓ cup olive oil

1 each sweet red pepper, yellow pepper, orange pepper, and green pepper, seeded and cut into triangles

2 cloves garlic, minced

1 cup Greek olives, pitted

¼ cup chopped fresh basil

freshly ground black pepper to taste

1 pound rotelle pasta, cooked according to package directions

½ pound fontina cheese, cubed

Heat the oil in a medium skillet, and stir-fry the peppers and garlic for about 3 minutes, until tender-crisp. Remove from the heat, and stir in the olives, basil, and black pepper. *The peppers can be prepared ahead and held at room temperature for 1 hour.*

Cook the rotelle, drain, and mix it while still warm with the peppers and olives. Cool slightly; stir in the cheese.

Serve at room temperature.

For other pepper recipes, see: Butternut Ratatouille; Cantonese Egg Foo Yung; Chicken, Garbanzo, and Pepper Stew; Kale with Sweet Red Pepper and Balsamic Vinegar; Kidney Beans with Sweet and Hot Red Peppers; Microwave Barley Pilaf; Mushroom and Barley Soup with Escarole; Stir-Fry Pork with Supervegetables; Picadillo Pumpkin in Shell; Paella with Brown Rice; Roasted Eggplant and Garlic Soup with Sweet Red Pepper; Shrimp with Apple and Celery; Skillet Cacciatore for Two, with Broccoli; Spiced Turkey with Shiitake Mushrooms; Sunshine Oat Bran Pizza; *Tonno* and Brazil Nut Salad with Sweet Red Pepper Dressing

PINEAPPLE

A TROPICAL TENDERIZER THAT PROMOTES STRONG BONES. A staple of Polynesian cuisine, the pineapple was first encountered by Europeans in the voyages of Columbus and, later, Sir Walter Raleigh to the West Indies, where they found the fruit—called *nana* (meaning "fragrance") by the inhabitants— used for food and winemaking. Although Hawaii once was the world's leading pineapple grower, Thailand currently produces more of this succulent tropical fruit.

Pineapple's reputation as a symbol of welcome dates back to this country's early seafaring days. New England captains, returning to their wives from voyages to tropical ports that might have lasted many months, would nail a pineapple to the front door when the "second honeymoon" was over and the family was ready to receive guests.

The pineapple contains a fair amount of vitamin C and is an especially rich source of easily assimilated manganese. Although it's generally understood that calcium is needed for strong bones, it's not as well known that manganese is also vital. In animal studies, a deficiency in manganese has led to osteoporosis, a crippling bone disease that afflicts postmenopausal women. Adding pineapple and pineapple juice to your diet is a good nutritional defense for your bones.

Fresh pineapple contains bromelain, an enzyme that breaks down protein (similar to papaya). Bromelain is an aid to digestion, so it makes a good dessert to conclude a big luau (or any heavy meat meal). This useful enzyme is also an enemy to any bacteria that may be lurking in your system.

Because of this fruit's enzyme content, gelatin made with fresh pineapple won't gel; canned pineapple doesn't have this effect. Less tender cuts of meat will be tenderized when marinated with the fresh fruit.

In the Market

Pineapples are available all year. Select a fruit that's plump and firm, not soft or bruised. Fresh-looking green leaves at the crown are a good sign, as are yellowed "eyes" at the base. An overall yellow color is not necessarily an indication of ripeness, however, since some ripe pineapples may have a greenish skin. A nice "pineappley" aroma is a better clue to ripeness. The larger the pineapple, the more of the fruit will be edible.

Canned pineapple is a pleasant-tasting, convenient product that's good to stock on your pantry shelves. Pineapple packed without sugar tastes better, especially in entrées, and is better for you. The processed fruit contains just as much manganese, but not as much vitamin C or bromelain—so the fresh fruit is still preferable.

In the Kitchen

Although a pineapple won't get any sweeter or riper after picking, it may be a bit juicier and less acidic if you leave it out on the counter for a day. After that, either use the fruit or refrigerate it for a day or two more.

Canned, sliced pineapple makes a beautiful upside-down cake, and crushed pineapple or pineapple chunks are nice to have on hand for salads and Asian dishes.

A compote presented in a hollowed-out pineapple shell looks exotic. Fresh pineapple chunks hold up well on skewers for barbecues; try them with shrimp and cherry tomatoes, or pork chunks basted with soy sauce.

Don't let the intricacies of preparing the spiny fruit put you off buying fresh pineapple. Just follow the easy directions in the first recipe in this chapter.

Fresh Pineapple Sauce

Makes about 3 cups.

Besides adding its fresh flavor to the recipe on page 236, this pineapple sauce has many intriguing uses. It's equally at home in desserts and in savory dishes; try it as a topping for frozen yogurt or as a pie filling.

> *1 fresh, ripe pineapple*
> *1 cup water*
> *¼ cup sugar or more*
> *2 tablespoons cornstarch*

With a sharp knife, cut off the top and bottom of the pineapple. Cut off the shell in strips down the sides. Remove the "eyes" by cutting away diagonal strips of the flesh. Quarter the pineapple and slice out the core.

Finely dice the remaining flesh of the pineapple. Put it in a medium-size saucepan with ½ cup of water and the sugar. Bring the mixture to a boil, reduce the heat, and simmer for 10 minutes, stirring occasionally.

Mix the cornstarch with the remaining ½ cup of cold water until there are no lumps. Stir it all at once into the pineapple, stirring constantly until the mixture bubbles and thickens. Simmer over low heat for 3 minutes.

Taste to correct the sweetening. You may want a little more sugar if the sauce is to be used in a dessert. *The sauce can be prepared ahead and refrigerated for a day or frozen in plastic containers for longer storage.*

Sweet and Sour Pork

Makes 4 servings.

Canned unsweetened pineapple can be used in this dish, but fresh pineapple is far superior.

4 boneless pork chops (about 1 pound), partially frozen

1 large onion, peeled

3 ounces fresh shiitake mushrooms

1 large carrot, scraped

one 10-ounce package frozen pea pods

2 tablespoons vegetable oil

1 teaspoon sesame oil

1 cup chicken broth

¼ cup each dry white wine, chili sauce, and soy sauce

3 tablespoons each rice vinegar and brown sugar

2 tablespoons cornstarch

1½ cups fresh or canned pineapple chunks

Prepare the vegetables: Slice the onion. Sliver the mushrooms, discarding the stems. Cut the carrot into thin flowers or slices. (To make flowers, cut away 5 very thin strips down the length of the carrot and then slice across into coins. The cutaway strips will define petals.) Put the frozen pea pods in a strainer and rinse them in cold water until they separate.

Trim the pork and slice it thin.

In a wok or 12-inch skillet, heat 1 tablespoon of vegetable oil over high heat and quickly fry the pork, stirring constantly. When it's cooked through, remove the pork with a slotted spoon. Add another tablespoon of vegetable oil and 1 teaspoon of sesame oil; fry the onion, carrot, and mushrooms together, until the onions are tender-crisp. The carrots will still be crunchy. Remove these vegetables.

Make the sauce: Deglaze the hot pan with ½ cup of the broth. Add the wine, chili sauce, soy sauce, vinegar, and brown sugar, and allow the mixture to simmer 1 minute. Stir the cornstarch into the remaining ½ cup of cold broth, add it all at once to the sauce, and stir constantly until the mixture bubbles and thickens. Simmer 2 minutes.

Stir the pork, stir-fried vegetables, pea pods, and pineapple chunks into the sauce and heat the dish through. Serve with hot unsalted rice.

If desired, accompany the dish with Hot Mustard Sauce *(see Basics).*

Cutlets with Fresh Pineapple Sauce

Makes 4 servings.

Pineapple sauce is a pleasing alternative to cranberry with turkey and chicken.

1 to 1½ pounds thinly sliced turkey or chicken cutlets

flour for dredging

2 or more tablespoons olive oil

2 large shallots, minced

4 large brown mushrooms, finely diced (about 1 cup)

salt and pepper to taste

½ cup dry white wine

1 cup fresh pineapple sauce (see recipe on page 234)

Flour the cutlets. Heat the oil in a 12-inch skillet, and sauté the shallots and mushrooms until they are golden. Remove the vegetables from the pan and reserve them.

Fry the cutlets in batches (don't crowd the pan!), adding more oil if necessary, until they are brown on both sides. Salt and pepper them, and keep them warm on a platter.

Deglaze the pan with the ½ cup of wine, allowing it to boil until reduced by half. Add the shallots, mushrooms, and pineapple sauce, and heat through. Pour the sauce over the cutlets and serve.

Baked Cod with Pineapple and Ginger

Makes 2 servings.

You'd never guess from the peppery "bite" of ginger that it's a real stomach soother. New findings in China and India suggest that this spicy root also stimulates the immune system to fight infections, like colds and influenza. Besides all that, the flavors of pineapple and ginger are made for each other, as you'll find out when you make this 5-minute sauce.

2 teaspoons vegetable oil

2 cod fillets (about ¾ pound)

one 8-ounce can crushed pineapple packed in its own juice

1 tablespoon each dry sherry (or dry vermouth) and soy sauce

1 tablespoon cornstarch

¼ cup chopped scallions

1 tablespoon minced fresh ginger (about 2 slices)

Preheat the oven to 400° F. Put 1 teaspoon of oil in a gratin dish that will just hold the fillets in a single layer; turn the fish over in the oil to coat both sides.

Drain the pineapple, reserving the juice. Add the sherry and soy sauce to the juice, and whisk in the cornstarch until smooth.

Put the remaining teaspoon of oil in a small saucepan and sauté the scallions until they begin to soften. Add the ginger and cook for about 30 seconds more. Add the pineap-ple, and when it begins to bubble, add the cornstarch mixture all at once, stirring until the sauce is thickened. Cook on low for 3 minutes, stirring often.

Pour the sauce over the fillets and bake them for 20 minutes, or until they flake apart easily with a fork.

Rice-Stuffed Cabbage Leaves with Pineapple-Tomato Sauce

Makes 6 servings.

After you've stuffed the outer leaves of a cabbage, you can use the inner portion for soup or a sauté. This dish also can be made with large outer leaves of escarole briefly blanched. Or try the sauce alone on broiled pork chops.

1 head of cabbage (about 2 pounds)

1½ teaspoons salt

2 tablespoons butter or low-cholesterol margarine

2 tablespoons olive oil

2 large onions, chopped

one 28-ounce can of Italian-style tomatoes with juice

½ teaspoon dried marjoram leaves

¼ teaspoon white pepper

½ of a fresh, ripe pineapple, diced (see directions for cutting in the first recipe in this section), or one 1-pound, 4-ounce can crushed pineapple, drained

2 cups cooked brown or white rice

3 ounces sliced low-fat ham, chopped

¼ teaspoon ground summer savory

½ cup boiling water

Bring a large pot of water to a boil. With a sharp, pointed knife, core the cabbage. Add 1 teaspoon of salt to the water and blanch the whole cabbage for 8 minutes. Remove it from the water without draining the pot. Use 2 large slotted spoons and great care in handling the cabbage head so that it doesn't drop into the pot and splash boiling water.

Carefully remove 14 outer leaves of the cabbage. (This is 2 more than you'll need, in case you tear a leaf or you find you have a little extra filling.) If any inner leaves seem too crisp to bend easily, use tongs to put them back in the boiling water for a minute or two. Cut away the thickest part of the center rib so the leaves will roll up neatly.

In a large skillet, heat the butter and oil, and sauté the onion until it is limp and yellow but not brown. Remove about half of it to a medium-size bowl.

Make the sauce: Add the tomatoes and marjoram, the remaining ½ teaspoon of salt, and the white pepper to the onion in the skillet. Simmer uncovered for 20 minutes, stirring occasionally and breaking up the tomatoes. (A potato masher works well.) Add the pineapple and cook 10 minutes longer.

Make the stuffing: Add the rice, ham, and savory to the onion in the bowl, and blend.

Stuff the leaves: Put about 3 tablespoons (or a scant ¼ cup) of filling in a leaf. Roll up from the rib end, folding in the sides. Repeat with the rest of the leaves.

Place the leaves seam-side down in an ovenproof serving dish. Spoon the sauce over the rolls. *The recipe can be prepared ahead to this point and refrigerated for several hours.*

Preheat the oven to 375° F. Drizzle the ½ cup of boiling water over all, cover tightly with foil, and bake for 1 hour.

Broiled Pineapple Slices

Makes 6 servings.

Lots of possibilities! Serve these tangy slices for brunch, or as an accompaniment to a pork or poultry entrée, or as a slimming dessert—if the last, top with a dollop of lime sherbet right in the center of each ring.

Honey was a "heal-all" medicine among the ancient Egyptians, used as an ointment for treating wounds and sores. Recent studies have shown that honey acts as an antibacterial agent in the intestines.

1 fresh, ripe pineapple (about 12 slices)
honey
cinnamon or ground ginger

With a sharp knife, cut off the top and bottom of the pineapple. Cut off the shell in strips down the sides. Remove the "eyes" by cutting away diagonal strips of the flesh. Use an apple corer to cut out the core from both ends. Slice the pineapple into rings.

Lay the rings on a buttered baking sheet (heavy steel) or the bottom of a broiler pan. Use a pastry brush to brush the slices with honey. Sprinkle with cinnamon or ginger.

Broil 4 inches below the heat on one side until lightly browned, about 3 minutes.

For other pineapple recipes, see the following: Carrot-Pineapple Snacking Cake; Jamaican Chicken with Sweet Potatoes; Pineapple Slaw; Pineapple Tabbouleh; Turnip Slaw with Pineapple and Mint

POTATOES

COMFORT FOOD MAKES A COMEBACK. Remember when nutritionists advised us to eat more meat and fewer potatoes? Meat protein, they said, would give us strength and energy; starchy potatoes would make us fat and lumpy. Even today that prejudice lingers in the deprecatory term *couch potato*.

Still, the public has never lost its love for this familiar, comforting vegetable, and recent reevaluation has not only exonerated the potato (and some other well-loved carbohydrate foods as well) from the charge of being fattening, it's also shown that there's some potent preventive medicine in the potato.

This isn't true just of the richly colored sweet potato, which anyone can see is fairly bursting with beta carotene, tagged by scientists and by the National Cancer Institute as a dietary defense against some cancers, particularly lung cancer. The plain old white potato, too, contains compounds known as protease inhibitors, which protect the body from the effects of viruses and carcinogens.

Are potatoes fattening? One cup of white potatoes mashed with milk has only 137 calories; a baked sweet potato has 161. A quarter-pound patty of regular ground beef, on the other hand, racks up 319 calories. (It makes me wonder how some fast-food places dare to use the label "dieter's plate" for a beef patty sans bun, a scoop of cottage cheese, and a slice of torpid tomato on limp lettuce.) Or if you prefer a quarter-pound serving of rib roast, the tab is going to be 418.

Is there real comfort in a potato? You bet! Researchers studying the effects of diet on depression have found that depressed people frequently crave carbohydrate foods—and *for good reason*. Eating carbohydrates boosts the level of the chemical tryptophan in the blood. Tryptophan speeds to the brain, where it's converted into the neurotransmitter serotonin. Serotonin, in turn, helps you to feel calm, relaxed, and cheerful. (It's thought that depression may in part be caused by lowered levels of serotonin.)

So when the winter blues arrive, it's time to fill the kitchen with the pleasing aroma of baking spuds. (Microwaved baked potatoes can't compare in this respect, since they steam instead of bake. No crisp skin, either.)

Potatoes have a hefty potassium content and a respectable amount of cholesterol-lowering fiber, which makes them a healthy-heart food, also. To preserve more of that potassium, bake or steam potatoes instead of boiling them. A white potato has almost twice as much potassium as a sweet potato.

Along with tomatoes and peppers, potatoes are native to the Americas; as early as 3000 BC tiny potatoes were being eaten raw or roasted by the natives of Peru; there they were "discovered" by Spaniards, who carried them to Europe for cultivation. Various settlers then brought the larger cultivated potato back to this continent.

In the Market

Although there are now more than 400 varieties of potato, we need only be concerned with a few general categories as they are divided by grocers: new potatoes, red potatoes, russets, and white potatoes, long or round.

New potatoes don't have to be tiny, just any freshly dug potatoes, large or small. They're available only from May to September.

Look for clean, firm, thick potatoes that are not shriveled, blackened, or sprouting. Avoid white potatoes that have greenish areas on the skin; that sickly color signals the development of a substance called solanine that can indeed make you ill.

Sweet potatoes, which are not botanically related to white potatoes, range in color from pale golden to deep orange. The orange sweet potatoes are often called yams, but actually the *true* yam belongs to a different genus entirely and is not sold in this country. Sweet potatoes are available from September to February; the orange so-called yams contain the greatest amount of beta carotene.

In the Kitchen

Less starchy new potatoes are ideal candidates for boiling and steaming; their firm texture is perfect for potato salads. Round red potatoes are delicious simply steamed in their jackets and sprinkled with fresh dill. Mealy-textured russet potatoes make the best baked potatoes. Long white potatoes, sometimes called Idaho potatoes, can be used for any purpose. Round white potatoes are good for mashing and frying.

Many people consider the skin of a crisp baked russet potato or a steamed red potato the best part. If skins are to be eaten, be sure to remove any incipient sprouts that may have appeared since you bought the potatoes; these also contain solanine.

Sweet potatoes are fairly perishable; they can be stored at room temperature for a short period of time. White potatoes can be stored for about two weeks in a cool, dark, dry place; if you buy them in a plastic bag, remove the bag before storing. All potatoes need air circulation.

Never, never store potatoes of any color in the refrigerator!

Jamaican Chicken with Sweet Potatoes

Makes 4 servings.

To cut down on fat, I routinely skin all chicken pieces. The easy way to do this is simply to put your fingers under the skin and tear it free. This works fine on thighs and breasts; legs will need additional cutting.

½ cup unbleached all-purpose flour

8 skinned chicken thighs

2 tablespoons vegetable oil or more

salt and pepper to taste

2 large sweet potatoes (about 2 pounds)

1 cup orange juice

½ cup juice from pineapple

1 bay leaf

1 cup canned pineapple chunks packed in own juice, no sugar added

2 bananas, cut into chunks

½ cup chopped unsalted peanuts

Put the flour on a sheet of wax paper. Coat the chicken pieces with the flour.

Heat the oil in a large skillet. Brown the chicken pieces on both sides over medium-high heat, adding more oil if necessary. Salt and pepper the chicken pieces.

Cut the potatoes into quarters. Add the potatoes, the orange and pineapple juices, and the bay leaf to the skillet. Bring the mixture to a simmer and cook, with the cover ajar, for 15 minutes, turning the chicken once. The potatoes should be tender and the chicken pieces cooked through.

Remove the chicken and potatoes, and keep them warm. Discard the bay leaf. The pan juices should be thick and syrupy; if not, cook over high heat until they're reduced to a sauce consistency. Add the pineapple chunks and bananas; heat through. Pour the fruit mixture over the chicken. Sprinkle the peanuts over the top.

Whipped Sweet Potato with Yogurt and Chives

Makes 4 servings.

Low-fat yogurt is an excellent substitute for the butter, cream, and/or whole milk that so often drenches the nutritious potato with fat and extra calories.

2 large sweet potatoes (about 2 pounds), baked and peeled

2 eggs, beaten, or ½ cup prepared egg substitute

⅓ cup plain yogurt (can be low-fat)

1 tablespoon each minced chives and minced fresh flat-leafed parsley

salt and pepper to taste

Preheat the oven to 375° F. Mash the sweet potatoes. Blend in the eggs. Add the yogurt and whip with a hand-held mixer or a masher until the potatoes are fluffy. (Do not use the food processor for whipping potatoes.) Add more yogurt if necessary. Stir in the chives, parsley, and salt and pepper.

Spoon the potato into an oiled 1½-quart casserole and bake for 30 minutes, until lightly browned on top. *If the casserole is made ahead and chilled, allow 10 to 15 minutes extra cooking time.*

Steamed Sweet Potatoes with Poached Cranberries

Makes 4 servings.

Here's a different way to "candy" sweet potatoes that simply adds more nutrition and no cholesterol. It's a riot of color, too!

> one 10- to 12-ounce package fresh
>   cranberries
> 1 cup sugar
> 1 cup water
> 1 cinnamon stick
> 2 large sweet potatoes (about 2 pounds)
> 1 tablespoon cider vinegar
> salt to taste

Wash and pick over the cranberries. Combine the sugar, water, and cinnamon stick in a deep saucepan, and bring the mixture to a boil; cook for 3 minutes.

Add the cranberries, and cook uncovered at a low boil, stirring often, for about 5 minutes, or until the berries have popped open but still retain their shape. Remove the cinnamon stick and set the poached berries aside to cool slightly (the sauce will thicken) while preparing the potatoes. *The cranberries can be prepared ahead; if chilled, bring them to room temperature before proceeding.*

Peel the potatoes and cut them into thick, even slices, 4 to 5 per potato. Steam them over 1 inch of water to which you've added the vinegar for 10 minutes, or until tender. Scoop them into a serving dish, salt them, and ladle some of the cranberries on top. *Leftover cranberries may be frozen.*

Lucy's Perfect Mashed Potatoes

Makes 4 servings.

Potatoes have to be mashed by hand and served as soon as they're ready, which is why, although it's a simple dish, you'll never find perfect mashed potatoes in a restaurant.

Because it's her favorite food, my daughter Lucy puts a lot of love and attention into preparing mashed potatoes—and great energy into the whipping! Recently, she's reformulated her recipe to use the low-cholesterol ingredients you'll see here—but these fluffy, flavorful potatoes are still superb!

6 medium potatoes (about 2 pounds)
1 tablespoon salt for the cooking water
¾ tablespoon unsalted margarine
¼ teaspoon salt
½ teaspoon pepper
¾ cup skim milk
paprika or minced parsley

Peel the potatoes, wash them carefully, and cut them into eighths. Put them in a deep, heavy saucepan, cover with cold water, and add 1 tablespoon of salt. Bring the water to a boil and cook the potatoes until they are quite soft, about 15 minutes.

Note: Overcooking makes mashed potatoes gluey; undercooking makes them lumpy. To test, insert a fork into the cooked potato; if it readily breaks into 2 pieces as you turn the fork, they're done.

Drain the potatoes. Place the pan back on the heat to dry them for a minute or two. With an electric range, you can use the heat that remains in the turned-off burner. With gas, you'll need to turn the heat on low. Shake the pan every few seconds to make sure the potatoes don't burn and that they dry evenly.

Add the margarine, the ¼ teaspoon of salt, and the pepper. Pour in about ½ cup of milk. Mash the potatoes by hand, using a potato masher. Add the remaining milk as needed to lighten the potatoes. When there are no more lumps, whip the potatoes by using the masher as if it were a whisk. (A hand mixer also can be used, but *never use a food processor*, which turns potatoes into glue.)

Serve hot, garnished with paprika or minced parsley.

Baked Yams with Amaretti Topping

Makes 6 servings.
Candied yams with a sophisticated flair.

6 medium yams (orange-fleshed sweet potatoes)

2 tablespoons brown sugar

2 tablespoons amaretto (almond-flavored liqueur)

4 tablespoons butter or low-cholesterol margarine, softened

¼ teaspoon salt

10 to 12 amaretti (imported almond cookies)

Bake the yams in a 400° F. oven for 45 minutes, or until tender. Scoop out the flesh and mash it with the brown sugar, amaretto liqueur, 2 tablespoons of the butter, and the salt. Spread the yam mixture in a 9-by-9-inch baking pan.

Pulverize the amaretti cookies between 2 pieces of wax paper; blend in the remaining 2 tablespoons of butter. Sprinkle the cookie crumbs on the yams.

Preheat the oven to 350° F., and bake the yams for 30 minutes.

Baby Red Potato and Artichoke Salad

Makes 6 to 8 servings.
I prefer potato salad with a vinaigrette rather than mayonnaise dressing. Not only is there less danger of its spoiling in warm weather, the sweetness of the potatoes and the tartness of the vinegar do nice things for each other.

1½ pounds baby red potatoes, about the size of pullet eggs or smaller (new white potatoes may be substituted)

1 tablespoon white vinegar

1 teaspoon salt

one 10-ounce package frozen artichoke hearts, thawed to separate

For the dressing:

¼ cup olive oil

2 tablespoons red wine vinegar

2 tablespoons minced fresh flat-leafed parsley

½ teaspoon Italian seasoning (see Basics)

1 clove garlic, pressed or very finely minced

salt and freshly ground black pepper to taste

Wash the potatoes well and cut off ½ inch of peel all the way around each one, but otherwise leave them unpeeled. Steam them over 1 inch of boiling water to which you've added the white vinegar and 1 teaspoon of salt until the potatoes are tender, 10 to 15 minutes.

Slice the thawed artichokes in half lengthwise and put them in a bowl. Combine the dressing ingredients in a jar, shake, and pour over the artichokes. Stir thoroughly.

When the potatoes are cooked, add them to the bowl and stir again. Chill for several hours, stirring once or twice. Taste to correct the seasoning; you may want more wine vinegar.

Sweet Potato Muffins

Makes 12 muffins.

When baking sweet potatoes for dinner, bake one extra to make these muffins the next day. With the aid of a food processor, this batter is especially quick and easy to prepare.

2 cups sifted unbleached all-purpose flour

1 tablespoon baking powder

½ teaspoon salt

2 eggs or ½ cup prepared egg substitute

1 medium sweet potato, baked and peeled (about 1 cup mashed)

⅓ cup sugar

1 cup milk (can be low-fat)

⅓ cup vegetable oil

2 tablespoons toasted wheat germ

½ teaspoon cinnamon

¼ teaspoon nutmeg

½ cup raisins

Preheat the oven to 400° F. Line a 12-cup muffin pan with paper liners.

Sift the flour, baking powder, and salt into a large bowl.

In a food processor, blend the eggs, potato, and sugar. (Or by hand, beat the eggs and mash the potato before blending with sugar.) Add the milk, oil, wheat germ, and spices; process or beat until smooth.

Pour the liquid mixture into the dry ingredients. Mix just enough to blend. Stir in the raisins. Divide the batter among the muffin cups; they'll be about two-thirds full.

Put the muffins in the oven, reducing the heat to 350° F. Bake in the top third of the oven for 25 minutes, or until they are lightly browned on top and dry inside. Serve warm or at room temperature.

Sweet Potato and Bourbon Soufflé

Makes 4 servings.

It seems that every Southern cook has a recipe for sweet potato pudding or pie in her repertoire. This is a reduced-fat version, and better yet, if you use low-cholesterol alternatives, it's guilt-free. *And*—a big plus—sweet potatoes are a rich source of lung-protecting vitamin A. Serve this sweet soufflé as a dessert.

> *1 pound sweet potatoes*
> *(2 medium or 1 very large)*
> *⅓ cup dark brown sugar*
> *½ teaspoon cinnamon*
> *¼ teaspoon each ground ginger and salt*
> *⅛ teaspoon allspice*
> *2 tablespoons melted butter or*
> *low-cholesterol margarine*
> *2 tablespoons bourbon*
> *2 egg yolks plus enough milk to make*
> *½ cup, or ½ cup prepared egg substitute*
> *2 egg whites*

Bake the potatoes at 375° F. until quite soft. Peel and mash or purée them with the sugar, spices, and salt.

Use a little of the butter to grease a 1½-quart soufflé dish or casserole. Preheat the oven to 350° F.

Blend the rest of the butter, the bourbon, the egg yolk and milk mixture (or egg substitute) into the potatoes, whipping to lighten.

Beat the egg whites until they are stiff. Fold them into the potato mixture and spoon the batter into the prepared dish. Bake for 45 minutes on the middle shelf, or until the top is browned and risen and the soufflé has shrunk slightly away from the sides of the dish.

Serve immediately, with a dollop of lemon sherbet or frozen vanilla yogurt to melt on top.

For other potato recipes, see the following: Aunt Catherine's Pepper, Onion, and Potato Omelet; Baked Bluefish with Potatoes; Broccoli Rabe and Potato Soup with Meatballs; Carrot and Sweet Potato *Tzimmes*; Cream of Pumpkin Soup with Parmesan Croutons; Colcannon; Fresh Codfish Cakes; Garlic-Roasted Potatoes; Homey Chicken Stew with Blueberry Dumplings; Jalapeño-Sweet Potato Bisque; Old-Fashioned Pork Stew with Whole Garlic Cloves; Pork Cutlets with Chestnuts and Sweet Potatoes; Scalloped Rutabaga and Potato; Vegetable Chowder with Shredded Spinach

RICE

STAPLE SEED OF A HEALTHFUL DIET. The cultivation of rice originated in India about 3000 BC but wasn't introduced to Europe until medieval times. Probably because the plant must be grown on water-submerged fields, rice never replaced wheat in Europe but remained a staple of many Eastern countries, the chief food of half the world's population today.

Rice that's processed to remove only the husks, called brown rice, contains 8 percent protein and is a source of important B vitamins (thiamine, niacin, and riboflavin), iron, and calcium. White rice, milled to remove the bran as well as the husk, is greatly dimin-ished in nutrition. *Enriched* white rice has been supplemented with some of the missing B vitamins and iron.

In any form, rice is a complex carbohydrate food that when eaten without supplementary protein, will encourage the brain to manufacture more serotonin, thus promoting a feeling of calm cheerfulness and relaxation. Rice is also a good source of choline, which enhances the memory-boosting neurotransmitter acetylcholine. And its B vitamins combat the effects of stress.

Rice bran, a component of brown rice that is removed when the rice is refined, is a cholesterol-lowering agent similar to oat bran.

Not only richer in nutrients and fiber than white rice, brown rice is more flavorful and makes a tasty complement to wild rice, which is really an aquatic grass. The usual ratio is three parts brown rice to one part wild rice. Fortunately, they both cook in the same amount of time.

As a seed food, rice contains protease inhibitors, substances thought to inhibit the formation of tumors. Its starch, like that of cooked potatoes, creates butyric acid, another cancer-fighting agent, in the intestines.

In the Market

Unrefined rice doesn't keep as well as its processed counterpart, so always smell brown rice before buying it; it should have a fresh and nutty aroma. If you buy brown rice in a "whole foods" market, where there's bound to be a faster turnover than in a regular supermarket, you're more likely to find a fresher product.

My favorite white rice is the Italian Arborio, which seems to me to have much more flavor than the dry, tasteless long-grain "converted" white rice that's the biggest seller in American supermarkets. "Instant" rice is even worse than converted, with all the taste and appeal of ground-up Styrofoam.

When you buy any of the ready-flavored rice products, the main "flavors" you're getting are salt, the acrid essence of dried onion, and bouillon. These expensive products (compared with plain bulk rice) always taste boringly the same, whereas if you season rice in your own kitchen, the flavors will be fresh, varied, and not entirely dependent on salt.

In the Kitchen

White rice will keep well in an airtight canister on the pantry shelf for about six months. Brown rice should be refrigerated (up to six months) or a rancid taste may develop.

You can cook up a nice pot of white rice in 12 to 20 minutes. Brown rice will take 45 minutes or so, however, so the sensible thing is to cook a big batch at one time and reheat as needed through the week. You can reheat rice in a few minutes in the microwave, or scoop it into a small-meshed strainer and reheat over simmering water; cover the strainer and pot with a lid.

To keep the grains separate, add a little oil to the cooking water. For fluffier rice, stir with a fork after cooking and let stand, covered, for 10 minutes.

Tomato Rice Soup

Makes 1 quart before adding the rice.

A soothing winter soup to serve in big mugs by the fireplace. Try it with a dollop of *pistou* swirled over the surface *(page 194)*.

> *1 tablespoon each butter, or low-cholesterol margarine, and olive oil*
>
> *1 onion, chopped*
>
> *1 carrot, sliced*
>
> *2 cups canned Italian tomatoes*
>
> *one 13-ounce can of chicken broth*
>
> *¼ teaspoon each dried thyme leaves and white pepper*
>
> *about 2 cups cooked brown rice (see Basics)*

In a large saucepan, heat the oil and butter, and sauté the onion and carrot until the onion is golden. Add all the remaining ingredients except the rice, and simmer, with the cover ajar, for 20 minutes.

Purée the soup in batches (hot liquids foam up) in a blender or food processor; the blender is better for liquid-based mixtures.

Put ⅓ cup of rice in the bottom of each bowl or mug, and pour the soup over. Swirl in the *pistou*, if using.

Paella with Brown Rice

Makes 6 servings.

This paella departs from tradition in several respects: It uses nutritious brown rice rather than white; there's little fat, since the chicken is skinned and no sausage is included; and it's baked instead of sautéed. The good part about baking paella is that the dish can be expanded without much fuss. Paella is served from the pan and needs only bread and salad to go with it. Orange and Onion Salad *(page 97)* is a pleasing accompaniment.

> *1 cup brown Basmati rice (another brown rice may be substituted, but not white rice)*
>
> *2 tablespoons olive oil*
>
> *6 skinned chicken thighs*
>
> *2 cloves garlic, minced*
>
> *1 large onion, chopped*
>
> *1 sweet red pepper, seeded and diced*
>
> *one 13-ounce can chicken broth*
>
> *one 1-pound can tomatoes, drained and chopped*
>
> *¼ teaspoon cayenne pepper*
>
> *¼ teaspoon saffron threads (optional but traditional)*
>
> *1 cup frozen peas, thawed enough to separate*
>
> *½ pound cooked, peeled, cleaned shrimp*
>
> *1 pound mussels in shells (see Note)*

Parboil the rice in boiling salted water for 20 minutes. Drain.

Meanwhile, in a Dutch oven, brown the chicken in hot oil and remove it.

Preheat the oven to 400° F. Lower the heat under the Dutch oven, and sauté the garlic, onion, and sweet red pepper until they are softened. Add the broth, tomatoes, cayenne, and saffron, and bring the mixture to a boil to dissolve the saffron. Spoon in the parboiled rice and top with the chicken.

Put the boiling paella into the oven and bake for 35 minutes. If most of the liquid has been absorbed and the rice is tender, go to the next step. If not, bake a few minutes more.

Stir the peas and shrimp into the rice, again putting the chicken on top. Lay the mussels over the chicken. Cover tightly and bake 10 minutes, or until the mussels have opened. If one or two haven't opened when the rest have, discard the closed ones.

Note: Careful preparation is necessary in cooking mussels, but don't let that stop you.

While stored in the refrigerator, mussels should be kept on ice (not in the freezer) and allowed to breathe; don't store them in airtight plastic.

If possible, buy cultivated mussels that have been cleaned of their "beards" (fibers along the edges of the shells) and are grit-free, requiring no soaking. They should be bagged and labeled with that information.

Otherwise, soak the mussels in cold water for an hour before cooking. Scrub the shells under running water with a stiff brush and pull off the beards.

Discard any that have cracked shells. Use only mussels that are closed or that close tight when you tap them, indicating the critter inside is alive.

Chinese-Style Fried Brown Rice

Makes 4 servings.

I like to keep some Chinese and Japanese teas on hand. In case I should decide to whip up an Asian dish, it's nice to accompany it with the right beverage. Green tea, which is not fermented as are black teas, has been the focus of recent Japanese studies. It's been shown that certain tannins found in green tea act against the formation of cancers in animals.

3 eggs or ¾ cup prepared egg substitute
2 tablespoons water
3 tablespoons vegetable oil
1 shallot, minced
½ sweet red pepper, finely chopped
2 scallions, sliced thin
1 teaspoon minced fresh ginger
2 slices low-fat ham, diced
3 cups cooked brown rice (see Basics)
2 tablespoons soy sauce

Whisk together the eggs and water. In a large skillet, heat 1 tablespoon of oil and sauté the shallot until it's softened but not brown. Pour the egg into the pan in a thin "pancake" layer and let it cook until it's set through, loosening the bottom a bit from time to time. Remove this thin omelet, roll it up like a jelly roll, and slice it thin. (If the omelet refuses to come out of the pan intact, it's no big problem; you're going to slice it into shreds anyway.)

Clean out the pan and heat the remaining 2 tablespoons of oil. Stir-fry the red pepper, scallions, ginger, and ham until the pepper is tender-crisp, about 3 minutes. Add the rice and stir-fry for 5 minutes, stirring occasionally.

Add the shredded omelet and heat through. Season with soy sauce.

Brown Rice Risotto with Asparagus and Porcini Mushrooms

Makes 6 servings.

Italian porcini ("little pig") mushrooms are my favorites, but, alas, only dried porcini are available in this country. If you want to substitute fresh mushrooms, choose the big brown portobello mushrooms, which are about the closest in texture and flavor.

1 large shallot, minced

*¼ cup dried porcini mushroom pieces
soaked in warm water for 30 minutes,
drained and chopped, or ½ cup chopped
fresh portobello mushroom
(1 medium-sized portobello)*

2 tablespoons olive oil

*⅞ cup brown rice (1 cup less
2 tablespoons)*

one 13-ounce can chicken broth

*2 tablespoons tomato sauce or 1 tablespoon
tomato paste*

one 1-pound bunch fresh asparagus

¼ cup grated Parmesan cheese

Microwave method: In a 2-quart casserole, microwave the shallot and mushrooms in the oil on high until sizzling, about 3 minutes. Stir in the rice to coat it with oil. In a saucepan, combine the broth and tomato sauce or paste, and heat to boiling on the range top. Pour the broth over the rice. Cover and microwave on high for 6 to 7 minutes, until boiling. Change the setting to medium, and continue to cook for 35 to 40 minutes, until the rice is just tender and the liquid has been absorbed.

Range-top method: Sauté the shallot and mushrooms in a heavy, deep saucepan, and stir in the rice. In a second saucepan, combine the broth and tomato sauce or paste, and heat to boiling. Add about 1 cup of the hot broth to the rice. Remove the remaining broth from the heat.

Cook the rice at the lowest possible simmer, partially covered, stirring frequently, until the liquid is almost all absorbed. Add half the remaining broth (which can be warm or at room temperature) and repeat the procedure. Pour in the last of the broth and cook until the rice is tender. Total cooking time should be about 40 minutes.

If all the broth is absorbed before the rice is cooked (a distinct possibility with brown rice, which takes so long to cook), add hot water a little at a time until the desired tenderness is reached.

Meanwhile, cut the tough ends off the asparagus and steam the stalks in a small amount of water in a covered skillet until just tender-crisp, 5 to 6 minutes. Cut the stalks into 2-inch pieces.

Stir the asparagus and cheese into the risotto and serve.

Brown Rice Pilaf with Fennel

Makes 4 servings.

There's no mystery to cooking brown rice; it simply takes a little longer than white rice, but it's much more nutritious, with lots of B vitamins to fight against stress.

> 2 tablespoons olive oil
>
> ½ cup each chopped onion and diced yellow pepper
>
> 1 cup chopped fennel, including some of the "hair"
>
> ⅞ cup long-grain brown rice (1 cup less 2 tablespoons)
>
> 2 cups chicken broth or part broth, part water
>
> ½ cup (4 ounces) canned Italian plum tomatoes, chopped
>
> ¼ teaspoon salt (optional)
>
> ¼ teaspoon pepper

Microwave method: Put the oil, onion, yellow pepper, and fennel in a 2-quart casserole, and microwave for about 3 minutes on high, until sizzling. Stir the rice into the vegetables until all the grains are coated with oil. Add the broth, tomatoes, salt, and pepper. Cover and microwave on high until the liquid boils, 7 to 8 minutes. Continue cooking on medium for 35 to 45 minutes, until all the liquid is absorbed.

Range-top method: Heat the oil in a large, heavy saucepan; sauté the onion, yellow pepper, and fennel until the vegetables are softened and beginning to turn golden. Stir in the rice to coat all the grains with oil. Add the broth, tomatoes, salt, and pepper. Bring to a boil, then reduce the heat to a low simmer, and cook, covered, for 45 minutes, or until all the liquid is absorbed.

Fluff the pilaf before serving.

Maple-Nut Rice Muffins

Makes 12 muffins.

A slightly crunchy muffin with a delightfully intense maple flavor.

> 1 cup whole-wheat flour
>
> ¾ cup sifted unbleached all-purpose flour
>
> 1 tablespoon baking powder
>
> scant ½ teaspoon salt
>
> 2 eggs or ½ cup prepared egg substitute
>
> ⅔ cup milk
>
> ½ cup maple syrup
>
> 5 tablespoons vegetable oil
>
> ½ teaspoon mapleine (maple flavoring, found in the spice section of the supermarket)
>
> 1½ cups cooked brown rice (see Basics)
>
> ½ cup chopped pecans or walnuts

Line a 12-cup muffin pan with paper liners. Preheat the oven to 400° F.

Sift the flours, baking powder, and salt into a large bowl. In another bowl, beat the eggs, milk, syrup, oil, and flavoring until blended. Pour the liquid mixture into the dry ingredients. Mix just enough to blend. Stir in the rice and nuts. Divide the batter among the muffin cups.

Bake in the top third of the oven for 20 minutes, or until they are lightly browned on top and dry inside.

Serve warm or at room temperature.

Spicy Brown Rice Pudding with Dates

Makes 6 servings.

Spices and flavorings have their chemical effects, just as foods do. Nutmeg, cinnamon, and vanilla, for instance, are all stimulants. Allspice is a relaxant, however, as is milk, so you'll come out about even with a dish of this spicy pudding.

2 cups cooked brown rice (see Basics)
½ cup chopped, pitted dates
3 eggs or ¾ cup prepared egg substitute
½ cup sugar
½ teaspoon vanilla
¼ teaspoon each allspice, cinnamon, nutmeg, and salt
2 cups scalded milk (can be low-fat)

Fluff the rice to separate the grains and put it into a buttered 2-quart casserole. Stir in the dates. Put the casserole into a larger pan. Preheat the oven to 325° F.

In a medium-size bowl, whisk the eggs with the sugar, vanilla, and spices until the mixture is light and well-blended. *Slowly* pour in the hot milk while continuing to whisk.

Stir the milk-egg mixture into the rice. Arrange the casserole and surrounding pan on the middle rack of the oven, and carefully pour boiling water into the larger pan to an inch from the top. Bake the pudding until a knife inserted near the center comes out clean. If you've used whole eggs, this will take from 45 minutes to 1 hour; if an egg substitute, it may take longer.

Let the pudding cool until it's just warm before serving. Serve with spoonfuls of vanilla yogurt, if desired.

For other rice recipes, see the following: Broccoli and Wild Rice Casserole; Gratin of White Turnips, Carrots, and Rice; Kidney Beans with Sweet and Hot Red Peppers; Lemon-Scented Broccoli Risotto; Rice-Stuffed Cabbage Leaves with Pineapple-Tomato Sauce; *Risi e Bisi*

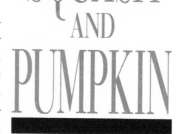

SQUASH AND PUMPKIN

PLUMP WITH VITAMIN A AND FIBER. Squash and pumpkins were widely cultivated in North America long before the coming of the Europeans; the Narragansett called the former *askutasquash*; the Iroquois name was *isquoutersquash*. Having been introduced to the sweet orange vegetables by the Native Americans, our forebears filled the hollowed-out pumpkins and squash with milk, eggs, and spices and baked them whole in slow ovens. Actually, that's pretty easy as well as showy, so I've included a recipe for Plymouth Colony pumpkin.

The orange winter squashes and pumpkins, in all their wondrous plump shapes, are powerhouses of the plant kingdom's vitamin A, beta carotene. Squash and pumpkin's bright orange color signals the presence of plenty of carotenoids, which have been shown to help fight cancer, colds, immune diseases, and night blindness. Both squash and pumpkin contain a good amount of fiber, too, for a second line of defense against the development of tumors.

In a report published by Graham A. Colditz et al. in the *American Journal of Clinical Nutrition* (January 1985), numerous previous studies were cited that "have shown that cancer risk is inversely related to the consumption of green and yellow vegetables." Particularly mentioned were lung, gastrointestinal, bladder, and colon cancers. The report was based on a study of more than 1,200 Massachusetts residents 66 years of age or older and demonstrated that those with the highest intake of carotene-containing vegetables had the lowest incidence of cancer.

Squash contains calcium for healthy bones, and pumpkin packs in some vitamin C for all-around tissue building and healing. Both pumpkin and squash are intensely rich in potassium for a healthy heart; a half-cup of squash will give you as much of that important mineral as a banana.

In the Market

The big nutritional winners among squash are the winter varieties: butternut, acorn, Hubbard, and spaghetti squash. They come into the stores in early fall, but they're such good keepers that you'll be able to buy decent ones all through the winter, just when you can use that vitamin A to help ward off colds.

Pumpkins, another fall vegetable, unfortunately seem to be reserved for decorative purposes and disappear from the stores after Thanksgiving. The occasional pumpkin pie is usually made from the canned vegetable. It's as if the public hasn't fully realized that one actually can cook the big round fellow that makes such a jolly jack-o'-lantern.

Whole squash and pumpkins are something of a mystery: As with melons, how can you tell what you're getting inside? In general, buy those that are heavy for their size, hard on the surface, clean, and free of cuts, cracks, and soft spots.

For cooking pumpkins, choose the small "sugar" variety (ask your grocer). A local farm stand may be the best supplier. Sometimes cooking pumpkins aren't sold in the supermarket's produce department but are used as part of their fall decor. I've bought a bunch of small pumpkins for my own culinary use right out of a supermarket's autumn display. It seems that the store's computer did after all have a per-pound price on those pumpkins arranged with sheaves of wheat.

In the Kitchen

Squash and pumpkins will keep quite well for a month or more in a cool, dry, airy place, such as an unheated attic.

Baking is about the easiest cooking method for squash and pumpkins. Ignore recipes that tell you to cook these vegetables cut sides down, because this will steam them and you'll lose that desirable nutty flavor. (For the same reason, don't cook them in the microwave oven.) Instead, bake them cut sides up. After cooling, baked squash will be a cinch to peel and can be used in any recipe that calls for cooked squash. You can also freeze any extra mashed squash for another occasion; pint containers are a convenient size.

After baking pumpkins, turn them upside down to drain, since they can be quite watery. When you want to use fresh pumpkin in pies, put the mashed vegetable in a saucepan over low heat and cook, stirring occasionally, until the desired dense consistency is reached.

Acorn squash, with those neat little hollows, seems to beg for stuffing. Even if nothing else is at hand, it will look elegant simply filled with creamed peas, but my favorite is a savory apple-raisin stuffing. ■■■

Acorn Squash Soup with Pastina

Makes about 2 quarts.

Pastina always makes me feel nostalgic; chicken soup with pastina used to be the standard fare for a childhood cold in my home. Here, that soup takes on a new color, enriched with puréed squash.

Evaporated *skim* milk is a healthful substitute for cream or whole milk in so-called cream soups.

> 2 acorn squashes
> 6 cups full-flavored chicken broth (canned, or see Basics)
> 1 large onion, finely chopped
> ½ cup evaporated skim milk
> ¼ teaspoon each dried rosemary and white pepper
> ½ cup pastina, cooked according to package directions

Cut the squashes in half, remove the seeds, and bake the halves, cut sides up, in a 375° F. oven for 45 minutes, or until tender. When cool enough to handle, scoop out the flesh and mash or purée it in a food processor or blender. *The squash can be prepared ahead and refrigerated until needed.*

Bring the broth to a boil in a large pot, add the onion, and cook until the onion is tender. Whisk in the squash, evaporated milk, rosemary, and pepper. Stir in the cooked pastina. Reheat to the simmering point and serve.

Cream of Pumpkin Soup with Parmesan Croutons

Makes 4 to 6 servings.

A comforting, rich soup with two great sources of beta carotene.

> one 2- to 2½-pound pumpkin
> 1 sweet potato (about ½ pound)
> 3 slices Italian bread, halved, or 6 slices French bread
> ½ teaspoon each cumin seed and celery salt
> ¼ teaspoon each dried cilantro and cayenne pepper
> ⅛ teaspoon ground allspice
> one 12-ounce can evaporated skim milk
> one 13-ounce can chicken broth
> 2 tablespoons butter
> grated Parmesan cheese
> paprika

Preheat the oven to 350° F. Pierce the sweet potato with a fork. Cut the pumpkin in half and scoop out the seeds. Put it in a baking pan, cut side up, with the sweet potato, and bake them for 1 hour, or until tender. During the last 10 minutes, add the Italian bread to the pan to dry it. *The recipe can be prepared ahead to this point; refrigerate the vegetables until needed.*

Peel and purée the pumpkin and potato in a food processor or blender, with all of the spices. With the motor running, add the evaporated milk and broth. (If using a blender, do this in batches and add some of the liquid called for in the recipe to each batch *before* beginning to purée.)

Heat the soup with the butter in a large double boiler over simmering water, whisking occasionally, until it is very hot. If the soup seems too thick, add broth or milk until you achieve the desired consistency.

Just before serving, sprinkle the slices of toast with Parmesan cheese and paprika. Melt the cheese under the broiler, and top each serving with a crouton.

Picadillo Pumpkin in Shell

Makes 6 servings.

A whole pumpkin takes a long time to bake, but the preparation of this spicy Cuban filling is quick and easy.

> one 3- to 4-pound "sugar" pumpkin
> (see Note)
> 1½ pounds ground turkey or
> very lean ground beef
> 1 slice whole-wheat bread, crumbed
> 1 egg or ¼ cup prepared egg substitute
> 1 onion, chopped fine
> 1 small sweet red pepper, diced
> 1 clove garlic, minced
> ¼ cup each chili sauce, dark raisins, and
> sliced stuffed green olives
> 1 teaspoon chili powder
> ½ teaspoon each ground cumin and salt
> ¼ teaspoon each ground cloves and pepper

Cut the top off the pumpkin and reserve it. Clean out the seeds and fiber. In a large bowl, mix the remaining ingredients.

Set the pumpkin in a round casserole that will hold it upright. Stuff the hollow with the meat mixture and cover it with the pumpkin top. Pour 1 inch of water around the pumpkin.

Bake at 350° F. for about 2 hours, or until the filling is cooked through, the pumpkin has darkened, and the flesh is tender when pierced with a fork. Cooking time varies with the thickness of the pumpkin flesh.

To serve, carefully place the pumpkin on a deep platter. Cut it in half, letting the halves fall filling side up, and drain off the accumulated juices. Then slice into wedges.

Note: Sugar pumpkins are a relatively small (2 to 6 pounds) variety of pumpkin. Developed for eating rather than decoration, they are sweeter and more flavorful. Ask the grocer; if they are unavailable, any pumpkin of the same size can be substituted.

Plymouth Colony Pumpkin in Shell

Makes 6 to 8 servings.

The Pilgrims cooked whole pumpkin in the shell, filling the hollow center with milk and spices, which makes this a really authentic Thanksgiving recipe. Although custard-filled pumpkin could be considered a dessert, I like to serve this dish alongside the roasted bird.

one 3- to 4-pound "sugar" pumpkin
milk
egg or prepared egg substitute
raisins
sugar
cinnamon
nutmeg

Cut the top off the pumpkin and reserve it. Clean out the seeds and fiber. Measure the hollow by filling it with water and pouring the water into a 2-cup measuring pitcher.

For every cup of filling needed, mix ½ cup of milk, 1 large egg—beaten—or ¼ cup of prepared egg substitute, ¼ cup of raisins, 1 tablespoon of sugar, ½ teaspoon of cinnamon, and ¼ teaspoon of nutmeg.

Set the pumpkin in a round casserole that will hold it upright. Pour the filling into the hollow and cover with the pumpkin top. Pour 1 inch of water around the pumpkin.

Bake at 350° F. for about 2 hours, or until the filling is set, the pumpkin has darkened, and its flesh is tender when pierced with a fork. Cooking time varies with the thickness of the pumpkin flesh. If you use the egg substitute, it may take a little longer to set.

Let the pumpkin stand for 15 minutes. If the filling is still a bit soft at the center, it will firm up during the standing time as the heat of the pumpkin continues to cook it.

To serve, slice in half, letting halves fall filling side up. Then slice into wedges.

Spaghetti Squash Romano

Makes 4 servings.

The delicate flavor of this squash makes possible a lot of delicious innovations. This is one of the simplest.

> *one 2- to 2½-pound spaghetti squash*
> *2 tablespoons olive oil*
> *1 tablespoon butter*
> *1 clove garlic, minced*
> *salt and pepper to taste*
> *¼ cup grated Romano cheese*

Preheat the oven to 350° F. Cut the squash lengthwise and scoop out the seeds. Place the halves cut sides up in a roasting pan. Add water to the depth of 1 inch. Bake for 45 minutes, or until fork-tender. As soon as the squash can be handled, use a fork to scrape out the flesh into strands and discard the skin. Put the squash in a casserole.

In a small skillet, heat the oil and butter, and sauté the garlic until just sizzling. Pour this mixture over the squash evenly. Add salt and pepper. Sprinkle with cheese. Bake until the cheese is melted and the squash is reheated, about 10 minutes.

Acorn Squash with Apple-Raisin Stuffing

Makes 4 servings.

This is a nice, easy dish to put into the oven when you're roasting a chicken.

> *1 large acorn squash (about 3 pounds)*
> *nutmeg for sprinkling and salt to taste*
> *1 cup plain breadcrumbs*
> *1 tablespoon melted butter*
> *1 tart apple, peeled and grated*
> *¼ cup raisins*
> *¼ cup finely chopped walnuts*
> *¼ teaspoon nutmeg*
> *¼ teaspoon cinnamon*
> *apple juice or water*

Preheat the oven to 375° F. Cut the squash into quarters; scoop out the seeds. Sprinkle the cut surfaces lightly with nutmeg and salt.

Mix together the remaining ingredients. Add apple juice or water, 1 teaspoon at a time, until the stuffing just holds together when pressed. Stuff the squash quarters, mounding the stuffing to use all of it. Push down any visible raisins, since they tend to overbrown.

Put the quarters into a baking pan with ½ inch of water in the bottom. Bake until tender, 45 minutes to 1 hour, without replacing evaporated water. Should the tops get too brown, cover the pan *loosely* with foil. (If the foil is sealed, the squash will steam rather than bake; baking gives a much nuttier flavor.)

Butternut Ratatouille

Makes 8 or more servings.

Butternut squash makes an interesting addition to a traditional French dish. This version is completely oven-cooked, using much less oil than is usual. Ratatouille is delicious served hot, cold, or at room temperature.

1 large eggplant

1 medium zucchini

1 medium butternut squash

2 green peppers, seeded

¼ cup olive oil

1 large onion, chopped

2 cloves garlic, minced

one 28-ounce can Italian tomatoes, drained

2 tablespoons minced fresh basil or 1 teaspoon dried

½ teaspoon salt or to taste

freshly ground black pepper to taste

¼ cup chopped fresh flat-leafed parsley

crusty French bread as an accompaniment (optional)

Peel the eggplant and slice it into rounds. Salt both sides and stand the slices in a colander to drain for 30 minutes. Rinse the slices, squeeze out the moisture, and pat them dry. Cut them into quarters. Slice the zucchini into half-rounds. Peel the butternut squash and cut it into chunks. Cut the peppers into strips.

Preheat the oven to 400° F. Combine the oil, green pepper, onion, and garlic in a large stainless steel or glass baking dish. Put the dish in the oven until the vegetables are sizzling but not brown. Add the eggplant and bake until it is softened, about 10 minutes.

Put the zucchini on top and bake 10 more minutes.

Add the squash, tomatoes, basil, ½ teaspoon of salt, and pepper; stir well, and continue to bake, uncovered, for 30 to 40 minutes. The vegetables should be very well cooked but still retain their shape, and the pan juices should be reduced.

Remove the dish from the oven and stir in the parsley. *The dish can be made ahead, refrigerated, and reheated in a skillet.*

Serve with crusty French bread.

Twice-Baked Butternut Squash with Pecans

Makes 6 servings.

This casserole is especially nice for a winter holiday meal because it's one dish you can get ready the day before things begin to get hectic in the kitchen. The recipe can be doubled or tripled, using more or larger casseroles.

1 butternut squash (about 2 pounds)
3 to 4 tablespoons brown sugar
a few dashes of ground cardamom or cinnamon
2 tablespoons butter or margarine
⅓ cup pecan halves

Preheat the oven to 375° F. Wash the squash and split it in half lengthwise. Scoop out the seeds and fibers. Place the halves, cut sides up, in a shallow baking dish. Add ½ inch of water to the dish. Bake the squash for 1 hour, or until quite tender. The water will boil away, but that's okay. Cool the squash completely.

Peel the squash and coarsely mash it with a fork. Put the mashed squash into a buttered round casserole, 2-quart capacity. Don't smooth the top; let it be slightly peaked like a meringue. Sprinkle with brown sugar and cardamom or cinnamon. Dot with butter or margarine. Arrange the pecans on the top. *The casserole can be prepared a day ahead and refrigerated until needed.*

Bake the casserole in a preheated 350° F. oven for 30 minutes, or until piping hot.

Pumpkin Flan

Makes 6 servings.

This flan is very much like a pumpkin pie, only much lighter, with a brown sugar glaze on top instead of a pastry crust on the bottom.

You'll need a nonstick, nonflammable coated metal pie pan for this dessert.

2 cups puréed fresh pumpkin (see previous recipe) or one 15-ounce can pumpkin

½ cup granulated sugar

1 tablespoon cornstarch

½ teaspoon each ground cinnamon and ginger

¼ teaspoon each ground nutmeg and salt

1 cup milk (can be low-fat)

2 beaten eggs or ½ cup prepared egg substitute

3 tablespoons molasses

1 tablespoon dark rum (optional)

½ cup sifted brown sugar

Preheat the oven to 325° F. Blend the pumpkin with the dry ingredients, except the brown sugar. Beat in the milk, egg, molasses, and rum. Pour the mixture into a 9-inch coated metal pie pan, and bake the flan for 45 minutes, or until a knife inserted at the center comes out clean.

Chill the flan. When ready to serve, heat the broiler and sprinkle the brown sugar evenly over the top of the flan. Heat just until the brown sugar melts and turns shiny.

Serve warm or cold in pie-shaped wedges.

Butternut Mincemeat Cookies

Makes about 4 dozen cookies.

Butternut squash, not butter, gives these soft spicy cookies their golden orange color. Try them with mulled cider on Halloween!

2½ cups sifted unbleached all-purpose flour

1 teaspoon baking powder

½ teaspoon each baking soda and salt

1½ cups mashed, cooked butternut squash

1 cup brown sugar

½ cup vegetable oil

2 eggs beaten or ½ cup prepared egg substitute

1 teaspoon cinnamon

½ teaspoon ginger

¼ teaspoon each nutmeg and ground cloves

1 cup prepared mincemeat

Preheat the oven to 350° F.

Grease a baking sheet.

Sift together the flour, baking powder, baking soda, and salt into a large bowl.

In another bowl, beat together all the remaining ingredients, except the mincemeat. Add the squash mixture to the dry ingredients and stir until blended. Fold in the mincemeat.

Drop the batter by tablespoons onto the prepared baking sheet. Bake for 12 minutes, in batches. Cool on wire racks.

Crostata di Zucca (Italian Pumpkin Pie)

Makes 8 servings.

To cook fresh pumpkin for this or any recipe, choose a small (two to five pounds) pumpkin, remove the seeds, and cut it into chunks. Put the unpeeled chunks, cut side up, in a roasting pan. If desired, sprinkle with cinnamon sugar *(see Basics)*. Pour a half-inch of water into the pan (don't add more during cooking) and bake the pumpkin in a 350° F. oven until tender, about 45 minutes. Turn the pieces upside down to drain while cooling (fresh pumpkin tends to be watery). Peel and refrigerate the pumpkin until needed.

1 uncooked 9-inch pie shell (see Basics) with a fluted edge

2 cups puréed fresh pumpkin or one 15-ounce can of pumpkin

¾ cup sugar

¼ cup stone-ground cornmeal

1 teaspoon cinnamon

½ teaspoon salt

2 beaten eggs or ½ cup prepared egg substitute

2 tablespoons rum (optional but traditional)

2 egg whites

½ cup chopped candied orange peel

¼ cup chopped candied citron (candied peel and citron are available in the baking ingredients section of the supermarket)

Preheat the oven to 400° F. Prick the pastry shell all over with a fork and bake it on the bottom shelf until it's cooked but still pale, about 10 minutes. Check the pastry while cooking; if part of the shell rises in a hump, prick it with a fork to allow steam to escape. Cool the shell.

When ready to cook the filling, preheat the oven to 350° F.

Mix the pumpkin with the sugar, cornmeal, cinnamon, and salt until the mixture is well-blended. Beat in the eggs and rum.

Use a little of the egg white to brush over the surface of the pastry shell. Beat the rest of the egg whites until they are stiff and fold them into the pumpkin. Stir in the candied fruit. Spoon the filling into the cooled pie shell.

Bake on the middle shelf of the oven until the filling is set, about 50 minutes. To test, insert a knife an inch from the center of the filling; it should come out clean. If the pastry gets too brown, lay a sheet of foil loosely over the pie; don't tuck it around the plate.

Cool the pie on a wire rack before cutting.

TOMATOES

BURSTING WITH RED-CHEEKED GOODNESS. My all-time favorite sandwich as a youngster was one thick slice of a perfectly ripe, fresh-from-the-garden beefsteak tomato slathered with mayonnaise on store-bought white bread. They weren't very filling, so I could easily down three of those oozing, inelegant sandwiches at a sitting. No tomatoes have ever tasted quite as good, except perhaps those I grow today in my small vegetable patch. Once you know how wonderful real tomatoes can taste, it's hard to settle for those anemic, square-sided pink tennis balls that stores try to pass off on consumers in winter.

On the other hand, when the peak season for fire-engine red, vine-ripened tomatoes arrives in your area, a tomato salad a day wouldn't be too much, especially not from a health standpoint. That red color has a special meaning healthwise—it signals the presence of lycopene, a carotene different from the beta carotene that's been mentioned so often in this book in connection with dark green and orange vegetables. Studies show that tomato's lycopene also may carry a protective factor against some forms of cancer.

Tomatoes are also a good source of vitamin C (although not a great source, like oranges). Older women who cut down on fat and increase their consumption of vitamin C foods may have a lowered risk of breast cancer.

Chock-full of potassium, tomatoes protect against strokes and heart disease. And when fresh tomatoes are out of season, canned tomatoes fill in nicely in the health department. Surprisingly, a cup of canned tomatoes, probably because it's denser, contains more vitamin C than a cup of fresh tomatoes.

When it comes to maximizing tomatoes, one thinks first of Italian cuisine, particularly southern Italian. The farther south you go in Italy, the more tomatoes, garlic, fish, pasta, and olive oil you'll encounter, which makes the tip of the boot the home of a five-star health cuisine. As you travel north, the more beef, butter, white rice, and refined grains are favored.

Fortunately, it's the southern Italian tomato-based dishes that have caught on most in this country. Youngsters especially seem to go for tomato-drenched pasta and pizza, and it's reassuring to know these foods are really good for them.

In the Market

In fresh tomatoes, round ones are best for salads, plum tomatoes for fresh sauce, and cherry tomatoes for snacks and hors d'oeuvre.

When you can't get real tomatoes, it's better to buy canned tomatoes—the imported Italian ones are excellent for sauces and soups—than to settle for gassed-to-ripeness tomatoes bred for travel and storage rather than taste. The one exception may be cherry tomatoes, so if you must have tomatoes in winter salads, go for the little guys, and let them ripen for a day or two at room temperature.

Since they travel from afar, watch out for dents in the imported-tomato cans and buy only those that are in perfect shape.

In the Kitchen

At home, finish ripening tomatoes at room temperature and use them up before you need to refrigerate them, because the warm-blooded tomato loses its sweet flavor when exposed to a chill.

Homemade tomato sauce with good olive oil and real, as opposed to desiccated, garlic is always the best, and even when you follow the same recipe, it seems to taste a little bit different each time. Store-bought sauce, on the other hand, is an invariable formula. Making tomato sauce doesn't have to be a long-simmering-and-stirring affair; a light sauce can be whipped up in a half-hour, in just the time it takes to put together a tossed green salad and cook the pasta.

Fresh Bruschetta

Makes 6 to 8 servings.

A hearty appetizer or a tasty accompaniment to a soup such as Mushroom and Barley Soup with Escarole *(page 36).*

2 ripe tomatoes, finely chopped
3 tablespoons extra-virgin olive oil
1 clove garlic, pressed
1 teaspoon minced fresh basil
salt and pepper to taste
6 slices Italian bread, ½-inch thick, or
8 to 10 of French bread
additional basil leaves as
a garnish (optional)

Mix together the tomatoes, olive oil, garlic, minced basil, salt, and pepper. Allow the mixture to stand at room temperature for about 1 hour, stirring once or twice.

Toast the bread until it's lightly browned. Divide the tomato mixture among the slices, spreading it over the tops. If desired, garnish each with a fresh basil leaf. Serve at once.

Pesto-Stuffed Cherry Tomatoes

Makes about 24 appetizers.

This colorful hors d'oeuvre combines some lovely fragrances of summer.

My mother, who was a wonderful cook, scorned hors d'oeuvre, calling them "appetite killers." She never wanted anything to interfere with her guests' enjoyment of the bountiful dinner she'd prepared for them. But I think she'd have approved of this one—it's pleasantly light, to stimulate rather than to quell the appetite.

2 pint cartons of cherry tomatoes

For the pesto:

2 cloves garlic, peeled
2 cups loosely packed fresh basil leaves
½ cup lightly toasted pine nuts
½ teaspoon salt
¼ teaspoon freshly ground black pepper
about ½ cup extra-virgin olive oil
¼ cup freshly grated Parmesan cheese
basil sprigs for garnishing

Cut off and discard the tops of the cherry tomatoes. Scoop out the pulp and seeds with a grapefruit spoon, and drain the tomatoes upside down on a wire rack.

Make the pesto. Rinse and thoroughly dry the basil leaves. In a food processor fitted with the steel blade, with the motor running, toss the garlic down the feed tube to mince it.

Stop the motor. Add the basil, pine nuts, salt, and pepper to the work bowl. Process until *very* finely chopped.

With the motor running, slowly pour the olive oil down the feed tube in a thin stream until the mixture reaches a pastelike consistency, neither too thick to drop off a spoon nor runny. You'll have to stop, stir, and check a few times.

Transfer the pesto to a bowl, and then stir in the cheese.

Shortly before serving, stuff the tomatoes with the pesto, and put them on a tray garnished with basil sprigs.

Crustless Tomato and Chili Quiche

Makes 12 servings.

This is a super company brunch dish! It can be prepared ahead of time, it doesn't need much watching or worrying, and the combination of tastes is delightful.

about ½ loaf stale Italian bread, sliced

one 4-ounce can Mexican green chilies, mild or hot, to taste

1 tablespoon butter

2 cups coarsely grated Monterey Jack or cheddar cheese

2 cups peeled diced ripe tomatoes or canned tomatoes, drained

1 avocado, diced

1 onion, chopped

6 eggs or 1½ cups prepared egg substitute

3 cups milk

salt and pepper to taste

If the bread isn't dry, put it in an oven set on 200° F. for about 30 minutes. In a food processor or by hand, chop or grate the bread into coarse crumbs. You'll need 4 cups of crumbs, loosely packed.

Dice the chilies. If they are hot ones, don't handle them with your hands. Dicing can be done with a knife and fork.

Butter two 10- or 9-inch pie pans. Sprinkle ½ cup of cheese on the bottom of each. Sprinkle 1 cup of breadcrumbs in each. Divide the chilies, tomatoes, avocado, and onion

between the pans. Sprinkle with the remaining breadcrumbs (1 cup each) and the remaining cheese (½ cup each).

Beat the eggs, milk, salt, and pepper until well-blended. Divide and pour the mixture over the quiches. Press the breadcrumbs down with the back of a spoon.

The quiches can be made 1 hour or so ahead to this point. When ready to cook, preheat the oven to 350° F.

Bake the quiches in the middle of the oven for 30 to 40 minutes, or until a knife inserted at the center comes out clean. Let them stand 10 minutes before serving, cut into wedges.

The Beautiful Tomato Salads of Summer

These salads should be made only with vine-ripened tomatoes that have never felt the chill of a refrigerator. First choice, of course, are homegrown tomatoes; second choice, authentic farm-stand tomatoes. It's okay to use tomatoes that still have a little green around the stem end, as farm tomatoes often do, if the rest of the tomato is red, ripe, and fragrant. "Vine-ripened" tomatoes sold in supermarkets aren't quite as juicy but will do. It's the marriage of tomato juice and olive oil that's so important to the first three of these salads.

There are few ingredients (which nevertheless are hotly disputed between Italian families) in a summer tomato salad, but as in a work of art, the whole is greater than the sum of its parts.

The Riccio Tomato Salad

Makes 4 to 6 servings.

6 medium vine-ripened tomatoes or 4 large (2 pounds), sliced not quartered

1 Vidalia or other sweet onion, peeled and ringed

salt to taste

⅓ cup olive oil

6 to 8 fresh basil leaves, snipped

fresh white Italian bread

Put the sliced tomatoes and onion rings in a flat vegetable serving dish. Sprinkle with salt. The salt encourages the tomatoes to exude juice. The slightly acidic tomato juice then replaces vinegar, combining with the oil into a mild vinaigrette.

Add the olive oil and basil. Stir gently with 2 forks. Let the salad stand at room temperature, stirring occasionally, for 30 minutes or so. Serve with bread for dipping in the accumulated juices.

The Papalia Tomato Salad

Makes 4 to 6 servings.

6 medium vine-ripened tomatoes or
4 large (2 pounds), sliced not quartered
2 cloves garlic, peeled and sliced
salt to taste
⅓ cup olive oil
10 to 12 fresh marjoram leaves, snipped,
or ½ teaspoon dried oregano
fresh white Italian bread

Put the sliced tomatoes and garlic in a flat serving dish. Sprinkle with salt. Add the olive oil and marjoram or oregano. Stir gently with 2 forks. Let the salad stand at room temperature, stirring occasionally, for 30 minutes.

You may remove the garlic slices or not, to your taste. Some people of robust digestion enjoy eating the garlic with the salad, and it's certainly good for them. Serve the salad with bread for dipping in the accumulated juices.

Tomato and Mozzarella Salad

Makes 6 servings.

6 medium vine-ripened tomatoes
(2 pounds), sliced
1 pound mozzarella cheese
(can be low-fat), sliced
2 cloves garlic, halved
salt and freshly ground pepper to taste
⅓ cup extra-virgin olive oil
10 to 12 fresh marjoram leaves, snipped,
or ½ teaspoon dried
marjoram leaves

Put the sliced tomatoes, mozzarella, and garlic in a flat vegetable serving dish. Sprinkle with salt and pepper. Add the olive oil and marjoram. Stir gently with 2 forks. Let the salad stand at room temperature, stirring occasionally, for 30 minutes or so.

Remove the garlic, and arrange the tomatoes and mozzarella in overlapping slices before serving.

Tomato and Salami Salad

Makes 6 servings.

*6 medium vine-ripened tomatoes
(2 pounds), sliced*

¼ pound hard salami, thinly sliced

¼ cup olive oil

2 tablespoons red wine vinegar

*2 tablespoons chopped fresh
flat-leafed parsley*

Arrange the tomatoes and salami so that the slices overlap in a flat vegetable serving dish. Drizzle with olive oil and vinegar. Sprinkle with parsley. Let the salad stand at room temperature, without stirring, for 30 minutes or so before serving.

Tomato and Artichoke Salad

Makes 6 servings.

*6 medium vine-ripened tomatoes
(2 pounds), sliced*

*two 14-ounce cans artichoke hearts,
drained and halved lengthwise*

4 scallions with the green tops, chopped

*salt and freshly ground lemon pepper
to taste*

⅓ cup olive oil

2 tablespoons red wine vinegar

*10 to 12 fresh oregano leaves, snipped, or
½ teaspoon dried oregano*

Put the sliced tomatoes, artichoke hearts, and scallions in a flat vegetable serving dish. Sprinkle with salt and pepper. Add the olive oil, vinegar, and oregano. Stir gently with 2 forks. Let the salad stand at room temperature, stirring occasionally, for 30 minutes or so before serving.

Tomato and Anchovy Salad

Makes 6 servings.

*6 medium vine-ripened tomatoes or
4 large (2 pounds), sliced not quartered*

*1 can of flat anchovies, separated,
rinsed in wine vinegar*

¼ cup olive oil

2 tablespoons red wine vinegar

*2 tablespoons chopped fresh
flat-leafed parsley*

Put the sliced tomatoes and anchovies in a flat vegetable serving dish. Add the olive oil, vinegar, and parsley. Stir gently with 2 forks. Let the salad stand at room temperature, stirring occasionally, for 30 minutes before serving.

Tomato, White Bean, and Tuna Salad

Makes 8 servings.

*one 20-ounce can Italian cannellini
(white beans), drained and rinsed*

*one 6½-ounce can of tonno (Italian tuna
packed in oil), drained*

*1 celery heart (just the pale inner part),
finely chopped, including leaves*

½ cup finely chopped sweet onion

¼ cup chopped black olives

*¼ cup each olive oil and
red wine vinegar*

½ teaspoon dried oregano

freshly ground black pepper to taste

*8 vine-ripened tomatoes
(about 2½ pounds)*

inner leaves of romaine lettuce

In a medium-size bowl, mix all the ingredients, except the tomatoes and lettuce. Allow the mixture to blend flavors by marinating it in the refrigerator for 30 minutes to 1 hour.

Cut the tops off the tomatoes; reserve them. Hollow out the centers and turn them upside down to drain.

Stuff the tomatoes with the filling and set the tops on. Line 6 bowls with lettuce leaves and place a stuffed tomato in each. If there is any extra filling, spoon it around the sides.

If the salads are not to be served within 30 minutes, refrigerate them.

For other tomato recipes, see the following: Baked Beans from the North End of Boston; Baked Pasta with Shiitake Mushroom Sauce; Basque Chicken with Almonds and Olives; Broccoli and Ziti Casserole; Butternut Ratatouille; Carrots with Tomatoes and Elbows; Cauliflower with Sun-Dried Tomatoes; Fresh Spinach Fettuccine with Bread Sauce; Greek-Style Shrimp with Shell Pasta; *Imam Bayeldi*; Kale with Tomato Risotto; Meat-Loaf "Pie" with Ricotta Filling; Molded Cauliflower with Spicy Carrot-Tomato Sauce; Orange-Scented Stuffed Eggplant; *Pasta de l'Estate con Noce*; Rice-Stuffed Cabbage Leaves with Pineapple-Tomato Sauce; Scallops with Vegetable Sauce; Shells with Tuna and Peperoncini; Skillet Cacciatore for Two, with Broccoli; Smothered Chicken with Peppers and Corn; Sole with Linguine; *Spezzatino di Vitello con Piselli*; Spinach Lasagna; Succotash with Tomatoes; Sunshine Oat-Bran Pizza; Take-It-Easy Minestrone; Tomato Rice Soup; Tuna Provençal; Two-Crust Whole-Wheat Broccoli Pizza; Vegetable Chowder with Shredded Spinach; Ziti *alla Siracusa*; Ziti with Cannellini Sauce

TURNIPS

A PREHISTORIC VEGETABLE THAT'S STILL SUPER. Anthropologists who have analyzed the remains of prehistoric dinners tell us that our remote ancestors liked to wrap the common white turnip in wild onions and steam the vegetables on flat rocks around the cave fire. It sounds tasty and probably was a comfort if the hunters failed to bring home the bacon.

The yellow turnip, also known as a rutabaga, is of much later origin. The Scandinavians developed it in the 1700s, which is why it's sometimes called the Swedish turnip.

White or yellow, turnips are cruciferous vegetables, members of the cabbage family, which means they contain chemical compounds, such as sulforaphane, that help to block the development of tumors. The National Cancer Institute recommends that we include lots of these cancer fighters in our diet. Rutabagas, as you may guess from the color, are also a rich source of vitamin A, which gives them a double-barreled shot against cancer.

In the Market

Because turnips are a cold-weather crop, the freshest ones will appear in markets from fall to the middle of winter. Think small when you think turnips. The smaller the turnip, the sweeter it will be. Look for purple tops no bigger than tennis balls, and rutabagas about five inches in diameter. Purple tops should not be shriveled, which indicates a loss of moisture. Rutabagas ought to feel heavy for their size.

Turnip greens, although not often available, are especially rich in vitamins A and C; they should be tender, unwilted, and moist. Braise them as you would any greens; they can be substituted for spinach in many of the recipes in the Greens chapter.

In the Kitchen

Turnips are full of moisture that evaporates rapidly at room temperature. Rutabagas are heavily waxed to prevent this, but purple-topped white turnips are not. They need to be kept in a humid part of the refrigerator. Packing them between heads of leafy greens in the vegetable crisper drawer should provide a climate that will keep white turnips fresh for a week. The waxed rutabagas, however, will keep a month in a refrigerator or cold room.

Turnips (except for tiny purple tops the size of large radishes) should always be peeled before cooking, because the peel will give a bitter flavor to the vegetable. This is a bit tricky with rutabagas, since a paring knife is liable to slip on the wax coating. To make the job easier and safer, first cut a slice off each end. Then pierce the rutabaga with a sturdy knife at the midpoint between root and stem and cut it in half. Stand a half rutabaga on this wide cut surface before proceeding to remove the rest of the peel.

About one-third of the turnip's cancer-fighting compounds are lost in cooking, although not the rutabaga's vitamin A. Fortunately, small white turnips are delicious raw as well as cooked. Add the raw slices to stir-frys and try them as part of a vegetable appetizer tray or grated into slaws. ■

Ragout of Lamb with Turnips and Carrots

Makes 4 servings.

Lamb and turnip, both strong flavors, mingle nicely with rosemary for a real country-style dish, perfect for a winter's evening by the fireside. Add a salad of mixed greens with a peppery vinaigrette and a good dark bread.

1½ pounds turnips (6 purple-topped) or 1 large rutabaga, peeled

4 carrots

1 tablespoon olive oil

4 large shoulder lamb chops (about 2 pounds), all visible fat removed

1 large onion, chopped

1 clove garlic, minced

½ cup chicken broth

½ cup tomato purée or sauce

½ teaspoon each celery seed and rosemary

salt and pepper to taste

Preheat the oven to 375° F. Cut the turnips into chunks (roughly the size of a large egg). Scrape the carrots and cut each into 2 pieces.

Heat the olive oil in a Dutch oven, and brown the chops, 1 or 2 at a time, on both sides. Remove the chops and sauté the vegetables until they are slightly browned. Add the onion and garlic, and sauté 1 more minute.

Put the chops on top of the vegetables. Add the broth and tomato purée. Sprinkle the celery seed and rosemary over all. Add salt and pepper. (With the addition of celery seed, salt becomes optional.)

Bake the ragout, covered, on the middle shelf of the oven for 1 hour, or until the meat and vegetables are tender. Most of the pan juices will have been absorbed into the turnips and carrots. If the casserole gets too dry toward the end of the cooking time, add a little more broth. *The casserole can be kept warm, covered, for 30 minutes.*

Scalloped Rutabaga and Potatoes

Makes 6 servings.

This is a delicious dish to put in the oven alongside a meat loaf. Nutmeg is particularly nice with turnip, giving it a chestnutty flavor.

one 1-pound rutabaga (yellow turnip)

2 large potatoes (about 1 pound)

2 tablespoons butter or low-cholesterol margarine

1 large shallot, minced

2 tablespoons flour

2 cups milk

¼ teaspoon each dry mustard, white pepper, nutmeg, and salt

2 tablespoons seasoned or plain breadcrumbs

additional nutmeg

Peel the rutabaga, slice it thin, and parboil the slices until nearly tender, about 10 minutes. Remove them with a slotted spoon to a 2-quart gratin dish.

Peel and slice the potatoes. In the same boiling water, parboil the potatoes until nearly tender, about 5 minutes. Drain and combine with the rutabaga, gently stirring to mix the vegetables evenly.

Preheat the oven to 375° F. Melt the butter in a saucepan and sauté the shallot until tender but not brown. Add the flour and cook the roux, stirring over low heat, for 3 minutes.

Heat the milk to scalding separately; this can be done easily in the microwave in a microwaveable measuring pitcher, 4 to 5 minutes on high.

Pour the hot milk all at once into the roux, stirring constantly over medium heat until the sauce is bubbling. Add the seasonings. Whisk until the seasonings are well-blended and the sauce is smooth. Pour the sauce over the vegetables, lifting them with a spatula so that the sauce will reach the bottom of the pan.

Sprinkle with crumbs and additional nutmeg. Bake for 35 to 40 minutes. The vegetables should be very tender, the sauce bubbly, and the top brown.

Gratin of White Turnips, Carrots, and Rice

Makes 6 servings.

A food processor makes short work of the necessary grating. You'll be surprised what a delicate flavor the turnips have in this dish.

> *3 to 4 purple-topped turnips*
> *(1 pound), peeled and grated*
>
> *3 carrots, scraped and grated*
>
> *1 tablespoon butter or*
> *low-cholesterol margarine*
>
> *2 tablespoons dry white wine*
>
> *2 cups cooked brown or white rice*
>
> *2 cups mornay sauce (see Basics)*
>
> *1 cup fresh breadcrumbs or*
> *½ cup unseasoned dry crumbs*
>
> *1 tablespoon grated Parmesan cheese*
>
> *paprika*

Preheat the oven to 375° F. Heat the butter in a large skillet, and stir-fry the turnips and carrots for about 1 minute. Add the wine, cover, and steam until the vegetables are reduced by half—this will take about 5 minutes. Watch that the pan doesn't dry out.

Mix the vegetables with the rice in a buttered gratin dish or glass baking pan about 2 inches deep—1½-quart capacity. Pour the sauce evenly over all. Sprinkle with the breadcrumbs, cheese, and paprika.

Bake until bubbly and brown, 35 minutes.

Rutabaga with Apple and Cardamom

Makes 6 servings.

No need for any butter in this smooth and spicy dish of puréed rutabaga.

> *one 1-pound rutabaga*
> *(yellow turnip), peeled*
>
> *1 cup applesauce*
>
> *½ teaspoon ground cardamom*
>
> *¼ teaspoon each cinnamon,*
> *white pepper, and salt*

Cut the rutabaga into 1-inch chunks and put them in a saucepan with water to cover. Bring to a boil and simmer for 20 to 25 minutes, until quite tender.

Drain and mash the rutabaga chunks, or purée them in a food processor. Blend well with the applesauce and seasonings. Serve hot. *The dish can be made ahead, refrigerated, and reheated.*

Turnip Slaw with Pineapple and Fresh Mint

Makes 4 servings.

A peppery, tart slaw of purple-topped turnips.

Mint has many medicinal uses, with peppermint being more powerful than spearmint. Native Americans used mint to cure respiratory ailments, and we all recognize the scent of the derivative menthol in cold remedies as well as in anesthetic rubs. Internally, mint is a digestive remedy. Folklore tells us that mint tea makes one cheerful, a claim that is as yet unproved—but worth a try!

1 pound purple-topped turnips, peeled and grated

1 cup fresh pineapple, finely minced, or one 8-ounce can crushed pineapple, undrained

3 tablespoons olive oil

1 tablespoon lemon juice

¼ teaspoon salt

2 tablespoons minced fresh mint (1½ teaspoon dried mint can be substituted, but the fresh herb is much better in this dish)

4 fresh mint sprigs for garnishing

The turnips and fresh pineapple are most easily prepared with a food processor. Combine all the ingredients, tossing well, and chill at least 1 hour to blend flavors. Garnish with fresh mint sprigs.

WHEAT

BREADBASKET OF NOURISH- MENT FOR MIND AND BODY. One of the ironies of progress, with the wealth and refinement it brings, is that basic good foods frequently get too refined to support optimum health. Poor peasants throughout history have eaten coarse brown bread, while the city folk got the pasty white refined stuff—along with a host of health problems that arise whenever the staff of life is missing its fiber and nutrients. Populations that rely heavily on rice are similarly weakened when their chief source of nourishment is refined to remove its bran.

Whole wheat, which contains both the germ and the bran, is a perfectly super source of the B vitamins, vitamin E, and insoluble fiber.

The B vitamins nourish the whole nervous system. A list of the mental problems that can be caused or worsened by a deficiency in one B vitamin or another reads like a psychiatrist's casebook: depression, overreaction to stress, general nervousness, chronic fatigue, and migraine headaches, to name just a few. Anyone who leads a stressful life (and who doesn't?) should be certain to get plenty of the B vitamins that whole grains provide.

The B vitamins are also active in providing the body with energy by converting carbohydrates to the body's chief fuel, glucose.

Vitamin B_6 stabilizes female hormones and also has been found to be effective in the reduction of symptoms of PMS, from fluid retention to acne.

As an antioxidant, vitamin E helps to prevent saturated fatty acids from breaking down in harmful ways. It protects the B complex vitamins against oxidation and retards the aging process of the cells, which is primarily due to oxidation. Vitamin E increases energy and stamina by enabling the body's muscles and nerves to function with less oxygen. And vitamin E nourishes the human body's reproductive system.

Grandma called it roughage, but we call it insoluble fiber. Unlike soluble fiber, which reduces cholesterol, insoluble fiber promotes the health of the intestines by increasing the stool's bulk and causing it to move faster through the body. Insoluble fiber relieves constipation and helps to prevent the disorders that go with it, like diverticular disease and hemorrhoids.

In the Market

Enriched white flour and bread made from it may return some of the B vitamins lost in the refining process but do nothing about the missing fiber. Still, when white flour is needed for particular recipes, *unbleached, enriched* are the words to look for. Whole-wheat cereals can give you some of the whole grain you need; two old-time favorites, shredded wheat and wheat flakes are good choices.

And don't overlook whole-wheat pastas! Supermarkets generally have one or two varieties; whole-food markets often have several.

In the Kitchen

Whole-wheat flour can replace some or all of the white flour in homemade breads, muffins, and certain cakes that don't require a superfine texture. A general rule is, seven-eighths of a cup of whole-wheat flour (one cup less two tablespoons) equals one cup of white flour. Whole-wheat flour should be refrigerated.

Whole-wheat pasta can be substituted for white in almost any recipe, including the many pasta recipes in this book.

Whole-Wheat Penne with Gorgonzola Sauce

Makes 4 servings as an accompaniment.
The sharp flavor of Gorgonzola stands up well to the assertive taste of whole-wheat pasta.

1 tablespoon butter

1 tablespoon flour

¾ cup hot milk

*1 wedge of Gorgonzola
(Italian blue cheese), crumbled,
about 6 ounces*

white pepper to taste

*½ pound whole-wheat penne
(tubular macaroni), cooked according to
package directions*

In a medium-size saucepan, melt the butter and stir in the flour. Cook the roux over very low heat, stirring occasionally, for 3 minutes; don't let the flour turn brown.

Add the hot milk all at once. Stir constantly while bringing the sauce to the point where it bubbles and thickens. Blend in the Gorgonzola until it has melted. Stir in the white pepper. *The sauce can be kept at room temperature for 30 minutes.*

Toss the penne with the sauce and serve immediately.

Pineapple Tabbouleh

Makes 6 to 8 servings.
A snacking salad that goes especially well with cold summer meals.

*one 20-ounce can crushed pineapple
packed in its own juice*

½ teaspoon salt

*1 cup fine-grain bulgur wheat (found in
the Greek foods section of the supermarket
or in whole-food and health-food stores)*

1 green pepper, finely chopped

1 cup chopped scallions

*¼ cup finely chopped fresh mint (¼ cup
chopped fresh parsley and 2 teaspoons
dried mint can be substituted)*

¼ cup olive oil

¼ cup fresh lemon juice

¼ teaspoon black pepper

lettuce leaves

Spoon the pineapple into a nonreactive wire strainer set over a 1-quart measure, saving the juice. Add water to the juice to measure 2¼ cups of liquid. Mix the liquid with the salt and bring it to a boil. Pour the liquid over the fine-grain wheat. Let the wheat stand for 1 hour.

Drain the wheat in a wire strainer, pressing out any excess liquid with the back of a spoon. Combine the wheat with all the remaining ingredients except the lettuce and mix well. Cover and chill. Add more lemon juice or salt, if needed. Serve on lettuce leaves.

Fennel Seed and Black Pepper Bread

Makes 8 servings.

A spicy bread that's equally good with hot, thick soup or with an entrée salad.

1 envelope dry yeast

1 teaspoon sugar

1 cup very warm water

1¾ cups whole-wheat flour

1½ cups unbleached all-purpose flour

¾ teaspoon salt

2 tablespoons olive oil

1 tablespoon fennel seeds

1 tablespoon coarsely ground black pepper (available on supermarket spice shelves— do not use whole black pepper)

Stir the yeast and sugar into the warm water. Let the mix stand for 5 minutes; the yeast should bubble up to show that it's active.

Combine the 2 flours and salt in the work bowl of a food processor fitted with the steel blade. Process just long enough to blend. Coat a medium-size bowl with a little of the olive oil; pour the rest into the flour mixture. Process to blend. With the motor running, pour the yeast mixture down the feed tube. Process 10 to 15 seconds, until the mixture forms a ball that cleans the sides of the work bowl. (If the flour does not adhere in a ball, add a little water, 1 teaspoon at a time.) Continue to process, counting 30 seconds, or until the dough is elastic and springy.

Alternatively, the ingredients can be combined in a bowl and the dough kneaded by an electric mixer's dough hook for 5 minutes or by hand for 10 minutes. The important factor is that the dough springs back when pressed.

Flatten the dough into a 15-inch circle, and sprinkle it with the fennel and pepper. Roll it up and knead it into a smooth ball. Place the dough in the oiled bowl, turning it to grease all sides, and cover it with plastic wrap. Let it rise in a warm place until double in bulk, about 1 hour and 30 minutes.

Punch the dough down and form it into a loaf. Place it in an oiled loaf pan. With a sharp knife, cut 6 diagonal slits, about 1 inch deep, in the top of the dough. Let it rise in a warm place until the dough reaches the top of the pan.

Preheat the oven to 375° F. Bake the bread in the middle of the oven for about 35 minutes. To test for doneness, lift the loaf and tap it on the bottom. It should sound hollow, and the bottom crust should be golden brown.

Remove the loaf from the pan and cool on a wire rack. Serve at room temperature.

Boston Brown Bread

Makes 2 loaves; the extra one can be frozen.

Steamed breads like this one were created by inventive New England cooks who didn't have ovens. Brown bread in its mold could be steamed in the same cauldron that was cooking a soup or heating water on the hearth.

Coffee cans (13-ounce size) work nicely as molds. The bread takes only a few minutes to mix up, but it will take 2 hours to steam—little watching is necessary, however.

Besides being the traditional accompaniment to baked beans, brown bread is a healthful breakfast food. It's delicious spread with cream cheese or toasted and buttered.

2 cups milk
2 teaspoons cider or white vinegar
½ cup dark molasses
⅔ cup raisins
1 cup whole-wheat flour
1 cup cornmeal
1 cup rye flour
1½ teaspoons baking soda
1 teaspoon salt

Butter the insides of 2 coffee cans. Sour the milk by stirring the vinegar into it and letting it stand for 10 minutes. Put the milk in a large bowl with the molasses and whisk to blend. Add the raisins.

In another bowl, mix the remaining dry ingredients. Add the dry ingredients to the milk mixture in 3 portions, blending after each.

Divide the batter between the coffee cans. Put a buttered piece of wax paper on top of the batter in each mold and top each can with a tent of foil held on by a large rubber band.

Put the molds in a large pan. If you have a flat rack, put it under the molds. Add hot water to reach three-quarters of the way up the sides of the molds; if the molds begin to float, you have too much water.

Bring the water to a simmer, cover with the lid, and steam the bread for 2 hours. (Watch that the water doesn't evaporate or boil fast enough to tip the molds. An occasional peek should do.) The bread is done when a cake tester inserted in the center comes out dry.

Lay the molds on their sides on a wire rack. When the molds are cool enough to handle, remove the bottom end of each can with a can opener, run a spatula around the bread inside, and gently push it out of the mold. Finish cooling the breads on the wire rack.

Whole-Wheat, Oatmeal, and Apple Muffins

Makes 12 muffins.

Not a morning person? Make these muffins ahead of time and heat them up in the microwave, about 1 minute on medium for 2 muffins.

1 cup whole-wheat flour
½ cup unbleached all-purpose flour
1 tablespoon baking powder
1 teaspoon cinnamon
½ teaspoon salt
1 cup uncooked oatmeal
½ cup brown sugar
(sifted so there are no lumps)
¾ cup milk
2 eggs or ½ cup prepared egg substitute
⅓ cup oil
1 Granny Smith (or other tart) apple,
peeled and diced small
cinnamon sugar (see Basics)

Line a 12-cup muffin pan with paper liners. Preheat the oven to 400° F.

Sift the flours, baking powder, cinnamon, and salt into a large bowl. Stir in the oatmeal and sifted brown sugar.

Mix together the milk, eggs, and oil.

Pour the liquid into the dry ingredients. Mix just enough to blend. Stir in the apple cubes. Divide the batter among the muffin cups. Sprinkle the tops with cinnamon sugar.

Bake in the top third of the oven for 20 minutes, or until the muffins are lightly browned on top and dry inside. Serve warm or at room temperature.

Pastiera

Makes 12 servings.

This traditional Italian Easter dessert incorporates wheat berries, the whole kernels of the grain. My version is crustless and offers low-cholesterol alternatives.

Canned, cooked wheat berries can be found in Italian and specialty food stores, or you can buy the uncooked berries in a health food store and cook them according to the instructions given in Basics.

unseasoned dry breadcrumbs
2 pounds low-fat ricotta cheese

5 eggs or 1¼ cups prepared egg substitute
¾ cup sugar
1 teaspoon grated orange zest
1 teaspoon grated lemon zest
½ teaspoon almond extract
1 cup cooked wheat berries
½ cup toasted slivered almonds
¼ cup diced candied orange peel

Preheat the oven to 325° F. Butter a 9-inch flan pan (a straight-sided, 2-inch-deep cake pan with a removable rim) and dust it with unseasoned dry breadcrumbs.

In a food processor or by hand, mix together the ricotta, eggs, sugar, grated zests, and almond extract until well-blended. Fold in the cooked wheat berries, ¼ cup of the almonds, and the orange peel. Pour the mixture into the prepared pan.

Bake in the middle of the oven for 1 hour and 30 to 45 minutes, or until the custard is set to within 1 inch of the center. Sprinkle with the remaining almonds during the last 10 minutes of cooking.

Cool completely on a wire rack. Remove the rim of the flan pan. Serve at room temperature or chilled.

For other recipes using whole wheat, see the following: Couscous with Figs and Raisins; Garlic Snacking Bread; Hot Onion Bread; Irish Brown Oatmeal Bread; Maple-Nut Rice Muffins; Strawberry Griddle Cakes; Two-Crust Whole-Wheat Broccoli Pizza

YOGURT

SUPER MILK FOR ALL AGES. Thought to have originated in Turkey, yogurt is milk, whole or skim, raised to nutritional heights by the addition of active cultures with rather formidable names like *Streptococcus thermophilus, Lactobacillus bulgaricus, and L. acidophilus.* These agents ferment the milk into a semisolid or solid food with yogurt's characteristic mildly sour flavor. While retaining milk's considerable protein and calcium content, yogurt with active cultures also imparts a number of health benefits not found in milk alone.

Adults sometimes lose their taste for milk or find they don't tolerate it well. Yogurt is an easily digested food that can be flavored in many different ways to appeal to those who, for one reason or another, don't drink milk. The amino acid tyrosine in protein-rich yogurt stimulates alertness chemicals in the brain, making it a wonderful busy-day snack.

Women especially benefit from the additional protein, often deficient in their diets, and from the calcium, which may reduce bone loss in postmenopausal women.

In test-tube studies, yogurt has stimulated human cells to produce more interferon, one of the body's infection-fighting agents. In animal studies, yogurt in the diet has been shown to reduce the amount of cancerous products that are produced by other intestinal bacteria.

One of the great things about yogurt cultures is the beneficial effect they have on the intestines. Yogurt is known for helping to prevent or control diarrhea caused by bacteria or by taking antibiotic drugs. Yogurt is itself an antibiotic that offers some protection from bacterial invaders like salmonella.

A recent study reported that a daily cup of yogurt containing the active culture *L. acidophilus* reduced the incidence of vaginitis (caused by the yeast infection candida) in susceptible women.

In the Market

In buying yogurt, it's necessary to read the label to be certain the yogurt does contain those infection-fighting cultures—not all brands do. You should see the words "active cultures." If you want a yogurt with *L. acidophilus*, a particularly beneficial culture, check the label for those words. And while you're reading, look for "nonfat" and "natural flavoring." Also check the "sell-by" date.

Plain unflavored yogurt in larger containers is really the best buy and the most versatile. It's so handy for use in salad dressings, dips, sauces, desserts, and baked goods. Then, when you want fruit-flavored, sweetened yogurt, it's a simple matter to mix in chopped fruit and honey.

In the Kitchen

Since yogurt is dated, you'll know exactly how long it may be kept in your refrigerator.

Although you may have read that yogurt can't be used in heated sauces because it will curdle, there is a way to do this. Blend a tablespoon of cornstarch into a half-cup of yogurt and whisk it into a cup of boiling liquid, such as chicken broth. The mixture will thicken without separating, for a guiltless nonfat sauce to replace those usually enriched with cream. Try this with a half-teaspoon of curry powder and a pinch of tarragon to make a terrific topping for plain chicken. ▬

Baked Swordfish with Tarragon Yogurt

Makes 2 servings.

For this dish, you'll need yogurt cheese *(see Basics)*, which is simply yogurt that has been drained of moisture in a cheesecloth-lined strainer for several hours or overnight.

1 tablespoon olive oil
¾ to 1 pound swordfish steak
½ cup plain nonfat yogurt cheese
1 teaspoon dried tarragon

Preheat the oven to 400° F. Spoon the olive oil into a baking dish and turn the swordfish steak to coat both sides. Layer the yogurt cheese over the fish; sprinkle with tarragon. Bake 20 minutes, or until cooked through.

Salmon Steaks with Cucumber Mint Sauce

Makes 2 servings, with some sauce left over.
This cool and spicy sauce perfectly complements the oily fish that are so good for you.

If you don't make your own seasoned crumbs, try whirling a good-quality dry herb stuffing mix (not a stovetop variety) in the food processor until it is reduced to coarse crumbs. For extra nutritional zip, add toasted wheat germ. This mild but flavorful mix will enable you to avoid the heavy garlic-powder taste of store-bought seasoned crumbs.

2 salmon steaks
olive oil
about 3 tablespoons seasoned crumbs
2 thick slices lemon

For the sauce:

2 cucumbers
1 clove garlic, pressed
1 cup plain nonfat yogurt
2 tablespoons chopped fresh mint or
1 teaspoon dried mint
¼ teaspoon each ground coriander and
white pepper

Peel the cucumbers and cut them lengthwise. Scoop out the seeds with a grapefruit spoon. Salt and drain the cucumbers for 30 minutes.

Rinse the cucumbers and squeeze out the excess moisture. Chop them fine. Mix them with the remaining sauce ingredients. Cover the sauce and chill it for at least 1 hour.

Rinse and pat dry the steaks. Brush both sides with oil. Place the steaks in a round, flat microwave-safe dish, thickest parts on the outside. Sprinkle with crumbs. Top with lemon slices, slightly squeezed over the crumbs.

Microwave on high for 8 to 10 minutes, or until the fish flakes easily. Alternatively, bake in a conventional oven for 20 minutes at 400° F.

Serve the steaks with cucumber mint sauce.

Tomato, Cucumber, and Scallion Salad with Blue Cheese Yogurt Dressing

Makes 6 servings.

A cool and beautiful salad with a nice crunch of scallions. Try this dressing another time as a super dip for raw veggies, such as broccoli and cauliflower, for example.

about 6 leaves of red leaf lettuce
6 medium tomatoes, sliced into rounds
2 small, crisp cucumbers, peeled and thinly sliced into rounds
one bunch thin scallions, chopped

For the dressing:

2 tablespoons olive oil
1 tablespoon red wine vinegar
1 teaspoon each Dijon mustard, celery salt, and dried dillweed
freshly ground black pepper to taste
1 cup plain nonfat yogurt
1/3 cup finely crumbled blue cheese

On a platter, make a bed of red leaf lettuce torn into bite-size pieces. Alternate overlapping slices of tomato and cucumber on the lettuce. Scatter the chopped scallions on top.

In a small bowl, whisk the oil, vinegar, mustard, celery salt, dill, and black pepper. Blend in the yogurt. Stir in the blue cheese.

Just before serving, stir the dressing again and pour it over the salad.

Strawberry Chambord Yogurt Parfaits

Makes 4 servings.

They're almost too pretty to eat—and so easy to make!

1 quart strawberries, washed and hulled
1/4 cup Chambord (raspberry liqueur, optional)
2 tablespoons sugar
2 cups vanilla nonfat yogurt

Reserve 4 perfect strawberries. Purée the remaining strawberries in a food processor or blender. Add the Chambord, if using, and sugar. (If the berries are very tart, you may need more sugar.) Chill until ready to serve.

In 4 parfait glasses or stemmed water goblets, alternate layers of yogurt and strawberry sauce. For a garnish, press one of the reserved whole berries onto the rim of each glass (as you would lemon for iced tea).

Note: You'll have about 3 cups of sauce; any extra sauce may be frozen.

Yogurt *Coeurs à la Crème*

Makes 4 servings.

Yogurt hearts are flavored with almond and surrounded with fruit in this fat-free version of the decorative French dessert. Just right for a Valentine's Day luncheon!

2 pounds plain nonfat yogurt
¼ cup sugar
½ teaspoon almond extract
1 cup sliced canned peaches, packed without sugar, drained
½ cup frozen whole raspberries, thawed
¼ cup raspberry jelly

Place a strainer over a deep bowl and layer it with a double thickness of rinsed cheesecloth. Mix the yogurt with the sugar and almond extract. Spoon it into the prepared strainer, cover with the extra cheesecloth, and let the yogurt drain in the refrigerator overnight.

Line 4 heart-shaped molds of ½-cup capacity (they don't have to be perforated molds) with rinsed cheesecloth, and divide the yogurt cheese among them, smoothing the tops. Refrigerate the hearts for 1 hour or more, then gently unmold them onto dessert plates. Discard the cheesecloth.

Mix the peaches and raspberries. Melt the jelly in a microwaveable bowl in the microwave, about 1 minute on high, or in a small saucepan over low heat. Blend the jelly with the fruit and spoon it around the yogurt cheese hearts.

Banana-Peach Frozen Yogurt

Makes about 1½ quarts.

Enjoy this high-nutrition, low-fat, but creamy dessert with a clear conscience. And there's no ice-cream maker needed for this easy treat!

2 very ripe bananas
1 cup drained canned peaches, packed without sugar (reserve juice)
1 envelope unflavored gelatin
½ cup juice from peaches
2 tablespoons lemon juice
½ cup sugar
¼ teaspoon salt
3 cups plain nonfat yogurt
2 egg whites
½ teaspoon almond extract

Purée the bananas and peaches in a food processor or blender.

In a saucepan, stir the gelatin into the peach and lemon juices, and let it soften for 5 minutes. Add the sugar and salt, and stir over low heat until the gelatin and sugar dissolve.

In a large bowl, blend the puréed bananas and peaches with the gelatin and yogurt. Pour the mixture into freezer trays or a loaf pan, and freeze until firm.

Turn the frozen yogurt into a large bowl. Break it into pieces, and add the egg whites and almond extract. Beat on high speed with an electric mixer until light and fluffy. Return to the pan and freeze.

Fruit Yogurts

Each of the following recipes makes about 1½ cups.

Want a change from the flavors in your grocer's dairy case? Just buy a 2-pound container of plain nonfat yogurt, and go creative!

Banana Cinnamon Yogurt

In a processor or blender, purée 1 banana with 1 tablespoon of honey and ⅛ teaspoon of cinnamon.

Blend in 1 cup of plain nonfat yogurt. Chill until the texture firms.

Tangerine Yogurt

In a bowl, whisk together 2 tablespoons of undiluted frozen apple juice concentrate, 1 tablespoon of orange marmalade, and 1 cup of plain nonfat yogurt.

Peel and remove the pith from 1 small seedless tangerine or clementine. Snip each segment into 3 pieces and stir into the yogurt.

Chill to let the flavors blend.

(The rest of the frozen apple juice can be put right back into the freezer.)

Cranberry Yogurt

Stir ½ cup of canned or homemade whole-berry cranberry sauce into 1 cup of plain nonfat yogurt.

Concord Grape Yogurt

Whisk ¼ cup undiluted frozen grape juice concentrate into 1 cup of plain nonfat yogurt.

Stir in ½ cup of halved, seeded Concord grapes (any grapes can be substituted).

Papaya Yogurt

Whisk 1 tablespoon of honey and 1 tablespoon of lime juice into 1 cup of plain nonfat yogurt.

Stir in ½ cup of finely diced, very ripe papaya.

Mango-Orange Yogurt

Whisk 1 tablespoon of honey and 1 tablespoon of frozen orange juice concentrate, undiluted, into 1 cup of plain nonfat yogurt.

Stir in ½ cup of mashed ripe mango.

For other yogurt recipes, see the following: Baked Chicken Breast with Yogurt Crust and Peaches; Cantaloupe Mousse; Frozen Mango-Banana Mousse; Red Cabbage Slaw with Dilled Yogurt Dressing

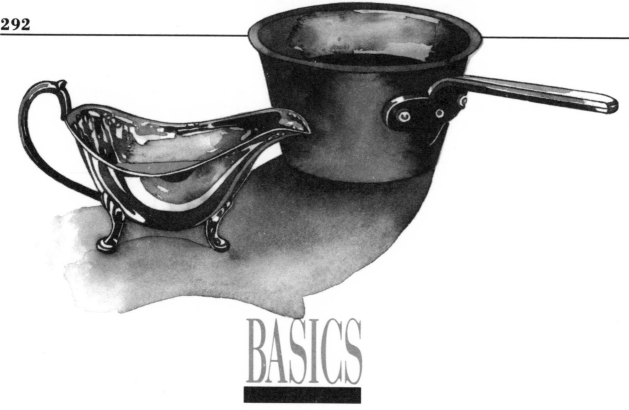

BASICS

**ALL-PURPOSE RECIPES OFTEN FOUND
IN INGREDIENTS LISTS**

All-Purpose Cooked Chicken

*Makes about 2 cups of cubed chicken
and 2 cups of broth.*

For chicken salad or any of the many dishes that use cooked chicken or just to tuck away in the freezer.

*2 pounds skinned chicken thighs
and/or breasts*
water to cover (about 1 quart)
1 large carrot, sliced
1 large onion, chopped
1 stalk celery, chopped
several sprigs of fresh parsley
*1 teaspoon mixed dried herbs—choose
from thyme, rosemary, basil, marjoram,
tarragon, and savory*
½ teaspoon salt
½ teaspoon whole peppercorns
1 bay leaf

Combine all the ingredients in a pot. If you don't have the carrot or celery on hand, you can proceed—but the onion is imperative.

Bring to a boil and simmer, covered, until the chicken is cooked through, 30 to 45 minutes. Let the chicken cool, covered, for 20 to 30 minutes, no more. Chill the chicken in the refrigerator in the chicken broth.

After you have removed the chicken for whatever dish you are making, reduce the broth to half by boiling rapidly. Strain and discard the peppercorns and solids. Use the broth for sauces, soups, and other dishes.

Full-Flavored Chicken Broth

Substitute a whole 3- to 3½-pound chicken, well-washed in cold, salted water, for the skinned thighs and breasts. Increase the water to 2 quarts. Substitute ¼ teaspoon of black pepper for the peppercorns, but don't add it until the soup is finished. Simmer with the cover slightly ajar, and increase the cooking time—1 hour to 1 hour and 15 minutes.

Remove the chicken; strain the broth. Chill the broth so that the fat rises and remove all of it.

Makes about 6 cups of broth and 2½ cups of chicken meat when all the bones and skin have been discarded. If you wind up with less than 5 cups of broth, add water to make up the difference, if the broth is to be used for soup. You can do this because the stock will be quite concentrated. If the broth is to be used for a sauce, however, don't add water.

Mornay Sauce

Makes about 2 cups.

I use grated Parmesan cheese in mornay sauce because it is one of the lowest of the hard cheeses in fat and cholesterol and is the highest in calcium. One ounce of Parmesan, however, contains sodium equivalent to ¼ teaspoon salt, so do not add salt to this sauce.

*2½ tablespoons butter or
low-cholesterol margarine
3 tablespoons flour
2 cups milk (can be low-fat)
¼ teaspoon white pepper
⅓ cup grated Parmesan cheese*

In a medium saucepan, melt the butter and add the flour.

Cook the roux over low heat for 3 minutes, stirring often, but don't brown it.

Heat the milk to scalding separately; this can be done most easily in the microwave in a microwave-safe measuring pitcher, 4 to 5 minutes on high.

Pour the hot milk all at once into the roux, stirring constantly over medium heat until the sauce is bubbling. Add the seasonings and cheese; whisk until smooth.

A Light Italian Tomato Sauce

Makes 2 to 3 cups, more than enough for 1 pound of pasta.

What makes it light? No heavy tomato paste to give this sauce an acidy taste.

¼ cup olive oil

1 clove garlic, minced

1 large can (2½ to 3 pounds) imported Italian plum tomatoes

1½ teaspoons dried basil

½ teaspoon each dried oregano and salt

¼ teaspoon black pepper or more to taste

1 dried whole, hot red pepper (chili) or ¼ teaspoon red pepper flakes

¼ cup finely chopped fresh flat-leafed parsley

Heat the oil in a large skillet. Sauté the garlic until it is softened but not brown. Add all remaining ingredients except the parsley. Cook uncovered, stirring occasionally, until a sauce consistency is reached, about 30 minutes. As the tomatoes soften, break them up with a fork. The finished sauce should be slightly chunky. There's no need to strain this sauce (or any tomato sauce, in my opinion).

Discard the chili pepper. Add the parsley and remove from the heat.

Note: A seeded, chunked green pepper is a pleasant addition; sauté the green pepper with the garlic.

Or add a can of well-drained anchovies with the tomatoes and omit salt.

A half-cup of pitted black olives and/or 1 tablespoon of drained capers would make nice variations.

Or add all of the above, in which case you will have made *Salsa Puttanesca*, a quick, spicy sauce so named because it was favored by Neapolitan ladies of the evening.

Oven-Cooked Italian Meat Sauce

Makes about 2 quarts.

This is a really rich meat sauce, sometimes called "gravy" by Italians, and shouldn't be confused with Bolognese sauce, with ground

beef. The meat is removed and served separately or saved for another occasion.

This version, without meat fat or chicken skin, is lighter than the traditional. If you want to make it lighter still, omit the pork and double up on the chicken.

Cooked in the oven, the sauce requires much less watching and stirring; it almost cannot burn, but it will stick just a bit around the edges. Don't worry; this is a plus! Stir the browned bits right into the sauce for a really authentic taste. Italian meat sauce should be simmered right to the point where it *might* have stuck on the bottom of the pan if not removed that instant. Remember, this one is called gravy. Just as we get real brown-gravy flavor from the browned bits around the roasting pan, tomato gravy, too, profits from that grilled (but not *burned!)* taste.

You might as well make a big batch; it freezes beautifully.

¼ cup olive oil

2 or more boneless pork cutlets (½ pound), every scrap of visible fat removed

½ pound chuck steak or a thick slice of beef shin

2 or more skinless chicken thighs

3 cloves garlic, pressed or very finely minced

three 28-ounce cans Italian tomatoes with juice

1 small can tomato paste plus ½ can water to clean out every last drop of flavor

1 or 2 dried, whole, hot red peppers (chilies)

1 teaspoon salt or more to taste

1 tablespoon dried basil

1 teaspoon dried oregano (optional)

½ teaspoon black pepper or more to taste

½ cup minced fresh flat-leafed parsley

Heat the oven to 400° F. Choose a large, heavy, nonreactive (not aluminum) metal roasting pan. A stainless steel lasagna pan will work well. Put the pan on the largest range-top burner, add the oil, and brown the meats on both sides. Add the garlic to the pan and turn off the heat. The garlic should sizzle but not brown.

Add all the remaining ingredients except the parsley, and bake on the middle shelf of the oven for about 1½ hours *after* the mixture begins to simmer, or until it's reduced to a sauce consistency. Stir 2 or 3 times, breaking up the tomatoes.

When the sauce is done, remove the meat with a slotted spoon and reserve it for another use. Be especially careful that no chicken bones fall back into the sauce.

Remove and discard the red peppers. Stir in the parsley.

Note: Italians would serve the meat after the pasta and before the main course in a typical 4-hour company dinner of several courses: antipasto, pasta, meat cooked in the gravy, a roast of some kind with vegetables, salad, and dessert. Meat cooked in tomato gravy can be dry from long cooking but makes tasty sandwiches when combined with some of the sauce, which is how I like to use them.

Arborio Rice

Makes about 2 cups.

When plain white rice is wanted, this is my favorite—far superior to all American "converted" or "five-minute" or "one-minute," or "boil-in-bag" types.

2 quarts water
1 teaspoon olive oil
½ teaspoon salt (optional)
1 cup Arborio rice

In a 3-quart saucepan, bring the water to a boil. Add the oil and salt, if using. Add the rice. Reduce the heat to medium, stir once, and keep at a lively simmer for about 12 minutes, or until cooked al dente. Drain well.

Return the rice to the warm pan, fluff it with a fork to separate the grains, and let it stand 2 to 3 minutes. Serve hot.

Brown Rice

Makes about 3 cups.

Cook exactly the same way as Arborio rice, but allow 40 to 50 minutes simmering time.

Roasted Peppers

4 thick-fleshed peppers, any color
salt to taste
1 clove garlic, sliced
olive oil

Broil the peppers about 1 inch from the heat source until slightly charred. Turn them and continue to broil until all sides have been cooked in the same manner. The finished peppers should not be completely blackened but should have charred spots here and there; this is what gives them a nice grilled flavor.

Put them in a bowl, *covered*, or in a closed plastic bag to cool. This will loosen the skins.

When they're cool, skin and seed the peppers. Cut into quarters or strips and salt them.

Pack the peppers in a pint jar with garlic. Cover with olive oil. The peppers will keep for 4 to 5 days, refrigerated. If some of the garlicky oil is left over, it's wonderful in salads.

Yogurt Cheese

A pint makes about 1 cup;
a quart makes 2 cups.

Yogurt cheese has the consistency of a creamy farmer cheese. Mix it with herbs and peppers as a savory substitute for cream cheese dips, or sweeten and surround it with fresh berries to make *coeurs à la crème*.

(See the Yogurt chapter for specific recipes.)

*1-pint or 1-quart container
of plain low-fat yogurt*

Line a strainer with a double thickness of cheesecloth that you have rinsed and wrung out. Place the strainer over a deep bowl. Spoon the yogurt into the cheesecloth, and let it stand, covered, in the refrigerator for 8 to 12 hours or overnight.

Drain off the whey and use the yogurt cheese according to the recipe instructions.

Whole-Grain Griddle Cake and Waffle Mix

Makes 4 batches.

If you enjoy having this "Sunday morning" mix on hand, you may want to double the recipe.

*2 cups unbleached all-purpose flour
1½ cups whole-wheat flour
⅓ cup sugar
3 tablespoons baking powder
1 teaspoon salt
1 envelope nonfat dry milk (makes 1 quart)
½ cup oat bran (uncooked hot cereal)*

Sift together the all-purpose flour, whole-wheat flour, sugar, baking powder, and salt into a large bowl. Stir in the dry milk and oat bran until very well blended. Store in a canister until needed.

To make 8 to 12 griddle cakes:

*¾ cup water
1 egg or ¼ cup prepared egg substitute
1 tablespoon butter or no-cholesterol margarine, melted
1¼ cups mix
1 cup blueberries or other fruit, diced (optional)
pure maple syrup*

Combine the water, egg, and butter; beat until blended. Stir the mix before measuring. Pour the liquid ingredients all at once into the measured mix, stirring until smooth.

Heat a nonstick griddle to 375° F. (or use a cast-iron skillet lightly coated with butter).

Add berries, if using. Stir more water, up to ¼ cup, into the batter if it seems too thick; the batter should pour readily from a spoon.

Bake the cakes until bubbles form on top. Turn them and brown on the second side. Serve with pure maple syrup.

To make 4 waffles:

*¾ cup water
1 egg or ¼ cup prepared egg substitute
3 tablespoons butter or no-cholesterol margarine, melted
1½ cups mix
2 egg whites*

Combine the water, egg, and butter; beat until blended. Stir the mix before measuring. Pour the liquid ingredients all at once into the measured mix, stirring until smooth.

Beat the egg whites until stiff; fold them into the batter.

Heat the waffle iron according to the manufacturer's directions. Spray the grids with a nonstick cooking spray.

Spoon about ½ cup of batter over the bottom grid; bake until it stops steaming. Do the same with the rest of the batter. If the cooked waffles are to be kept warm until all are ready, arrange them in a single layer on a baking sheet in a warm oven. Stacking the waffles makes them soggy.

Serve with a cooked fruit sauce— blueberry or raspberry—or pure maple syrup.

Easy, No-Cholesterol Pastry

*Makes enough for 1 double-crust pie
or 2 single-crust tarts or pies.*

This is not the flaky butter-and-lard pastry of past generations, but on the plus side, it's not only guiltlessly no-cholesterol, it's the easiest to mix and roll out of any pastry recipe ever. And that's a lot of pluses!

When baking juicy pies, put them in the bottom third of the oven so that the bottom crust will be crisped before it gets soggy (pizza is baked the same way). Unfilled pie shells and deep-dish pies, on the other hand, should be cooked on the top shelf to facilitate browning the visible pastry. Fresh-fruit pies in which the fruit won't exude its juice until the pie is almost done should be cooked on the middle shelf; you don't want the top to get *too* brown before the fruit is tender.

2¼ cups unbleached all-purpose flour
*½ to 1 teaspoon salt (the lesser amount
will work, if you're cutting down)*
½ cup vegetable oil
⅓ cup cold skim milk

Mix the flour and salt together with a fork. Measure the oil and milk into a cup. Pour the liquids all at once into the dry ingredients, mixing with a fork until just blended.

The above measurements usually produce a perfect pastry, but since the consistency of flour can vary, you may want to add a bit more milk (a teaspoon at a time) if the pastry seems too dry, or pat in more flour if it seems too wet.

Form the pastry into 2 balls; flatten each slightly. Roll out half of the pastry between 2 sheets of floured wax paper or plastic wrap into a 12-inch circle. Handle gently to avoid toughening the pastry. As you roll, turn the pastry over, paper and all, from time to time, and straighten out wrinkles in the bottom paper.

Peel off the top paper and fit the dough, bottom paper side up, into a tart or pie pan. Remove the second sheet of paper.

After filling the pastry, do the same with the top crust. Seal the edges as you usually do.

To bake a single-crust pie or tart shell for an already-cooked filling, such as a pudding, preheat the oven to 400° F. Prick the pastry shell all over with a fork and bake it on the bottom shelf of the oven until it's golden brown, about 12 minutes. Check the pastry while cooking; if part of the shell rises in a hump, prick it with a fork to allow steam to escape. Cool the shell before filling.

Note: This dough doesn't freeze well.

Low-Cholesterol Margarine Pastry

*Makes enough for 1 double-crust pie
or 2 single-crust tarts or pies.*

This pastry is similar in texture to traditional butter-and-lard pastry, and it handles well.

2½ cups unbleached all-purpose flour

½ to 1 teaspoon salt

*⅔ cup low-cholesterol unsalted margarine
(if you can't find unsalted margarine, use
regular and reduce the salt to ¼ teaspoon)*

½ cup water or more

Mix the flour and salt together. In a food processor with on/off turns of the motor, or using a pastry cutter, cut in the margarine until the mixture resembles coarse crumbs. If using a processor, transfer the mixture to a bowl.

Pour the water into a small pitcher, and add 2 ice cubes. Sprinkle the water by tablespoons over the flour, mixing lightly with 2 forks after each addition. After 6 tablespoons have been added, use your fingers instead of forks to mix in the remaining 2 tablespoons. This will enable you to feel when the right amount of moisture has been added and the pastry will form a ball. If needed, more water can be added, cautiously, by the teaspoonful.

Divide the pastry into halves and pat the halves into circles the size of bread plates. Roll out half the pastry on a floured surface into the desired size. As you roll, use a spatula to loosen the pastry and turn it from time to time, dusting the new side with flour. Do everything gently to avoid toughening the pastry.

Fit the dough into an 8- or 9-inch pie pan. Chill the shell while rolling out the top. After filling the pie, place the top sheet over the filling, and trim and seal the edges as usual.

To bake a single-crust pie or tart shell, follow the directions given in the previous recipe.

Pastry Cream

Makes about 1¼ cups.

This versatile filling is "creamy" and delicious, and it can be low-cholesterol when made with an egg substitute. When not enriching pie crusts or cake layers, pastry cream (flavored with vanilla and almond) also makes a nice custard pudding simply to eat with a spoon.

> *2 tablespoons cornstarch*
> *1 cup milk (can be low-fat)*
> *2 egg yolks or ⅓ cup prepared*
> *egg substitute*
> *¼ cup honey, slightly warmed*
> *⅛ teaspoon salt*
> *flavoring (see Note)*

In a medium-size saucepan, stir the cornstarch into the milk until there are no lumps. Whisk in the eggs, honey, and salt. Cook over medium direct heat, stirring constantly, until the mixture bubbles and thickens. Lower the heat and cook 1 minute longer. Remove from the heat and stir in the flavoring.

Let the pastry cream cool before using it as a filling, then chill it in the refrigerator until set.

Note: The basic flavoring is 1 teaspoon of vanilla extract and ½ teaspoon of natural almond extract. Substitutions depend on the recipe in which the pastry cream is to be used. Instead of vanilla and almond, you may want to use one of the following flavors: 1 tablespoon liqueur or dark rum, 2 tablespoons of a sweet wine such as Marsala, or 1 tablespoon lemon juice with ½ teaspoon grated lemon zest.

To make 1½ times the recipe, use the following measurements: 3 tablespoons cornstarch, 1½ cups milk (can be low-fat), 3 egg yolks or ½ cup prepared egg substitute, ⅓ cup honey, and a scant ¼ teaspoon salt.

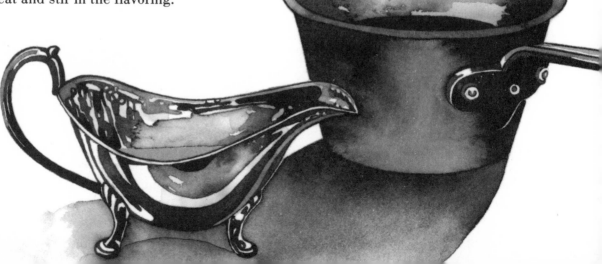

Poached, Peeled Chestnuts

Good fresh chestnuts come into the market just before Thanksgiving and are gone (or too dry) by the time Christmas is over. To be certain that I have the best possible chestnuts for holiday dishes (such as turkey stuffing), I buy them early, cook and peel them by the following method, and freeze them in one-cup batches in small plastic bags. It's such a production that I always do a big batch at one time so that I have extras for other dishes through the winter. I also enlist help in peeling them. "Many hands make light work."

> *chestnuts (any amount)*
> *water to cover*
> *1 or 2 bay leaves*

Wash the chestnuts thoroughly. With a small sharp knife, cut an X in the top of each. Put them in a deep, heavy saucepan and add the bay leaf. Add enough water to cover.

Bring the water to a boil; lower the heat to a sustained simmer and cook the chestnuts, uncovered, for 20 minutes. Do not drain.

Let them stand for 5 to 7 minutes. Then cool the chestnuts until they can be handled, scoop them out with a slotted spoon one at a time from the still-hot water. Peel off the outer shell and the inner membrane. As long as the chestnuts are quite warm, this will be easy, so if they cool off too much, reheat them in the cooking water, but not to the boiling point.

I recommend playing holiday music and being comfortably seated at the kitchen table while doing this job.

If you'd simply like to snack on chestnuts, they *can* be roasted "on an open fire," just as the song describes. Cut Xs in a half-pound, make a single layer of chestnut in a cast-iron skillet with the bay leaf and a tablespoon of vegetable oil. Place the skillet in hot coals, and shake it from time to time, using a double pot holder. When they smell delicious, they're probably done. (No fireplace? Roast them in the oven at 350° F.)

You can sometimes find peeled chestnuts in the can in specialty stores. But they're a lot more expensive, and you'd miss all this fun.

Whole-Wheat Berries

Makes about 3 cups.

1 cup whole-wheat berries
4 cups water
⅓ cup sugar (optional)

Put the whole-wheat berries and water in a slow cooker. Cook on low for 6 to 8 hours, or until they are tender but crunchy. If wheat berries are to be used in a dessert, add the sugar during the last hour of cooking.

Alternative method: Soak the wheat berries in water overnight. Drain them and put them into a heavy deep saucepan with the water. Simmer over low heat until tender, about 2 hours, stirring occasionally to prevent sticking—if necessary, add more water. Add the sugar, if using, during the last 15 minutes of cooking time.

Drain and rinse the wheat berries to remove the extra starch.

They may be frozen in 8-ounce containers until needed.

Fresh Ginger Syrup

Makes about 2 cups.

Along with its uses as an ingredient, this syrup makes a delightful fresh ginger ale. Combine 1 or 2 tablespoons of syrup with 8 ounces of chilled seltzer water or plain water.

A teaspoon of ginger syrup is also a refreshing sweetener for hot tea. You might like to take this stomach soother with you when you travel. Recent studies have shown that ginger helps to prevent motion sickness *even better* than the leading over-the-counter drug.

1 pound fresh ginger root, peeled
3½ cups water
1½ cups sugar

Mince the ginger in a food processor. Combine with the water, bring to a boil, and simmer, uncovered, for 5 minutes. Cover and let stand overnight.

Strain the mixture through double cheesecloth, squeezing to get all the liquid; discard the solids. Combine the juice with the sugar, bring to a boil, and simmer over medium heat until reduced to 2 cups, about 15 minutes.

The syrup will keep for 2 weeks or more, in the refrigerator.

Seasonings

Italian Seasoning: Mix 2 tablespoons dried parsley, 2 tablespoons dried basil, 2 teaspoons dried marjoram, 1 teaspoon dried oregano, and ½ teaspoon rosemary leaves *or* fennel seeds.

Store in spice jars for up to 6 months.

Garlic and Herb Oil: Mix ½ cup olive oil with 1 crushed clove garlic and ¼ teaspoon of each of the following herbs: dried oregano, basil, marjoram, thyme leaves, and rosemary.

Let the flavors blend before using. Keep refrigerated. The oil may solidify, but a few minutes at room temperature will restore it.

Hot Mustard Sauce: Put about 2 tablespoons dry mustard (which is hot mustard—sold in the spice section of the supermarket) in a small dish and add water a few drops at a time until a sauce consistency is reached.

Seasoned Breadcrumbs: Use a food processor to convert stale bread into fresh, fine breadcrumbs. For every 2 cups of crumbs, add 1 clove of *finely* minced garlic, 2 tablespoons grated Parmesan cheese (optional), and 1 teaspoon Italian seasoning (or any favorite herbs). Layer the crumbs in a baking pan; bake at 200° F. for 1 hour, or until pale golden but not brown; turn off the heat and leave in the oven for another hour.

Cinnamon Sugar: Mix ⅓ cup sugar with 2 tablespoons cinnamon. Store in a shaker.

Vanilla Sugar: Store 1 or 2 vanilla beans in a pint jar of sugar for a week or more to develop flavor. As you use this flavorful sugar, keep adding more sugar to the jar. One vanilla bean lasts a good long time!

ACKNOWLEDGMENTS

With love and thanks to my family—to my husband, Rick, who helps to evaluate every recipe and who is always lavish with praise and gentle with criticism; to my daughter, Lucy-Marie, for her special contributions, and to my son-in-law, Frank, for his loyal assistance; to my son, Charlie, whose fussiness about vegetables always sparks creative effort; and to all, including the entire Riccio family, for their abiding interest in the goodness of food.

With warmest thanks to everyone at Time Warner who helped to make this book a reality—and especially to my editor Liv Blumer for her continued enthusiasm and support of this project and for her discriminating skill in editing the manuscript; to Jack Maley for his heartening interest; to copyeditors Barbara Quarmby and Tony Pordes for their expert finishing touches; and to artist Bobbi Tull for her wonderful illustrations.

With appreciation to literary agent Blanche Schlessinger for her acumen and finesse and especially for her encouragement.